Fiscal Zoning in Suburban Communities

Fiscal Zoning in Suburban Communities

Duane Windsor
Rice University

LexingtonBooks
D.C.Heath and Company
Lexington, Massachusetts
Toronto

Library of Congress Cataloging in Publication Data

Windsor, Duane.
    Fiscal zoning in suburban communities.

    Includes bibliographical references and index.
    1. Zoning—New Jersey. 2. Fiscal policy—New Jersey. 3. Local taxation—New Jersey. 4. Discrimination in housing—New Jersey. 5. Housing—New Jersey. I. Title.
HT169.72.N5W55   336.749   78-20632
ISBN 0-669-02751-0

International Standard Book Number: 0-669-02751-0

Library of Congress Catalog Card Number: 78-20632

To my parents

Contents

List of Tables

Acknowledgments

This study has benefited greatly from the assistance provided by several individuals. I have employed data sets assembled for other purposes by Patrick Beaton, Robert W. Burchell, Lynne B. Sagalyn, and George Sternlieb (director), all former colleagues at the Center for Urban Policy Research of Rutgers University. The first sections of chapter 5 of this study draw heavily on earlier work published with Franklin J. James, also formerly at the Center for Urban Policy Research.

This book developed from doctoral research at Harvard University. I am indebted to the members of the dissertation committee for their guidance and suggestions, especially H. James Brown and David Harrison.

The use of computer facilities for much of the data analysis in this study was provided by the Graduate Program in Urban and Regional Planning at the University of Iowa. Typing and reproduction were provided by the Jones Graduate School of Administration at Rice University. The manuscript was typed by Mary Rydzewski and Delores Richardson.

None of these individuals or organizations is responsible for any errors of commission or omission remaining in this study.

1 Fiscal and Zoning Reform

There is mounting pressure for thorough reform of both state-local fiscal systems and municipal land use regulation.[1] The source of this reform movement is concern that low- and moderate-income households cannot obtain access to suburban jobs, housing, and education and are adversely affected by both artificial shortages in low-cost housing and fiscal disparities in tax base between suburbs and central cities created by suburban zoning practices. Exclusionary zoning ordinances are believed to maintain economic and racial segregation, distort metropolitan housing markets, and influence the spatial distribution of the property tax base.

It is argued that there is a considerable disparity between the locations of job growth (found in suburban areas) and low-cost housing (confined to central cities) in metropolitan areas. There is a growing belief that (whatever the actual motives of suburban municipalities and their voters) suburban land use and growth management practices may maintain that disparity and hence metropolitan racial and income segregation. The prevailing policies are believed to restrict the availability of low-cost housing in suburban areas, separate job growth from low-cost housing, and consequently increase both the housing and commuting costs of poorer (including minority) households. It is also argued that such policies are linked to substantial fiscal disparities among communities (particularly poor central cities compared with wealthy suburbs) in terms of tax base, tax effort, and demand for public services. As a result, leaving the financing of public services such as education in the hands of local governments, including wealthy suburbs practicing exclusionary zoning, may violate basic standards of equal opportunity or equal protection for both taxpayers and service recipients. The linchpin of the pressure for fiscal and zoning reform is the assumption that exclusionary zoning practices result largely from the fiscal implications to suburban taxpayers of various types of ratables under the prevailing system of local property taxation. Fiscal and zoning reform are thus linked. The purpose of this study is to investigate that assumption.

This reform movement has led to a tremendous upheaval recently in the relations between state and local governments. This upheaval has taken two forms. The first is a revolution in the financing of public education in several states, traditionally funded by local government through property taxation with state assistance. The second is a continuing controversy over the rights and obligations of local governments in the regulation of land development and the management of population growth. Both issues have been hotly contested in

1

federal and state courts, as well as in state legislatures. The battle over fiscal and
zoning reform has been fought out in seven landmark (and now famous) cases:
Robinson, Mt. Laurel, and *Madison* (New Jersey Supreme Court); *Ramapo* (New
York Court of Appeals); *Petaluma, Warth v. Seldin,* and *Arlington Heights* (U.S.
Supreme Court).

In August 1971 the California Supreme Court invalidated local property
taxation as a mechanism for financing public education in *Serrano v. Priest* (a
case concerning Los Angeles County).[2] The *Serrano* principle was rapidly
adopted by state or lower federal courts in Minnesota (October 1971), Wyoming
(December 1971), Texas (December 1971), Arizona (January 1972), and New
Jersey (January 1972). By that time, similar suits had been filed in a total of
thirty-one states.[3] In January 1972, however, the *Serrano* principle was rejected
by a New York trial court,[4] citing two earlier federal opinions that had also
refused Fourteenth Amendment equal protection attacks on school financing.[5]
Then the U.S. Supreme Court overturned the decision made by a three-judge
federal court in *Rodriguez v. San Antonio Independent School District.*[6] The
Supreme Court concluded that public education was not a "fundamental
interest" nor school district wealth a "suspect classification" under the Fourteenth Amendment. The school financing mechanism in Texas (which involved
about 50 percent state aid in addition to local property taxation) was
specifically upheld.

The status of local land use regulation is even more confused. The
Pennsylvania Supreme Court has invalidated exclusionary zoning practices,
especially those based on the desire to avoid the fiscal burdens of population
growth.[7] The U.S. Supreme Court, however, has refused to overturn similar
ordinances in *Warth v. Seldin*[8] and *Arlington Heights.*[9] The latter case was
remanded to the Seventh Circuit for reconsideration under the Fair Housing Act
of 1968. The appeals court subsequently ruled that the act is applicable and that
effect rather than intent is sufficient for federal jurisdiction.[10] A similar ruling
had previously been made by the Eighth Circuit.[11] The U.S. Supreme Court has
also permitted municipalities to prevent housing stock conversion to higher
densities.[12] New York courts have approved the Ramapo growth management
scheme designed to regulate fiscal burdens (although avoidance is not permitted).[13] The federal courts have done the same in *Petaluma.*[14]

These controversies have been perhaps most virulent in New Jersey.
Between 1973 and 1976 the New Jersey Supreme Court reached two divisive
and far-reaching decisions. A long series of *Robinson* opinions resulted in the
eventual adoption of a new policy for state aid to public education funded by an
income tax.[15] The supreme court held repeated hearings on *Robinson* as the
state legislature struggled to develop an acceptable replacement for local
property taxation in financing public education. In May 1975 the court
intervened in the legislative process and ordered a provisional reallocation of
state aid funds for the 1976-1977 school year. Although the state legislature

adopted a new Public School Education Act in September 1975, which was approved in an extraordinary advisory hearing by the supreme court, the state legislature failed to adopt a full funding provision by the court's deadline. In May 1976 the supreme court enjoined every state, county, and local official from expending any funds for the support of public schools (excepting certain fixed costs), unless full funding was enacted for July 1 (the beginning of the next school year). This injunction was dissolved in June, when an income tax was adopted by the legislature. In the meantime all public schools in the state had remained closed.

Following the precedent of the Pennsylvania cases, *Mt. Laurel*[16] and *Madison*[17] flatly declared exclusionary zoning to be unconstitutional. These cases invalidated land use policies adopted on fiscal grounds as exclusionary in character and cast doubt on the acceptability of growth management schemes and environmental arguments for zoning restrictions. In the Municipal Land Use Law of 1975 the state legislature ordered the redrafting of all municipal land use regulations. The law required all 567 municipalities to adopt new regulations by January 31, 1977. The requirement appears to have entailed the massive rewriting (even if simply revised) of all zoning, subdivision, site plan, and official map ordinances. A "land use element" had to be adopted in the master plan before any of these ordinances could be rewritten.[18]

The New Jersey Supreme Court, which is now the cutting edge of fiscal and zoning reform, appears to have accepted a particular theory of fiscal zoning in its decisions. This fiscal motive theory[19] argues that exclusionary zoning policies are adopted by suburban communities largely due to specific fiscal pressures arising from the prevailing system of local property taxation. The supreme court has adopted two strategies to counter such zoning behavior. The Mt. Laurel strategy, as modified in *Madison,* forbids fiscally motivated exclusion and compels least-cost zoning[20] (in place of specific fair share housing plans based on regional needs) as an affirmative obligation to provide vacant land for the construction of low-cost housing. The Robinson strategy seeks, in part, to alleviate the fiscal pressures believed to underlie suburban resistance to income and racial integration. (The Robinson strategy was adopted primarily for reasons having to do with the state's constitutional obligation to provide public education. Here we are concerned only with the relationship between state aid and local zoning policies.)

The controversy in New Jersey is of general interest. New Jersey is simply at the forefront of the national debate over fiscal and zoning reform. It provides a highly valuable case study for the examination of this problem. In the face of executive, legislative, and popular opposition, the state supreme court has adopted coordinated strategies of fiscal and zoning reform in *Robinson, Mt. Laurel,* and *Madison,* which include revamping state aid to education, levying an income tax, and completely reorienting local land use regulations. A virtually unique collection of information is available for an evaluation of fiscal and zoning reform in New Jersey at the municipal level. The results in New Jersey may have general implications for the national controversy over such reform.

My concern with this problem is twofold. First, how can we influence local zoning behavior to open suburban housing opportunities for low- and moderate-income households or at least improve housing supplies and prices on their behalf? In other words, will suburban zoning practices (and hence the supply and cost of low- and moderate-income housing) be affected by state policies that require increased state aid to education and least-cost zoning in place of exclusionary zoning? To answer these questions, we need to know the relationship of suburban zoning to the supply and cost of such housing and the role of local fiscal motives in the adoption of zoning practices. Second, the fiscal motive theory involves an important issue. What role does the local public sector play in maintaining income and racial segregation in metropolitan areas? The answer may do much to shape our attitude toward local property taxation and land use regulation.

It is not my objective to attack the *Robinson, Mt. Laurel,* and *Madison* decisions. On the contrary, I am in deep sympathy with their purpose, which is to improve educational, housing, and employment opportunities for the poor. However I am dubious about the likely effect of the Robinson strategy and the Mt. Laurel strategy on suburban housing markets. I shall not argue that *Mt. Laurel* and *Madison* should not have struck down fiscally motivated exclusionary zoning. Rather I shall suggest that the Mt. Laurel strategy may have been tied to a seriously mistaken analysis of the fiscal considerations involved in local land use policies and to a misunderstanding of the effect of those policies on suburban housing markets. While the Robinson strategy has other useful goals, it may well thwart the Mt. Laurel strategy. This conflict of public policies based on possible misinformation deserves closer study than it has received.

Notes

1. See Ira D. Heyman, "Legal Assaults on Municipal Land Use Regulation," *Urban Lawyer* 5 (Winter 1973):1-24.

2. Serrano v. Priest, 96 Cal.Rptr. 601, 487 P.2d 1241 (August 1971, *modified on denial of rehearing,* October 1971).

3. Donald G. Hagman, "Property Tax Reform: Speculations on the Impact of the Serrano Equalization Principle," *Real Estate Law Journal* 1 (Fall 1972):115-135.

4. Spano v. Board of Education, 68 N.Y.Misc.2d 804, 328 N.Y.S.2d229 (1972).

5. McInnis v. Shapiro, 293 F. Supp. 327 (N.D. Ill. 1968), *aff'd,* McInnis v. Ogilvie, 394 U.S. 322 (1969); Burruss v. Wilkerson, 310 F. Supp. 572 (W.D. Va. 1969), *aff'd,* 397 U.S. 44 (1970).

6. Rodriguez v. San Antonio Independent School District, 337 F. Supp. 280 (W.D. Tex. 1971), *rev'd*, 411 U.S. 1 (1973).

7. National Land and Investment Co. v. Kohn, Appeal of Easttown Township, 419 Pa. 504, 215 A.2d 597 (1966); Appeal of Girsh, 437 Pa. 237, 263 A.2d 395 (1970); Appeal of Kit-Mar Builders, 439 Pa. 466, 268 A.2d 765 (1970).

8. Warth v. Seldin, 495 F.2d 1187 (2d Cir. 1974), *aff'd*, 422 U.S. 490 (1975).

9. Metropolitan Housing Development Corp. v. Village of Arlington Heights, 517 F.2d 409 (7th Cir. 1975), *aff'd* 429 U.S. 252 (1977).

10. 588 F.2d 1283 (7th Cir. 1977).

11. United States v. City of Black Jack, Mo., 508 F.2d 1179 (1974).

12. Village of Belle Terre v. Boraas, 416 U.S. 1 (1974).

13. Golden v. Planning Board of the Town of Ramapo, 30 N.Y.2d 359, 285 N.E.2d 291 (1971), *appeal dismissed*, 409 U.S. 1003 (1972).

14. Construction Indus. Assn. of Sonoma County v. City of Petaluma, 375 F. Supp. 574 (N.D. Cal. 1974), *rev'd*, 522 F.2d 897 (9th Cir. 1975), *cert. denied*, 424 U.S. 934 (1976).

15. There were seven supreme court opinions in Robinson v. Cahill: 62 N.J. 473, 303 A.2d 273 (April 3, 1973); 63 N.J. 196, 306 A.2d 65 (June 19, 1973), *cert. denied*, 414 U.S. 976 (October 23, 1973); 67 N.J. 35, 335 A.2d 6 (January 23, 1975); 67 N.J. 333, 339 A.2d 193 or 69 N.J. 133, 351 A.2d 713 (May 23, 1975); 69 N.J. 449, 353 A.2d 129 (January 30, 1976); 70 N.J. 155, 358 A.2d 457 (May 13, 1976); 70 N.J. 464, 360 A.2d 400 (June 15, 1976). There were two trial court opinions: 113 N.J.Super. 223, 287 A.2d 187 (January 19, 1972); supplemented at 119 N.J. Super. 40, 289 A.2d 569 (March 30, 1972).

16. Southern Burlington County N.A.A.C.P. v. Township of Mount Laurel, 336 A.2d 713 (1975), *appeal dismissed and cert. denied*, 423 U.S. 808 (1975).

17. Oakwood at Madison, Inc. v. Township of Madison, 117 N.J. Super. 11, 283 A.2d 353 (1971), *cert. granted*, 62 N.J. 185, 299 A.2d 720 (1972), *remanded*, 128 N.J.Super. 438, 320 A.2d 223 (1974); 72 N.J. 481, 371 A.2d 1192 (1977).

18. William Miller, "The New Jersey Land Use Law Revision: A Lesson for Other States," *Real Estate Law Journal* 5 (Fall 1976):138-154.

19. This term is taken from Eric J. Branfman, Benjamin I. Cohen, and David M. Trubek, "Measuring the Invisible Wall: Land Use Controls and the Residential Patterns of the Poor," *Yale Law Journal* 82 (January 1973):490.

20. This term is taken from Randall W. Scott, "New Jersey Supreme Court Requires Rezoning for Least Cost Zoning," *Practicing Planner* 7 (March 1977):8-9, 33.

2 The Fiscal Motive Theory of Suburban Zoning

It has been widely argued that many suburban communities in major metropolitan areas practice *exclusionary zoning*, by which is meant the employment of local land use controls to exclude lower-income and minority households from suburban communities. As Schafer points out, there are two methods of practicing such exclusion. The first method, which he calls direct exclusion, is simply to forbid the construction of or conversion to low-cost housing types, such as apartments or small homes. The second method, which he terms indirect exclusion, is to raise the cost of available housing by various restrictions or requirements. Since direct exclusion on economic or racial grounds is unconstitutional, exclusion must operate indirectly through the price mechanism.[1] According to this argument, suburban communities employ land use controls to raise housing costs beyond the means of lower-income households. It is generally thought that such land use practices restrict the supply of lower-cost housing in suburban areas and produce price rises throughout metropolitan housing markets.

By their very nature, land use controls have exclusionary effects. The purpose of zoning is to exclude or restrict various land uses (and at least indirectly land users). The difficult question to determine in any zoning decision is whether public considerations are sufficiently important to justify the likely exclusionary effects of the zoning policy under review. Moreover, a wide variety of techniques can be used to produce such exclusionary effects. It is well recognized that zoning ordinances, subdivision regulations, and building codes can give at least indirect control over a community's land use patterns, housing costs, growth, socioeconomic composition, and fiscal situation. Such regulations are public interventions into the land and housing markets that will typically lead to supply restrictions and price distortions. In consequence, some kind of economic exclusion through the raising of housing costs will occur and may be linked in turn to racial exclusion by the income distribution of racial groups in metropolitan areas. The Douglas Commission report places the blame for income segregation in metropolitan areas squarely on suburban exclusionary zoning.

The abuses that such a multiplicity of governments works on a metropolitan area are many, and we need not list them all here. One is the discriminatory zoning that suburban towns adopt. Zoning, which is barely a body of law, very effectively keeps the poor and those with low incomes out of suburban areas by stipulating lot sizes way beyond their economic reach. Many suburbs prohibit or severely limit the construction of apartments, townhouses, or planned unit developments which could accommodate more people in less space at potential savings in housing costs. Even where apartments are allowed, they often are limited as to size of dwelling unit, effectively keeping out families with children who would presumably place a burden on school budgets.[2]

The Fiscal Motive Theory

The fiscal motive theory of suburban zoning underlying the Mt. Laurel strategy of the New Jersey Supreme Court is founded on two closely related hypotheses accepted in the *Mt. Laurel* and *Madison* cases. The first, which I will call the *exclusionary zoning hypothesis,* assumes that exclusionary zoning practices are sufficiently widespread in suburban areas to have significant allocative and distributional effects on regional housing markets (which violate the constitutional rights of low- and moderate-income households). In other words, the removal of exclusionary zoning practices will significantly improve housing supplies and prices for such households, while promoting a more equitable distribution of local tax base. Such zoning has been identified in terms of particular land use policies that have been widely adopted by suburban communities. The principal exclusionary devices identified in *Mt. Laurel* and *Madison* are (1) excessive zoning for commercial and industrial uses to attract tax base, (2) as much exclusion or restriction of apartments as possible to keep out lower-income households, and (3) large minimum lot and building requirements to force up the cost of single-family housing permitted.

The second, which I will call the *fiscal zoning hypothesis,* assumes that exclusionary zoning practices are at root fiscally motivated and ignore regional housing needs (without constitutional or statutory justification). As a result, fiscal and exclusionary zoning are virtually synonymous. On examination, this hypothesis divides into two arguments. The first argument is that exclusionary zoning practices are fiscally designed, as opposed to other possible motivations. The New Jersey Supreme Court carefully sidesteps the issue of whether any nonfiscal motives are involved in suburban zoning. The second argument is that these fiscal incentives are due specifically to the prevailing system of local property taxation. According to this hypothesis, the restrictive practices of excessive commercial and industrial zoning, apartment exclusion, and large minimum requirements have important fiscal consequences under local property taxation. Presumably such policies will maximize local tax base per household and hold down public service costs so as to minimize property tax rates for a given quality of services. This hypothesis is clearly stated in *Mt. Laurel* and *Madison*; it seems to be tacitly accepted in *Robinson.*

The generally accepted doctrine is that suburban municipalities practice fiscal zoning rather than exclusionary zoning. In other words, the exclusionary effects of local land use controls result from strong fiscal incentives that arise specifically from local property taxation.[3] According to this view, exclusionary zoning practices are produced by the fiscal environment of suburban communities.[4] Fiscal zoning is aimed at reducing the number of schoolchildren on the one hand (holding down service costs) and inflating the market value of new housing on the other (increasing revenues at given tax rates) because education is the principal component of the local public sector.

It is typically believed that multifamily or low-cost development contributes higher service costs (due to pupils and household size per dwelling unit) than tax revenues (due to low market value per dwelling unit). Hence suburban municipalities restrict or exclude such housing types. They compete for expensive housing and commercial or industrial ratables. The latter are presumed to produce substantial tax revenues but few residents or schoolchildren and hence only limited expenditures. Suburban officials and voters are presumed to scrutinize the fiscal implications of alternative development possibilities and then to design their land use policies so as to minimize service costs and maximize revenues while holding tax rates constant. By concentrating the property tax base in expensive residential or commercial and industrial ratables, fiscally motivated exclusionary zoning creates, or at least maintains, income segregation and fiscal disparities.

If local zoning has such fiscal incentives, then fiscal reform to reduce reliance on local property taxation should help relieve suburban dependence on fiscally designed land use controls. Thus zoning reform has been linked to a prior reform of state-local fiscal systems to eliminate the alleged fiscal incentives for economic exclusion. The New Jersey Supreme Court has apparently embraced this view. *Mt. Laurel* and *Madison* forbade the use of various zoning practices presumably founded on fiscal considerations; *Robinson* altered the funding of public education and forced legislative adoption of a state income tax.

The Legal Controversy in New Jersey

The New Jersey Supreme Court has become the principal judicial proponent of the fiscal motive theory. Its recent landmark cases *Robinson*, *Mt. Laurel*, and *Madison* are linked by the theory. The court has treated fiscal zoning and exclusionary zoning as equivalent. *Robinson* attributes disparities in the tax base to fiscal zoning in order to show that differences in property tax ratables per pupil and the resulting tax effort required to fund public education are unjustifiable. *Mt. Laurel* and *Madison* attribute income segregation to such zoning. Although these two decisions do not require fiscal reform (leaving the matter of state-local fiscal relations to the state legislature), they specifically condemn local property taxation as promoting exclusionary zoning. The close connection of these three cases is strong evidence that a coordinated strategy of fiscal and zoning reform has been adopted by the New Jersey Supreme Court.

The Mt. Laurel strategy forbids certain specific exclusionary devices and requires least-cost zoning. The objective is to strike at both economic segregation and fiscal disparities in property tax base. The Robinson strategy seeks, in part, to alleviate the underlying fiscal pressures behind suburban adoption of exclusionary zoning practices. The New Jersey Supreme Court assumed that the Mt. Laurel strategy would significantly improve access to suburban housing, employment, and public services for low- and moderate-income households, thus partly relieving fiscal disparities among municipalities in conjunction with state aid to education under the Robinson strategy. (As we shall see, the supreme court has substantially changed the grounds for the Mt. Laurel strategy between the *Mt. Laurel* and *Madison* decisions.)

Mt. Laurel and *Madison* are explicit in their presumption of the fiscal motive theory. While less explicit, *Robinson* is ultimately founded on the argument that local property taxation for public education is unconstitutional, because property tax ratables bear no reasonable relationship to number of pupils. (Moreover, the resulting wealth-based educational financing scheme was not ameliorated by existing or proposed state assistance formulas.) In effect, though the *Robinson* opinions never quite said so, the implicit premise was that exclusionary zoning based on strong fiscal incentives under local property taxation underlies the differing distributions of wealth and pupils.

The Mt. Laurel Strategy

The focal point of the recent controversy in New Jersey over state assumption of local functions and the adoption of a state income tax is the fiscal impact of the various types of land development typically permitted or excluded by municipal zoning ordinances in suburban New Jersey. The principal theme of *Mt. Laurel* and *Madison* is that fiscal zoning in developing suburban communities is inherently exclusionary in character and hence unconstitutional.[5] The failure to consider regional housing needs in conjunction with the explicitly fiscal design of the Mt. Laurel and Madison ordinances was the decisive factor.[a]

> In pursuing the valid zoning purpose of a balanced community, a municipality must not ignore housing needs, that is, its fair proportion of the obligation to meet the housing needs of its own population and

[a]*Madison* was originally appealed to the New Jersey Supreme Court before *Mt. Laurel*. However, Madison amended its zoning ordinance before the appeal had been heard. In accordance with its rules of procedure, the supreme court remanded the case to superior court, because an amended zoning ordinance constituted a new proceeding that must be heard initially by the trial court. Hence *Mt. Laurel* was decided by the supreme court before *Madison,* but the former opinion incorporated the superior court decision in the latter. Therefore the superior court opinion in *Madison* by Justice Furman is dealt with first, as the background for *Mt. Laurel.* The supreme court opinion in *Madison* involves an important modification of the Mt. Laurel strategy.

of the region. Housing needs are encompassed within the general welfare. The general welfare does not stop at each municipal boundary. Large areas of vacant and developable land should not be zoned, as Madison Township has, into such minimum lot sizes and with such other restrictions that regional as well as local housing needs are shunted aside.[6]

The principal foundation for including housing needs in the general welfare was the 1967 declaration of the state legislature that there was a "severe housing shortage" in New Jersey.[7] Justice Furman held that, "the ordinance under attack must be held invalid because it fails to promote reasonably a balanced community in accordance with the general welfare, unless it is defensible on some other ground."[8] The bulk of the superior court opinion in *Madison* concerns his rejection of fiscal and environmental considerations raised by the defendant municipality to justify the zoning ordinance.[b]

Justice Furman concluded that, "the underlying objective of the ordinance . . . was fiscal zoning, zoning as a device to avoid school construction and other governmental costs incident to population expansion. Housing needs of the region were not taken into consideration in its enactment. . . ."[9] He rejected that purpose, arguing, "Fiscal zoning *per se* is irrelevant to the statutory purposes of zoning."[10] In other words, the fiscal effects of community development are not included or excluded under the general welfare requirements of the state constitution or enabling legislation but regional housing needs are.[11] Furman held that the test for the validity of a local zoning ordinance does not turn on fiscal grounds at all. "In any event, the Madison Township zoning ordinance must stand or fall not as fiscal zoning. The test must be whether it promotes reasonably a balanced and well ordered plan for the entire municipality."[12] On remand of the case from the supreme court, a fair-share housing plan based on regional housing needs was required.

Without the rigidity of a mathematical formula this court holds that Madison Township's obligation to provide its fair share of the housing needs of its region is not met unless its zoning ordinance approximates in additional housing unit capacity the same proportion of low-income housing as its present low-income population, about 12%, and the same

---

[b]Madison Township is located in rapidly developing Middlesex County in central New Jersey. Justice Furman found that the 1970 zoning ordinance was explicitly designed to curb population growth and stabilize the local property tax rate. In a fairly large township, which was about 30 percent vacant, the ordinance restricted new multifamily units to between five hundred and seven hundred units, with no more than two hundred units to be built annually. Multifamily construction was to be at a maximum density of twelve units per acre and no more than 20 percent were to be two-bedroom units. Single-family districts were zoned for one- and two-acre minimum lots with minimum building sizes of 1,500 and 1,600 square feet. A developer filed suit, not only against the ordinance for practicing exclusionary zoning, but also against the enabling statute (Zoning Act of 1928, NJSA, 40: 55:30 et seq.) on the grounds that it did not include regional housing needs as a standard for determining general welfare, which was required under the 1947 Constitution. *Oakwood at Madison, Inc. v. Township of Madison*, 283 A.2d 353 (1971).

proportion of moderate-income housing as its present moderate-income population, about 19%. The amended zoning ordinance under review falls palpably short and must be struck down in its entirety.[13]

The New Jersey Supreme Court took essentially Furman's position in *Mt. Laurel.* (In a note the opinion argued that intention or motive was not at issue; only the effects need be examined in land use controls.)[14] However fiscal zoning—demonstrated by restrictions on number of school-age children and provisions raising house values—was held to be impermissible economic exclusion.[c] "The conclusion is irresistible that Mount Laurel permits only such middle and upper income housing as it believes will have sufficient taxable value to come close to paying its own governmental way."[15] The supreme court concluded that such fiscal zoning was widespread in suburban New Jersey. "It is also entirely clear . . . that most developing municipalities, including Mount Laurel, have not met their affirmative or negative obligations, primarily for local fiscal reasons."[16]

Exclusionary zoning practices were assigned to fiscal motives. "There cannot be the slightest doubt that the reason for this course of conduct has been to keep down local taxes on *property* (Mount Laurel is not a high tax municipality) and that the policy was carried out without regard for non-fiscal considerations with respect to *people,* either within or without its boundaries."[17] Fiscal zoning policies in developing suburban municipalities were explicitly attributed to the reliance on local property taxation in New Jersey.

> This policy of land use regulation for a fiscal end derives from New Jersey's tax structure, which has imposed on local real estate most of the cost of municipal and county government and of the primary and secondary education of the municipality's children. The latter expense is much the largest, so, basically, the fewer the school children, the lower the tax rate. Sizeable industrial and commercial ratables are eagerly sought and homes and the lots on which they are situate are required to be large enough, through minimum lot sizes and minimum floor areas, to have substantial value in order to produce greater tax

---

[c]Mount Laurel Township is located in Burlington County near Philadelphia. The 1964 zoning ordinance provided 4,121 acres for industrial use (2,800 acres more than in 1954 and about 29.2 percent of the total area, of which only about 100 acres had been occupied). An additional 169 acres (1.2 percent) were zoned commercial (most of which were occupied). Another 10,000 acres were zoned single-family detached. Townhouses and apartments were strictly excluded. Quarter- to half-acre lots were required in vacant single-family districts. Since much of the single-family land was in fact developed, the bulk of vacant land was zoned for industrial use (with specified performance standards). Average housing value in 1971 was $32,500. There were four approved Planned Unit Development arrangements in existence for at least 10,000 multifamily units. The approvals stipulated that one-bedroom units would be limited to two school-age children. The number of two-bedroom units was restricted; and developers were required to pay school costs for children in excess of an average of 0.3 per multifamily unit. In addition, various amenities, certain public facilities, and low-density development were required. *Mt. Laurel,* 336 A.2d 713 (1975).

revenues to meet school costs. Large families who cannot afford to buy large houses and must live in cheaper rental accommodations are definitely not wanted, so we find drastic bedroom restrictions for, or complete prohibition of, multi-family or other feasible housing for those of lesser income.[18]

The supreme court offered no specific solution to this fiscal problem: ". . . relief from the consequences of this tax system will have to be furnished by other branches of government. It cannot legitimately be accomplished by restricting types of housing through the zoning process in developing municipalities."[19] The court greatly constrained the limits for local land use controls.

> As a developing municipality, Mount Laurel must, by its land use regulations, make realistically possible the opportunity for an appropriate variety and choice of housing for all categories of people who may desire to live there, of course including those of low and moderate income. It must permit multifamily housing, without bedroom or similar restrictions, as well as small dwellings on very small lots, low cost housing of other types and, in general, high density zoning, without artificial and unjustifiable minimum requirements as to lot size, building size and the like, to meet the full panoply of these needs.[20]

The essential strategy envisioned in *Mt. Laurel* and the superior court decision in *Madison* is fair-share housing based on regional housing needs. Specific exclusionary devices are forbidden, and specific zoning policies are required. That strategy is considerably modified by the supreme court in its later *Madison* decision, which abandons fair-share housing plans for least-cost housing that must be achieved through least-cost zoning. No specific formulas for fair-share housing are required, because it is evident that "municipalities do not themselves have the duty to build or subsidize housing."[21] Moreover it is clearly difficult to determine regions and fair shares. The supreme court determined that compliance could be more easily obtained by compelling substantial overzoning to drive down land costs and by preventing any impediments to the construction of public housing. The court also fell back from an expectation of new private or public housing construction to a reliance on the filtering process.

> Nothing less than zoning for least cost housing will, in the indicated circumstances, satisfy the mandate of *Mount Laurel*. While compliance with that direction may not provide *newly constructed* housing for all in the lower income categories mentioned, it will nevertheless through the "filtering down" process . . . tend to augment the total supply of available housing in such manner as will indirectly provide additional and better housing for the insufficiently and inadequately housed of the region's lower income population.[22]

The Robinson Strategy

The basic thrust of the *Robinson* opinions was that property tax ratables and pupils are distributed inequitably among school districts. The supreme court found specifically that ". . . the amount of taxable real property within a district is not related to the number of students within it," and that ". . . it is clear also that State aid does not operate substantially to equalize the sums available per pupil."[23] Prior to *Robinson,* about 67 percent of school funds in New Jersey came from local property taxes, 28 percent from state aid, and 5 percent from federal aid.[24]

In school year 1971-1972 state aid to public education was distributed under the State School Incentive Equalization Aid Law of 1970, popularly known as the Bateman Act. The vast bulk of pupils (over 1 million) were located in school districts where expenditure varied between $800 and $1,200 per pupil. But 97,208 pupils were in districts spending less than $800, and 245,601 pupils were in districts spending more than $1,200. In terms of district wealth, 171,224 pupils were in districts having under $20,000 equalized valuation per pupil; 188,887 pupils were in districts having over $60,000.[25] Even with state aid, the variation in property tax rates can be easily imagined. Between 1960 and 1973 the average cost per pupil rose about 150 percent, from $405 to $1,012. The average school tax rate rose about 40 percent, from $1.43 to $2.03 per $100.[26]

It is not difficult to document the existence of substantial fiscal disparities among both municipalities and school districts in New Jersey. The evidence in *Robinson* deals solely with school districts and fails to examine tax effort in relationship to expenditures and tax base, except to observe that average school tax rates have been rising since 1960. We can reveal some additional considerations by a simple examination of county averages, aggregated over municipalities and school districts, for a comparison of local functions. Fiscal data on municipal and school functions are reported in table 2-1. The twenty-one counties in New Jersey have been ranked by total property tax rate, from lowest to highest. Then equalized valuation, equalized tax rate, local tax expenditure, state aid, and number of persons serviced are reported (on a per pupil basis for school districts and a per capita basis for municipalities).

For both school districts and municipalities a fourfold difference exists in taxable wealth between the richest and poorest counties. It is evident that taxable wealth is not distributed alike for school and municipal purposes. The underlying factors for this variation may be systematic. The basic reason is probably the relative concentration of population in urban counties and of school-age children in suburban counties. The poorer counties are concentrated in the suburban rings around New York City (Hudson, Essex, and Monmouth) and Philadelphia (Camden, Burlington, Cumberland, and Warren) and in the rural south of the state (Gloucester and Salem).

Even including state aid, there is considerable variation in expenditure per pupil and per resident. This variation is much greater for municipal functions (about six to one) than in public education. Expenditures do not vary strictly with wealth, although in general wealthier communities spend more and poorer communities spend less. Municipal expenditures are highest in the urban or industrial counties (except in the unusual case of Ocean). Although state aid rises with the decline in taxable wealth, it does not appear to offset the basic pattern set by local tax collections. State aid to education varied between $150 in Bergen and $307 in Salem. Rural counties like Cape May (which includes a Standard Metropolitan Statistical Area), Ocean, and Hunterdon received relatively higher aid per pupil than other wealthy counties. When ranked by valuation, state aid rises sharply, from $211 to $307 below about $35,000 equalized valuation. State aid for municipal functions is very low compared with aid for education, varying between $3 and $25 per capita. Such aid went primarily to urban and industrial counties.

Economic Models of the Fiscal Zoning Mechanism

Municipal zoning has been subjected recently to analysis by urban economists interested in the effects of local land use controls on resource allocation and income distribution in metropolitan areas.[27] This analysis has focused on how the local public sector influences metropolitan housing markets and residential segregation by income and race. In part, this interest is due to concern over the disparity between the locations of job growth and low-cost housing in metropolitan areas and over the role of land use controls in creating or maintaining both that disparity and fiscal differentials among local governments. However, there is also a growing consensus among urban economists that the Tiebout hypothesis may be defective on a number of grounds.[28] The critical problem in any theory of public expenditure is to determine a basis for the optimal allocation of resources between the private and public sectors. The economist uses individual preferences in the form of demand functions as a standard for determining efficient resource allocation in the private sector. By purchasing commodities in the marketplace (so much at some price per unit), consumers must necessarily reveal their preferences. In the case of public goods, however, taxpayers may rationally conceal their true preferences for public expenditures in order to avoid payment of taxes.

Tiebout solved this nonrevelation problem by observing that in a spatial economy (such as a metropolitan housing market), a household's selection of a residential community (with its specific package of public services, taxes, and community amenities) could be interpreted as revealed preference for public goods.[29] By physically moving to a particular residential location, the taxpayer necessarily reveals his preferences for public expenditures and tax levels. Local

Table 2-1
Average Fiscal Data for New Jersey School Districts and Municipalities by County (1970)

County	1970 Total Property Tax Rate	School Districts (Per Pupil Data)					Municipalities (Per Capita Data)				
		1969-1970 Equalized Valuation	1969-1970 Tax Rate	1969-1970 Tax Expenditure	1970-1971 State Aid	September 1970 Resident Enrollment	1970 Equalized Valuation	1970 Tax Rate	1970 Tax Expenditure	1970 State Aid	1970 Population
Cape May	$2.64	$87,230	$0.88	$768	$190	11,254	$16,484	$0.99	$164	$10	59,554
Bergen	2.90	55,333	1.81	1,002	150	174,229	10,347	0.64	67	4	898,012
Middlesex	3.02	36,330	1.96	712	182	128,481	7,995	0.50	40	6	583,813
Union	3.10	48,367	1.85	895	152	104,781	9,331	0.76	71	8	543,116
Passaic	3.13	39,971	1.64	656	188	88,426	7,671	0.83	64	11	460,782
Ocean	3.13	46,041	1.94	893	211	48,890	10,797	0.50	54	3	208,470
Somerset	3.17	40,413	2.21	893	187	49,523	10,089	0.39	40	5	198,372
Morris	3.18	43,606	2.17	946	182	91,170	10,368	0.53	55	4	383,454
Hunterdon	3.24	39,915	2.45	978	209	17,723	10,147	0.21	22	6	69,718
Salem	3.38	20,206	2.09	422	307	15,553	5,208	0.24	13	12	60,346
Burlington	3.39	23,418	2.32	543	288	78,038	5,656	0.37	21	5	323,132
Warren	3.42	31,513	2.20	693	232	16,976	7,241	0.30	22	8	73,879
Gloucester	3.69	22,684	2.52	572	286	42,945	5,641	0.42	24	5	172,681
Sussex	3.79	38,910	2.37	922	198	20,158	10,117	0.47	48	6	77,528
Monmouth	3.86	33,716	2.47	833	227	108,403	7,956	0.61	49	5	459,379
Mercer	3.91	35,632	2.10	748	223	55,487	6,504	0.79	52	16	303,968
Atlantic	4.04	35,227	1.72	606	224	35,117	7,067	1.27	90	9	175,043
Cumberland	4.08	20,654	2.23	461	300	28,528	4,855	0.57	28	11	121,374
Camden	4.28	25,801	2.35	606	253	96,257	5,443	0.82	45	11	456,291
Hudson	4.96	35,152	1.82	640	211	91,581	5,284	1.83	97	25	609,266

Essex	5.01	34,346	2.23	766	216	178,949	6,609	1.57	104	16	929,986
New Jersey	3.57	38,172	2.02	771	207	1,482,469	7,894	0.79	63	10	7,168,164

Sources: Total property tax rate and school district data (with the exception of 1969-1970 tax expenditure) are taken from New Jersey Education Association, *Basic Statistical Data of New Jersey School Districts, 1971 Edition* (Trenton, N.J.: July 1971), Research Bulletin A71-2, p. 32, reprinted with permission. Municipal data are calculated from New Jersey Department of Community Affairs, *Thirty-Third Annual Report of the Division of Local Government Services, 1970: Statements of Financial Condition of Counties and Municipalities* (Trenton, N.J.: 1971). Population data are taken from 1970 Census of Population and Housing.

Notes: School fiscal year is July 1 through June 30; municipal fiscal year is January 1 through December 31. Total property tax rate includes county, school, and municipal functions and tax exemptions for veterans and senior citizens. Tax expenditure for 1969-1970 is calculated from equalized valuation and tax rate for school districts. Equalized valuation per capita for 1970 is calculated from 1969-1970 equalized valuation per pupil and 1970 population. Tax rate for 1970 is calculated from equalized valuation and tax expenditure for municipalities. Tax expenditure is computed from property tax levies for local municipal purposes and does not include tax levies for veteran and senior citizen exemption.

land use controls lie at the heart of the Tiebout mechanism for solving the dilemma of how to allocate resources in the public sector where no market solution exists because "free riders" do not reveal their preferences. The essence of this Tiebout mechanism is that population size is ultimately limited by congestion costs in the provision of public services. A U-shaped average cost curve (which can be due to some fixed factor of production such as the amount of land available to a community) is mathematically required in order to produce a minimum for determining optimum size. This straightforward argument acquires considerable power when demand for public services is related to household income.[30]

A number of economists have demonstrated that land use controls theoretically permit the achievement of Pareto-optimal provision of public goods by local governments.[31] There are two particularly important versions of this fiscal zoning mechanism. The first is a formulation by Hamilton, which White terms neutral zoning; the second is White's reformulation as fiscal-squeeze zoning. The distinction is essentially between pricing of public services to new residents to cover the marginal cost imposed on the community and pricing to extract a fiscal profit from newcomers. "The particular policy under which newcomers pay exactly the marginal cost of their public services will be called *neutral zoning*. The policy under which they pay more than their costs will be called *fiscal-squeeze zoning*."[32]

The Hamilton Neutral Zoning Model

Hamilton has been a principal proponent of the fiscal motive theory and its implications for fiscal reform. The Hamilton approach is aimed at two objectives. In his view the proper strategy by which to attack suburban exclusionary zoning is not to forbid the various exclusionary land use controls, as was done in *Mt. Laurel* and *Madison*. Rather he argues that reforming local public finance as was done in *Robinson* will help to eliminate the strong fiscal incentives producing exclusionary zoning. His studies indicate that the fiscal reform he has in mind is the use of compensatory state aid for public education to poorer school districts.

> Reform, I believe, should not focus on the institution of zoning, but on the larger institution of local public finance. So long as local governments have a fiscal interest in manipulating land use, they will make a valiant effort to find a way of doing so. The tool can be zoning, building codes, selective granting of sewer permits, and so on. A legislative or judicial attack on local land use controls has two major defects in my view. First, local control over land use is so pervasive and ingrained that the probability of meaningful reform seems remote, particularly if it concentrates on a single exclusionary instrument like

zoning. Second, local land use controls perform nonfiscal roles which may be useful. Prohibition of only fiscally motivated zoning strikes me as a futile exercise.[33]

The second objective is to reconstruct the Tiebout hypothesis. In Hamilton's neutral zoning formulation, fiscal zoning is designed to keep out free riders by using minimum house value (established indirectly through restrictive zoning requirements) in a purely residential community to insure that new households pay exactly the marginal cost of their local public services. No household is permitted to move into the community unless it purchases enough housing and land to maintain the average tax base per household. Without zoning in a world where the local public sector is financed through property taxation, any household could reduce its property tax payments by simply moving into a wealthy community through minimum expenditure on housing (if we ignore transportation costs and developer preferences). Ideally the zoning ordinance would simply state this minimum house value as a direct capital-consumption requirement. But zoning does not directly regulate house value. Minimum zoning requirements exercise greater control over land than over housing value, which includes both land and capital. One implication is that very large lots may be needed to insure the appropriate minimum house value.[34]

Fiscal zoning directed toward a minimum house value introduces a system of prices for local public services into the Tiebout model. A toll or head tax that covers the marginal cost of public services is charged each entering household. This toll is collected through the minimum housing value set in the zoning ordinance.[35] Given a sufficiently large number of jurisdictions, zoning will convert the property tax into a price mechanism for local public services, based strictly on the benefit principle without any efficiency losses.[36] Neutral zoning has no effects on the housing market, according to Hamilton's analysis, because households trade off housing costs and taxes in their residential location decisions.

The White Fiscal-Squeeze Zoning Model

The Hamilton formulation is restricted to the allocation branch of the local public budget. White reformulates his original model to incorporate the distribution branch. Fiscal-squeeze zoning is designed to redistribute income from newcomers to present residents by overcharging the former for local services. Zoning ordinances not only set minimum house values through restrictive requirements to cover the marginal cost of public services but also permit suburban municipalities to exercise some degree of monopoly power as suppliers of building sites with desirable characteristics. If so, house values can be set higher than is required to cover the marginal cost of public services.

The White model must be strictly delineated from the original Hamilton formulation. The two models approach fiscal zoning quite differently. In the context of the Tiebout hypothesis, Hamilton was constrained to neutral zoning, under which newcomers cannot be exploited fiscally; the objective is rather to prevent the fiscal exploitation of present residents. With the assumption of some monopoly power over the supply of vacant land, fiscal exploitation may be practiced by present residents, if they can coordinate sufficiently to pursue their common fiscal interest and adopt such land use policies.

With the introduction of fiscal exploitation under monopoly power, the theory of fiscal zoning also becomes more complicated. Communities may engage in strategies more sophisticated than simple fiscal-squeeze zoning. Such strategies may aim to maximize the wealth of present residents in housing or vacant land by making either commodity scarce. A scarcity zoning policy is more complicated in its fiscal effects than one of fiscal-squeeze zoning. Fiscal, scarcity, and externality effects are involved. The fiscal effect involves capitalization of fiscal-squeeze transfers; the scarcity effect involves housing value changes due to supply increases with new construction; the externality effect involves the neighborhood effects on housing values of new construction.

Price Effects of Zoning Restrictions

White's analysis of fiscal-squeeze zoning is straightforward. The principal fiscal mechanism involved is a hidden tax on multifamily development that functions in the following manner. (To stick closely to the White model, let us suppose that we have a given market price and demand function for residential land that is not zoned by use categories and an inelastic supply of land for agricultural purposes. The market price in this instance ignores locational price differences and is the price of land of a given quality at a given distance from the central business district of a metropolitan area.) Equilibrium in the aggregate (total) residential land market is due to the relative price adjustments in the underlying submarkets for multifamily (which could also be called rental or lower-valued) and single-family (which could also be called owned or higher-valued) housing.

The introduction of zoning restrictions that reduce the amount of vacant land available for multifamily development and create minimum lot size categories for single-family development affects this equilibrium. Exclusionary zoning ordinances typically restrict the supply of apartment land and create separate submarkets of large and small lots for single-family housing. The result of fiscal-squeeze zoning is to alter land prices from what would be produced by market forces without zoning or by neutral zoning. Zoning restrictions on apartment use would be expected to drive up the price of such land. At the same time the price of single-family land would be driven down. The price per acre should be lowest for large lots.[37] The precise changes in price for each submarket due to supply restrictions on apartment and small single-family lots depend on the price elasticities and cross-elasticities of demand for land for various uses.[38]

Ohls, Weisberg, and White concluded that it is not possible to predict a priori the effect of such zoning restrictions on aggregate land value in individual communities.[39] To raise the aggregate value, the elasticity of demand for apartments must be less than the elasticity of demand for single-family housing and sufficiently inelastic that the rise in the value of apartment land will be greater than the fall in the value of single-family land. White shows that there seems to be contradictory evidence on the elasticity of demand for apartment land.[40] While it is conceivable that fiscal zoning would permit aggregate land value to be increased, the Ohls article concludes that zoning probably has the effect of lowering aggregate land value. The rise in apartment values is not expected to match the decline in single-family values.[41]

White points out that most suburban communities do not act as discriminating monopolists; rather they zone largely for a single lot size category.[42] This result implies that the wealth of the community held in land will decline with zoning restrictions. One result of restrictive zoning practices is to reduce the price per acre of land assigned to single-family uses. If we cannot assume under the fiscal motive theory that suburban communities act as discriminating monopolists in order to maximize fiscal-squeeze transfers, then we must assume that large lots maximize such transfers and are zoned for that purpose (obviating the need for price discrimination).

Assuming that such exclusionary zoning practices are widespread in metropolitan areas and can be enforced by suburban communities against newcomers, the allocative and distributional effects should be marked. White's principal conclusion is that "fiscal zoning . . . causes the market to undersupply low-value housing. The situation has effects on the entire metropolitan area."[43] We can place more emphasis on this conclusion by combining it with the one reached on land values. "Assuming that the community's fiscal zoning regulations are still in effect, only high-value houses can be built. Under zoning, therefore, a shortage of lower-value housing persists, while high-value housing is oversupplied on artificially low-value land."[44] It is through this precise mechanism that exclusionary effects should arise from fiscal considerations in local zoning policies, assuming the fiscal motive theory to be valid.

Fiscal zoning should lead to exclusion of lower-value housing types through land use restrictions. Industrial promotion policies will be pursued to the point where undesirable environmental effects offset desirable effects on the tax base. Both policies will be intended to obtain higher average tax base per household. Such fiscal zoning practices should result in a restriction of the total supply of lower-cost housing in a metropolitan area and presumably a rise in the price of such housing over the no-zoning situation.[45] The ultimate product of such zoning practices should be a significant degree of income segregation within metropolitan areas, because of the close correlation of housing value and income.[46] Hamilton makes this argument explicit. "The theoretical and empirical evidence on the segregation effects of fiscal zoning indicates 1) that it makes neighborhoods more homogeneous, and 2) that it increases the concentration of poor people in central cities."[47] Such income segregation may be linked to racial segregation, depending on the pattern of income distribution by race.

The exclusionary zoning hypothesis requires a demonstration that exclusionary zoning practices are not only widespread but also binding in their effects on land markets; moreover, such practices must not be simply a reflection of developer preferences (and thus indirectly of market demand). The fiscal zoning hypothesis assumes a simple and straightforward linkage between land uses and property taxes. This linkage, however, involves a number of specific conditions. First, the local public sector significantly affects income segregation and is an important consideration in residential location choices by households. Second, nonfiscal considerations—such as income and racial segregation, negative externalities from higher density development, or preservation of suburban life-style— are not very important. Third, voters and local governments can readily compute the fiscal effects of alternative development proposals. Fourth, single-family housing is fiscally superior to multifamily housing, and such superiority rises with lot size. (For the moment we may lay aside the problem of commercial and industrial ratables to focus on the fiscal strategy of purely residential communities, which is the approach taken by both Hamilton and White.)[48]

If these conditions are valid, then the Robinson strategy of increased state aid to public education ought to relieve the fiscal pressures for exclusionary zoning practices. As a corollary, the Mt. Laurel strategy of forbidding such practices ought to increase suburban housing opportunities for low- and moderate-income households, particularly as fiscal opposition to such households is reduced by state aid. These policy implications are the critical consideration in any evaluation of the fiscal motive theory. The precise issue at stake in the *Mt. Laurel* and *Madison* decisions is whether the adoption of least-cost zoning in developing municipalities will in fact affect suburban housing markets. The fiscal motive theory leads to an expectation that the Robinson strategy of increased state aid to education designed to correct for fiscal disparities after the fact will also relieve the fiscal incentives for exclusionary zoning before the fact.

An Alternative View of Fiscal Zoning

The fiscal motive theory has been enormously persuasive, although by no means entirely unchallenged.[49] The essential thrust of the theory is that specific fiscal incentives arising directly from local property taxation are responsible for exclusionary zoning practices. The rational consumer will presumably maximize utility given income and the prices of all available commodities. Since this hypothesis ordinarily implies the purchase of cheaper commodities when available (for the typical consumer), suburban voters will seek to minimize their property tax rates. Minimization of tax rates evidently requires industrial promotion and exclusion of lower-value housing types.

On closer examination, however, the fiscal motive theory reveals itself to be highly complicated. Moreover, its policy implications for fiscal and zoning reform may be quite sensitive to the underlying assumptions or conditions. This theory of suburban fiscal zoning contains a number of critical conditions that must be shown to be valid if we are to accept the theory as formulated and especially its policy implications. This position is different from one that would assert that there are not important fiscal motives in suburban zoning practices. On the contrary, such fiscal motives are given at least widespread lip service. Rather I am taking the position that these fiscal motives are different from, and more complicated than, those assumed in the simple fiscal motive theory.

If so, both the Mt. Laurel strategy and the Robinson strategy may be based on too simplistic a view of suburban fiscal concerns. The effects of least-cost zoning and state aid to public education are likely to be very different from those predicted, if the purpose of such policies is to improve suburban housing opportunities for low- and moderate-income households. The fiscal motive theory, as presently formulated, will not necessarily give the proper corrective policies. The Mt. Laurel strategy will not build low- and moderate-income housing in suburban municipalities. (It may or may not have much effect on the filtering process in the existing housing stock.) The Robinson strategy may thwart—not reinforce—this least-cost zoning policy. One empirical study of the fiscal motive theory suggests that fiscal reform may not affect exclusionary zoning practices.[50]

A similar position has been taken by the New Jersey County and Municipal Government Study Commission. Its report concluded that current state aid to municipalities has little effect on fiscal incentives and that state aid to school districts (at that time the Bateman program prior to *Robinson*) reinforced fiscal incentives to zone out multifamily housing. "State aid to education . . . tends to reinforce the local interest in maximizing the property tax revenues that are generated with each additional pupil."[51] The commission report doubts that increased state assistance would alter this picture very much.

> There is no strong evidence to suggest that any generalized changes in the fiscal rules would be likely to influence officials' thinking about the relative advantages of multifamily versus single family development. Since, for example, single family homes contain on the average far more school children per unit than do most apartments, *a school aid program, while reducing deficits from multifamily development, may in fact reduce deficits from single family homes even more!* . . . The removal of school costs, as well as that share of property tax payments

previously going to support of the educational system, substantially reverses the relative advantages of the two housing developments.

As a result, if the state does assume all educational costs, or adopts a substantially equivalent policy, an awareness of the advantages to be gained from single family development could lead many municipalities to discourage apartment construction even more strenuously than they do today, or to relegate it to the most undesirable areas, those considered unsuitable for single family construction. If fiscal policy, therefore, is to have a positive effect on the development of multi-family housing, it may well be necessary to develop a new series of fiscal policies explicitly targeted at the multifamily housing development.[52]

Assumptions of the Fiscal Motive Theory

Hypothesis 1: The Exclusionary Zoning Hypothesis. The basic assumption of the exclusionary zoning hypothesis that local governments do in fact widely practice restrictive zoning must be demonstrated empirically. If such practices are not widespread, the Mt. Laurel strategy and Robinson strategy are misdirected. The same is true if such practices are widespread but do not particularly affect metropolitan housing markets. However the argument by Hamilton and White is somewhat hypothetical. They associate observed patterns of metropolitan income segregation and suburban zoning. Their models demonstrate that income segregation may arise from fiscally designed exclusionary zoning practices. Even if it can be shown that such practices are sufficiently widespread, there are still two problems with this demonstration. First, it assumes that private developers will build suburban housing for low- and moderate-income households. Second, it assumes that suburban zoning restrictions are actually binding and do not simply reflect developer preferences.

Condition 1-1. There must be at least a demonstration that exclusionary zoning practices as defined are sufficiently widespread to influence metropolitan housing markets and produce the predicted allocative and distributional effects. *Madison* and *Mt. Laurel* rely solely on the state legislature's declaration of a statewide housing shortage in New Jersey.

Condition 1-2. A second condition of the exclusionary zoning hypothesis is that local zoning restrictions are binding on the one hand and do not reflect developer demand (which in turn presumably reflects market demand) on the other. Not only must suburban communities be attempting to practice fiscal zoning, but such a strategy must also be successful. In other words, it is local zoning practices that control community development and land use patterns. The lack of low- and moderate-income housing in suburban areas is attributable to such practices. Relaxation of land use controls should lead developers to construct such housing, due to a reduction in the costs of production through least-cost zoning as forecast in the Mt. Laurel strategy.

Hypothesis 2: The Fiscal Zoning Hypothesis. This hypothesis argues that the adoption of exclusionary zoning practices by local governments is largely forced by specific fiscal incentives under the prevailing system of local property taxation. The hypothesis asserts that such fiscal incentives lead to industrial promotion policies and exclusion of lower-valued housing. In other words, commercial or industrial ratables and large-lot homes produce the most favorable fiscal balances, and hence lowest property tax rates, for suburban communities.

Condition 2-1. It must be shown that the spatial location of income groups is affected significantly by the local public sector. A principal implication of the fiscal motive theory is that spatial patterns of income segregation in metropolitan areas are influenced by local fiscal variables. Another way of attacking this problem is to show that fiscal considerations influence the residential location decisions of households. Because direct exclusion is unconstitutional, restrictions must operate through metropolitan housing supplies and costs to affect spatial location. There are, after all, other possible explanations for observed patterns of income and racial segregation or for the lack of suburban housing opportunities for lower-income and minority groups.

Condition 2-2. Taxpayers and local governments understand or can compute the fiscal stakes of zoning decisions. Moreover the fiscal preferences of taxpayers are translated into public policy. Zoning policies are typically the result of a governmental process and do not reflect simply the aggregation of voters' preferences. In most states voters do not directly address local land use policies in referenda. Often they do not even elect zoning commissions. Land use policies are determined by the government. Thus this hypothesis assumes that the fiscal stakes of zoning decisions are well known to the voters and that local governments know or can readily compute the costs and revenues of development alternatives (and the property tax implications to the voters). If local governments did not adopt land use policies to minimize property taxes, such governments would be removed from office as an electoral sanction.

Condition 2-3. The fiscal zoning hypothesis specifically implies that single-family housing is fiscally superior to multifamily housing. Moreover, this fiscal superiority should rise with lot size for single-family housing. As a result, suburban communities will exclude multifamily housing and zone most residential land for a single-lot size. As White shows, communities practicing fiscal-squeeze zoning should set larger minimum lot sizes than those practicing neutral zoning, because fiscal-squeeze transfers should rise with lot size.

Condition 2-4. The fiscal zoning hypothesis involves the assumption that nonfiscal considerations are either not particularly important in the local zoning process or are somehow computed into property tax rates. In other words, there is no "fiscal veil" of public rhetoric concealing real (ulterior) motives at work in zoning policies. Taxpayers simply compute the property tax implications of land use alternatives and act primarily on that information in order to minimize their property taxes. Given demand for public services, tax rate minimization is the principal consideration in local zoning policies.

Hypothesis 3: The Robinson Strategy. Given the validity of the exclusionary zoning hypothesis and the fiscal zoning hypothesis, the fiscal impact of state aid to public education should be in favor of multifamily housing and smaller lot sizes by relieving the burden of public education on local property taxation, a burden that suburban communities now attempt to avoid through exclusionary zoning practices.

The Exclusionary Zoning Hypothesis

Measuring the extent and impact of exclusionary zoning practices implies that we have a well-defined and widely accepted understanding of the effects of public policies on the operation of housing markets. There is, on the contrary, considerable judicial controversy over the problem of exclusionary zoning. While the New Jersey Supreme Court has assumed that exclusionary zoning practices are widespread in suburban communities, have significant allocative and distributional effects, and are fiscally motivated, the U.S. Supreme Court has reached a very different conclusion in the *Warth* and *Arlington Heights* cases. In both decisions the U.S. Supreme Court held, in effect, that exclusionary zoning was not involved. *Warth* turned on the issue of whether local zoning ordinances have any effect on housing costs at all that significantly affects low- and moderate-income households. The Supreme Court concluded, in effect, that economic segregation was the result of market forces rather than land use controls. *Arlington Heights* turned on the issue of whether apartments generate negative externalities that affect the property values of single-family homes and are properly subject to municipal regulation on that basis.

We may need to distinguish sharply between the effects of zoning on housing costs for poorer and richer households. *Warth* asserts that income distribution determines economic segregation in metropolitan areas. Low- and moderate-income households are excluded by their income, not by the changes in housing costs induced by suburban zoning ordinances. Such ordinances may well increase housing costs in suburban areas but not necessarily at the direct expense of the poor in terms of suburban housing opportunities that they would otherwise have.

Developers rarely build unsubsidized housing affordable by low- and moderate-income households. Most low-cost housing is supplied by the filtering process in the housing market, whereby housing prices decline over time as the quality of the housing stock is decreased by aging and depreciation.[53] (*Warth* does not address the problem of filtering.) The real effect of suburban zoning ordinances on such households is probably not through restrictions on the construction of new housing, but on the price of existing housing through restrictions on the total supply of low-cost housing. We know much less about the effect of zoning policies on the filtering process than on new residential construction.[54] It is therefore open to question whether the Mt. Laurel strategy of least-cost zoning will have much impact on housing prices for low- and moderate-income households.

It is debatable how binding suburban zoning ordinances are in practice. For instance, in New Jersey only about 5 percent of vacant land is zoned multifamily, but almost half of all residential building permits are for such construction. Two devices are regularly used to control multifamily development. First, most units are approved under zoning variances. Second, such units are restricted to one and two bedrooms. In other words, multifamily construction is not prevented, but it is closely regulated by an essentially nonzoning process.[55] (These bedroom restrictions may simply reflect developer preferences for smaller apartment units to place more rental units on each site.) Schafer cites some similar evidence from two studies about the Boston metropolitan area on both minimum lot and apartment zoning, which indicates that land use controls have relatively little effect on the housing market independent of income distribution or demand and supply factors.[56]

Fiscal Incentives in Suburban Zoning

The fiscal motive theory rests on an implicit assumption that voters and local governments can reasonably conduct a policy of fiscal optimization in the control of land development. In other words, the fiscal implications of industry, apartments, and single-family lot sizes are directly calculable. There are undoubtedly fiscal considerations involved in local land use controls. But these fiscal incentives for the adoption of exclusionary zoning practices are more complicated than generally assumed and interact with important nonfiscal considerations. These factors may be too complicated to permit much in the way of fiscal optimization. The fiscal motive theory assumes that industrial promotion and single-family zoning are, relative to multifamily development, fiscally superior strategies for suburban communities. Based on this assumption, the Hamilton and White expositions (as well as the New Jersey Supreme Court) concluded that suburban communities will adopt those zoning ordinances that are fiscally optimal in the sense of minimizing property tax payments for their present residents. By that same reasoning, state aid to public education should reorient their fiscal incentives toward multifamily development.

We actually know very little about the fiscal implications of land development and population growth. The vast bulk of the fiscal-impact or cost-revenue literature consists of specific case studies. The basic problem with such case studies is that too many variables are involved that are dependent on a community's revenue and expenditure structure, population characteristics, economic base, and other particularistic factors.[57] A typical fiscal-impact study estimates the costs and revenues of a specific housing proposal for a particular community with given tax base, tax rates, and zoning ordinance. Barring exceptional circumstances, such a detailed examination of a particular housing, land use, or annexation proposal cannot be readily extended to other proposals, even in the same community.

In addition to the consideration that community characteristics vary widely, the household size and school multipliers and public service costs required for cost-revenue calculations must usually be obtained separately in each community by field surveys or from other studies with only weak justification for the transfer other than practical necessity. Therefore general conclusions are difficult to derive about the fiscal impact of land development from studies of particular communities. There is no general model of fiscal-impact analysis applicable to all situations. There is little reason to presume that suburban communities can easily practice fiscal zoning.[58]

Much of the evidence cited in the *Mt. Laurel* and *Madison* cases deals with the fiscal pressures generated by substantial population growth in suburban communities. Such evidence actually confuses two different fiscal problems or policies. The first policy is one that seeks to stop growth as such—regardless of the source of growth. The second policy is one that seeks to restrict growth to fiscally favorable land uses. The two problems are analytically distinct. *Mt. Laurel* and *Madison* lump these two policies together under the rubric of fiscal zoning. While both policies may well be fiscally motivated, this study will attempt to show that lumping them together as though fiscal zoning were a single problem with a single solution is a mistake.

Hamilton and White carry this confusion into their economic models of zoning. White argues that "*fiscal zoning* refers to zoning motivated by fiscal rather than efficiency conditions."[59] That definition covers everything in the fiscal sense, if fiscal incentives are not simple and straightforward. Any land use policy with fiscal implications then falls under the rubric of such fiscal zoning (and White discusses four different policies). The definition simply categorizes all zoning strategies as either fiscal or externality in character.

It is highly debatable that the fiscal implications of population growth can be assigned to multifamily development or single-family development or, for that matter, that commercial and industrial ratables can be treated independently of their population implications. It is population growth itself and the type of population involved in growth that are really at stake in suburban zoning battles. The linkage to particular land uses or housing types is a weak one, especially for the purpose of fiscal and zoning reform. It is also highly debatable that multifamily development is fiscally inferior to single-family development. The conventional wisdom on both issues can be challenged. As chapters 4 and 5 demonstrate, the relative fiscal impacts of multifamily and single-family development depend critically on whether we are talking about people, housing units, or acres of land. One of the basic problems in evaluating fiscal and zoning reform is determining the proper way of measuring the fiscal implications of alternative land uses.

The New Jersey County and Municipal Government Study Commission reached two conclusions about suburban reaction to multifamily development. First, it found that citizens, civic leaders, and local officials were opposed to multifamily construction. But citizens and civic leaders were much more opposed than officials, who largely perceived their constituents to be hostile to such construction. Second, it found widespread misperception of the relative fiscal impacts (as analyzed by the commission staff) of single-family and multifamily residential development. Such misperception was considerably stronger among citizens and civic leaders than among officials, who were much closer to the commission's findings. The principal implication of the commission's report was that fiscal balance is not the major issue in and of itself. Rather fiscal balance is intertwined with other factors that strongly influence suburban decisions on multifamily housing developments. Local officials in particular were found to have a favorable attitude toward the fiscal impact of multifamily development.[60]

Leaving aside any nonfiscal concerns, a different fiscal strategy, compounded of three considerations, is pursued by suburban communities. First, zoning ordinances are designed to reduce the fiscal uncertainty of land development rather than to maximize fiscal gain. In this sense communities are willing to accept neutral zoning in preference to fiscal-squeeze zoning. Second, zoning ordinances are designed to restrict population growth per se; the fiscal implications of such growth are different from those measured directly by cost-revenue techniques. Third, zoning ordinances may be designed to extract compensation for anticipated negative externalities and loss of environmental amenities. This compensation covers some nonfiscal considerations, which may include preferences for income and racial segregation.

It is a misnomer to characterize the Madison and Mt. Laurel ordinances as fiscal zoning in the sense commonly meant. The ordinances may actually ignore the directly calculable cost-revenue implications of land development. They focus instead on growth management and are designed to avoid the expected scale effects of substantial population growth; the negative externalities of multifamily development; the loss of environmental amenities; and the admission of lower-income (and perhaps racial minority) groups defined in terms of taste and externality as well as fiscal factors.

Let us look at White's fiscal-squeeze zoning model more closely. Her model for computation of the fiscal-squeeze transfer (*FST*) is stated as follows[61]

$$FST = t\, Q_A\, (P_L + E_A) - C_A\, Q_A - PCT \cdot Q_A$$

where

t = property tax rate

Q_A = number of acres developed

P_L = price of land per acre

E_A = price of improvements per acre

C_A = direct costs of public services per acre

PCT = environmental cost of land development per acre, defined as a pollution-compensating transfer

When we examine this model, we find two different fiscal problems being combined under the category of fiscal zoning. The model reduces to the argument that

$$FST = (R - C)\, Q_A - PCT \cdot Q_A$$

where R is the fiscal revenue and C is the fiscal cost per acre. It will be seen at once by the fiscal specialist that part of this formal model is identical with the kind of calculus commonly used in municipal cost-revenue or fiscal-impact analysis by local governments. Cost-revenue analysis is a set of techniques widely used to compute the costs and revenues imposed on the municipal fisc by development proposals.[62] Net revenue means that property tax rates can be reduced as ratables are added to a community (assuming that average costs do not change); net cost means that property tax rates must be raised. The second part of the model is completely different. Pollution-compensating transfers in effect require a fiscal compensation for the opportunity costs of community development.

The fiscal impact of land development calculated in the $(R - C)$ section of the White model actually combines a number of different fiscal considerations, which include (1) the immediate cash-flow implications of land use decisions, (2) the scale effects of population growth (which are mistakenly associated with multifamily or high-density development), (3) public-goods zoning problems associated with poor households, (4) the location of new development with respect to facilities and infrastructure having excess capacity, and (5) development standards for public services. In other words, five separate problems involve fiscal effects, which may well be different in character.

Cost-Revenue Zoning. The first consideration is, of course, the immediate cash-flow effects of specific housing types as calculated in the typical fiscal-impact model (which is incorporated in White's fiscal-squeeze transfer equation). However, as we shall see, this typical model may not actually measure the true costs of land development. The most important or critical assumption that underlies the cost-revenue model is that governing cost-allocation procedures. In order to compare more than a few municipalities (with different zoning ordinances, subdivision regulations, tax base and rates, service costs, growth pattern, housing mix, and population characteristics), it is necessary to use an average cost-allocation procedure. The data problems involved in a marginal (or incremental) cost-allocation procedure would be insurmountable, because exhaustive case studies would be required in each municipality. Under average costing new residents are charged the average or per capita cost of providing public services; under marginal (or incremental) costing new residents are charged those additional costs associated with their consumption of public services. Marginal and average costs may not be the same for a given development proposal.

In general, however, due to the almost insurmountable problems of incremental cost analysis, fiscal-impact studies have stuck to the average-cost approach. There is a plausible argument for this practical necessity: average costing may be more appropriate for long-range planning of residential development (assuming that the community is growing, which is the general scenario for cost-revenue analysis). A growing community that does not expand its capital facilities is simply subsisting from old capital—sooner or later, it must accept further expenditures due to depreciation, obsolescence, and lack of capacity. These necessary costs of expansion due to long-term growth cannot be strictly attributed to the new residents who happen to arrive at the time of expansion.[63]

Muller and Dawson argue that increases in local expenditures tend to proceed in a series of steps with threshold values.[64] As a result, a number of small developments would produce much the same result as a single large development, but the cost-revenue computation might well be different under a separate measurement for each development. In principle one ought to lump the small developments together, averaging their impact. In some facilities incremental costs will be greater than average (where capacity has already been reached); in others incremental costs will be lower than average (where excess capacity exists). But in the long run as a community grows, the overall pattern sticks to the projected average costs that would be expected from population size and growth, regardless of the source of the growth.

Chapter 5 indicates that fiscal zoning based on such an average-cost model is not necessarily exclusionary in character. On the contrary, garden apartments (at least those of one and two bedrooms) are found to be widely profitable in suburban New Jersey, especially on a per acre basis, even compared with single-family housing on large lots. Doubt can be cast even on the alleged fiscal efficiency of single-family zoning controls. The zoning ordinances of many suburban municipalities appear to violate these cost-revenue considerations.

There are four basic problems with the average-cost methodology. These problems make it difficult to measure fiscal impact using standard cost-revenue techniques. Housing type has a complicated relationship to these fiscal consider- ations. First, the average-cost method ignores the scale effects of population growth on the costs of public services. The average methodology may break down as a forecasting device under the pressure of substantial population growth, which affects tax rates, service costs, and tax base. The average method assumes that tax rates and service costs remain constant (or that their time path can be forecasted accurately). Rapid growth makes it difficult to assess fiscal impact because average data become unreliable.

Second, just as suburban communities demand additional compensation for multifamily development (which White measures as pollution-compensating transfers), they also anticipate greater and different costs to be imposed by low- and moderate-income households (regardless of housing type). They treat richer and poorer households differently because different costs are expected. This problem is separate from the issue of household size and number of school-age children (which is also expected to be higher for such households). If two households had exactly the same composition, suburban communities would anticipate different costs according to the income, education, and other characteristics of the household. Third, the average method implicitly assumes that public facilities, infrastructure, and services are uniformly available regard- less of the location of the proposed development. Facilities and infrastructure may, in fact, be overloaded or have considerable excess capacity in particular locations. Fourth, fiscal impact depends in part on the development standards for public services imposed by a community. These development standards may vary arbitrarily by housing type and lot size.

The Fiscal Stakes of Suburban Growth Management. A development proposal showing a break-even fiscal balance might in fact create a positive or negative cost-revenue impact because both service costs and tax rates may be increased by scale diseconomies of population growth (scale economies would lower both). The cost-revenue computation will not include these scale effects. Population growth should not be confused with scale effects.[65]

These scale effects are improperly associated with multifamily or high-density development, producing a misleading impression that regulation of housing type (rather than population growth and density) is the focus of municipal zoning practices. Growth management is the policy or objective; regulation of housing type through land use controls is the instrument. Suburban communities oppose growth and density per se, as well as any fiscal implications of growth and density. The scale effect results from population, not from housing. While housing affects how much and what kind of population is permitted in a community, that fact does not mean that a cost-revenue study will accurately include the fiscal consequences of population growth.

At some point the average assumptions employed in cost-revenue analysis will break down and be overshadowed by the scale effects of a growing population. Tax rates and service costs do not remain constant with community development. Chapter 5 employs estimates of household size and number of school-age children for garden apartments and large-lot homes in six counties of New Jersey (see table 5-1). We can extrapolate these household multipliers per dwelling unit to 1,000 units and 100 acres. For garden apartments household size varies between 2.4 and 2.6, with from 0.17 to 0.28 school-age children. For large-lot homes household size varies between 4.0 and 4.7, with from 1.5 to 1.9 school-age children. For 1,000 units the scale effects of population growth may be much more serious for large-lot homes with their higher household multipliers. Garden apartments would produce about 2,500 residents and 170 to 270 children depending on the county. Large-lot homes would produce about 4,000 to 4,600 residents and 1,500 to 1,900 children.

This example is, however, somewhat artificial. It assumes that a particular municipality has unlimited vacant land and can expand the number of dwelling units at will. The 1,000 single-family homes would cover more than 2,000 acres. For New Jersey communities the amount of available vacant land is essentially fixed. We can employ 100 acres for comparison. (Platting coefficients are 14 apartments and 0.43 homes per acre.) Garden apartments will produce enormous population growth compared with large-lot homes. We would anticipate about 3,500 residents and 240 to 390 children in garden apartments. But 100 acres would yield only 200 residents at most and 60 to 80 children in large-lot homes. This example should make it clear that the fiscal impact of a housing type depends on the context. Single-family zoning controls restrict population growth and hence the scale effect; multifamily development speeds that scale effect.

Expenditure patterns appear to be strongly dominated by population size and growth rate.[66] Community development will typically result in higher tax rates, rising expenditures per capita, and declining taxable valuation per capita. The implication is that suburban communities could see fairly obvious fiscal stakes in managing or preventing growth, different from those of cost-revenue decisions relating to particular land uses or housing types. Fiscal-impact studies ignore the long-term growth implications of particular land development proposals by assuming constant tax rates and service costs. Residential zoning controls affect housing density for a fixed supply of vacant land and hence affect both population size and growth rate.

The following example illustrates this argument. We would term a problem in growth management the different fiscal impacts of adding 1,000 or 10,000 persons to a community. This difference would be expected to be relatively large, both per capita and in total. But it would make much less difference fiscally whether we housed 1,000 or 10,000 in a single large multifamily development, a single large residential subdivision, a series of smaller multifamily developments, or a series of smaller residential subdivisions. What really matters are their numbers, demographic and socioeconomic characteristics (particularly the proportion of school-age children) and the specific location of the development. The scale effect results from the difference between an additional 1,000 or 10,000 persons, not from the particular housing type (which does affect the proportion of school-age children).

It would be easy to misinterpret these results as implying that single-family housing should show fiscal outcomes superior to those of multifamily housing under conditions of substantial population growth. The real problem is that we may too easily confuse fiscal zoning (which will involve scale effects at some point) with growth management. Fiscal zoning deals with land use decisions in terms of the fiscal implications of housing type and the role of nonresidential ratables in the tax base. It is aimed directly at controlling the composition of the tax base. Growth management deals more broadly with the scale effects of population growth, employing both zoning (as a tool for density control) and capital investment (as a regulator of developable land supply).

Multifamily development permits higher population densities per acre and thus produces scale effects sooner than single-family development. Indeed, development of sufficiently low density may prevent serious scale effects from appearing at all if vacant land is limited. Capital investment by local governments is usually lump sum in character and occurs at particular population or density thresholds. As a result, heavy capital expenditures tend to occur at particular times and not to be spread out. At some times there is overload on facilities and infrastructure; at other times there is excess capacity. The result is to influence decision makers away from such developments.

It appears that local officials attempt to postpone investment in capital facilities and infrastructure to hold down tax rates as long as possible (which is growth management rather than fiscal zoning in the strict cost-revenue sense). One easy way of doing so is to exclude large-scale development (often multifamily in character, but a large subdivision would be treated similarly), in favor of smaller proposals (whether single-family or multifamily is largely immaterial, since local officials regard multifamily development favorably on fiscal grounds). One would expect local officials to treat large-scale residential subdivisions similarly, but these occur much less often than multifamily development.[67]

Public-Goods Zoning. Fiscal zoning involves a complicated relationship among housing type, housing density, household size and age composition, and the socioeconomic characteristics of the household (assuming that we are holding constant for the moment the fiscal implications of population growth and other relevant factors). The service costs per capita and per pupil may vary by the income and social class of households (which in turn may be related to housing value and age composition). The classic example is, of course, the household living in public housing, to which there is probably the most suburban resistance.

Mills and Oates label the fiscal strategy involved (as distinct from the problems of discrimination or externalities) public-goods zoning, by which they mean controlling the characteristics of newcomers to regulate demand for public services.

Mills and Oates specifically differentiate between the strategies of public-goods zoning and fiscal zoning but hint at the possible difficulty of distinguishing their fiscal effects empirically. These two strategies are mixed together in reality.[68] For example, poor households may be likely to have both more school-age children (which is a central consideration in fiscal zoning) and children for whom compensatory education is required (which is a central consideration in public-goods zoning).

Density, Location, and Development Standards. The other two problems with the average-cost method are best considered together with housing density. The fiscal motive theory assumes that average service costs rise with population density. This relationship, however, is a matter of considerable debate, culminating in *The Costs of Sprawl* (a study conducted by the Real Estate Research Corporation for the Council on Environmental Quality, the Environmental Protection Agency, and the Department of Housing and Urban Development), which concluded that both the private and public costs of development decline with density.[69] While a study by Wheaton and Schussheim indicates considerable variation in service costs with density of development and attributes cost differences largely to density and housing type, a study conducted for the Massachusetts Department of Commerce found that lot size, at least, had little effect.[70] The New Jersey County and Municipal Government Study Commission reached much the same conclusion, attributing cost differentials to population size and growth rate rather than to housing type.

Kain reviewed a number of such cost studies, including the Wheaton-Schussheim and Massachusetts reports.[71] He rejected the argument that public service costs vary significantly with housing density per acre. Kain suggests that the critical cost factors are the location of new development and development standards. These considerations outweigh density and housing type. Kain argues that cost studies tend to confuse density, location, and standards.

One of the critical difficulties is that such studies often change development standards with density. At low densities fewer and lower-quality services are assumed; at higher densities more and higher-quality requirements are imposed. Development standards have been relatively neglected in the debate over fiscal zoning, because they are typically found in subdivision regulations rather than in zoning ordinances. Development standards can raise housing costs, just as do zoning controls. Perhaps more important, development standards can also determine the allocation of costs between the public and private sectors. Cost-revenue studies deal only with public costs, which may result from the particular development standards imposed.

Kain also strongly emphasizes the importance of the location of development with respect to existing facilities and infrastructure having excess capacity. He argues that two separate problems have been confused under the rubric of urban sprawl. The first problem is the choice between low-density and high-density development, which is the subject of *The Costs of Sprawl*. The second is the spatial distribution of development. Scattered growth may in fact take maximum advantage of existing facilities and infrastructure. Where such facilities exist, the cost of development is actually lowered.[72]

Nonfiscal Incentives in Suburban Zoning

The fiscal motive theory lays aside nonfiscal considerations as being of secondary or subordinate importance. This view may be too simplistic. The courts are beginning to discover that identifying the motives underlying zoning ordinances is a difficult proposition. A particular zoning policy may well have exclusionary (income and racial segregation), fiscal (governmental costs and revenues), externality (including tastes as well as property values), economic (income and employment), population density, and population growth effects simultaneously. If so, it may prove extremely difficult to work back from an observed effect to the motives for adoption of the particular zoning policy under review.

Zoning has traditionally been based on land use compatibility derived from the legal doctrine of nuisance. This nuisance doctrine asserts, in essence, that external economies and diseconomies (neighborhood effects) in land markets prevent achievement of Pareto optimality. Zoning invokes the governmental process to divide land into compatible districts or zones that constrain the market mechanism. Externalities and zoning constraints have effects on market values and investment decisions. An external economy presumably increases the market value of property and hence investment. An external diseconomy presumably decreases the market value of property and hence investment. Zoning is intended to classify those property features that impose negative externalities (external diseconomies) and to determine appropriate district boundaries for each classification in order to move the market toward Pareto optimality.[73]

> *Externalities zoning* refers to zoning which deals with the external effects—positive or negative—that one resident's use of land in a community may have on neighboring uses of land. The action of the private land market may not lead to an economically efficient outcome under these conditions and standard Pigovian pricing of the externality may be difficult. . . . Externalities zoning normally segregates land uses by broad categories of users, on the assumption that similar land uses have no (or only small) external effects on each other whereas dissimilar land uses may have large effects.[74]

Such externalities or neighborhood effects are laid aside in the fiscal motive theory (except as new construction affects the value of present dwellings in the same area). The general argument is that while the legal justification for zoning is the public regulation of such externalities, the motives for the adoption of the particular zoning policies found in suburban communities are fiscal. "The motives for zoning have from the beginning been primarily fiscal, but the legal justification of zoning as a limitation on the rights of private property has always been couched in externalities terms."[75]

There appears to be little evidence that such external diseconomies exist significantly in urban land markets; at least some doubt has been thrown on this doctrine and has not yet been satisfactorily refuted.[76] However, many home-owners in suburban communities are likely to regard both industry and multifamily housing as generating negative externalities or neighborhood effects. It may not be necessary for the adoption of land use controls for actual property losses to be incurred, only for homeowners to be fearful of such loss or even simply to have preferences against industry and multifamily housing.

The *Arlington Heights* opinion deals with the problem of apartment externalities. Homeowners may view apartments as generating various externalities affecting both property values and preferences in addition to the problem of public service costs. Externality and fiscal considerations may be mixed together in the exclusion of apartments. The 1962 zoning ordinance of Arlington Heights, Illinois, was found to rest on two purposes acceptable to the U.S. Supreme Court. The first was the protection of local property values thought to be dependent on existing land use classifications. The other was the use of multifamily zones to serve as a buffer between single-family and nonresidential zones.

> Many of the opponents, however, focused on the zoning aspects of the petition, stressing two arguments. First, the area always had been zoned single-family, and the neighboring citizens had built or purchased there in reliance on that classification. Rezoning threatened to cause a measurable drop in property value for neighboring sites. Second, the . . . apartment policy . . . called for . . . [multifamily] zoning primarily to serve as a buffer between single-family development and land uses thought incompatible, such as commercial or manufacturing districts.[77]

White concluded that, ". . . fiscal zoning policies do not in general lead to the same pattern of land use as externalities zoning policies."[78] However, distinguishing between the two in practice is more difficult. Ohls, Weisberg, and White attached the caveat to their analysis of supposedly fiscal zoning practices that such practices could result from negative externalities between apartments and single-family homes.[79] Consider for instance two matters that presumably ought to be of importance to suburban communities in the determination of zoning policies. The first is income and racial segregation. Even if it is true that suburban voters are concerned with the fiscal implications of income and racial integration, are we to assume that no other considerations are involved in their support of restrictive zoning practices? It is not even necessary to assume that suburban voters discriminate against the poor or racial minorities (although they may). Externalities may be a matter of preferences, rather than of actual property damages.

The issue of discrimination or preferences as a motive in local zoning policies seems to be entirely ignored in the studies and court cases dealing with fiscal zoning. The judicial opinions literally lay aside this issue. Attributing motivation for restrictive zoning practices to fiscal considerations, *Mt. Laurel* and *Madison* strike at exclusionary effects rather than any alleged motive of racial or economic discrimination. The two opinions are perfectly explicit in so stating. The cases invalidate exclusionary zoning judged on the basis of a regional comparison between housing needs and housing supply. (Housing needs and housing demand are not necessarily the same thing.) The defending municipalities in both cases cited in justification of their zoning policies fiscal and environmental reasons that were rejected by the New Jersey Supreme Court. The opinions in consequence struck hard at the doctrine of fiscal zoning and dismissed environmental considerations out of hand as a rationale for exclusion of apartments and restrictive single-family controls.

Yet it is hard in the midst of the continuing controversy over school and residential integration to accept at face value this neglect of possible discriminatory motives. It is unlikely that any defendant municipality would admit to such motives. It is equally unlikely that a state supreme court altering the very foundations of local public finance and land use regulation would openly accuse officials and voters of such motives. Hamilton does not examine racial segregation in his empirical studies. He takes the position that, "of course, there are other motivations for exclusionary zoning (such as the desire to avoid racial mixture), but the fiscal incentive to exclude poor people is strong enough to have marked effects on the way metropolitan areas are organized."[80] Schafer, however, points out that fiscal zoning ought to operate by definition on income differentials. In other words, poor whites as well as poor blacks should be excluded by fiscal zoning. On the contrary, income segregation is markedly different by race in the fifteen largest SMSAs examined by Schafer. He concludes that this difference cannot be explained by exclusionary land use controls.[81]

Of course, such evidence does not prove discrimination. It is possible in principle that self-exclusion is the motivating force in both racial and income segregation. But this evidence does indicate that, whether discrimination or self-exclusion is at work, considerations of race are involved in household location. Race appears to cut across income-segregation patterns. If so, the neat world of fiscal zoning in which no mention of race occurs must be regarded as simplistic. It is possible that exclusionary zoning is simply an indirect device for racial and income segregation without reference to the fiscal implications that are discussed in public debates and judicial proceedings. It is also possible that economic segregation is determined fully by income distribution and developer response to market demand in the complete absence of the local public sector. Exclusionary zoning practices may serve other motives. Solving the problem of intention is more difficult if tastes are compounded with overt discrimination.

There is a second nonfiscal consideration of great importance—the preservation of suburban life-styles. Suburban voters are deeply concerned over the loss of their semirural (nonurban) environment, open space, and other amenities commonly associated with suburban living. Population growth (especially high-density and multifamily growth) implies an increasingly urban environment. The utility losses imposed on present residents by the disappearance (or reduction in quality) of such amenities are not directly reflected in the property tax rate (except in the sense that tax rates may rise with population growth) or in the cost-revenue studies typically conducted by local governments to evaluate land use decisions.

White touches on these concerns in the guise of pollution-compensating transfers, by which she means that voters demand fiscal compensation for the loss of such amenities. Such compensation is not fiscal zoning in the strict sense, although revenue is collected to cover costs. Strictly speaking, these costs are the opportunity costs of development (that is, the loss of the best alternative use of vacant land), not the direct costs of delivering public services. A sharp distinction should be drawn between these two types of costs. According to White's model, fiscal-squeeze transfers cannot be bid down to zero by supplier competition because suburban communities prefer land vacant over development at zero transfer.[82] The pollution-compensating transfer is defined as a payment that will make the community indifferent on environmental grounds to a particular development proposal. In other words, tax revenues must be high enough to cover the direct costs of local public services and the opportunity costs of land development.

Tax revenue for public service costs can be computed directly, at least in principle. White treats pollution-compensating transfers on the same basis. However such transfers may incorporate tastes and externalities affecting property values as well as the true opportunity costs of population growth. They are partly subjective in character. Pollution-compensating transfers are not simply some indirect cost of environmental impact that can be computed and incorporated into property tax payments. If anything, they are more uncertain than the fiscal impact of alternative housing types, because they include nonfiscal considerations that are translated, in effect, into a demand for compensation that is very different from fiscal zoning. By fiscal zoning I mean the immediate cash-flow implications of alternative land uses under the property tax system. Demand for compensation against environmental impacts, externalities, and tastes should be treated separately (as White does in her formal model). White, however, defines as fiscal zoning any zoning policy with fiscal rather than efficiency objectives. She has thus combined fiscal, externality, and preference considerations.

The importance of such nonfiscal considerations is strongly emphasized by the New Jersey County and Municipal Government Study Commission. The commission report argues that suburban communities do not practice any strict form of fiscal zoning. Negative externalities are expected from multifamily development; positive externalities are expected from single-family development. As a result, single-family and multifamily housing are treated differently.

> We know of no municipality in which the fiscal standards established for single family houses are at all close to those set for multifamily development. Outside of the relatively loose fiscal standards implicit in large lot zoning and large floor area requirements (which are rarely established on a systematic basis to ensure a break-even or profit-making development) municipalities appear to accept single family housing on the assumption that the social benefits to be derived from having a community of homeowners are more significant than the specific fiscal credits or deficits that will occur. Presumably, the opposite reasoning process takes place when multifamily development is evaluated: are the fiscal benefits adequate to make up for what they perceive as the potential social and political harm that will occur as a result of the multifamily development?[83]

The New Jersey County and Municipal Government Study Commission makes a mistake in dealing with this issue. The report concludes that municipalities employ a "fiscal double standard" in dealing with multifamily development.[84] This term is misleading. Suburban communities presume that single-family housing adds to the community's environment and status, and that multifamily housing both subtracts from the community's environment and status and produces negative externalities. A single fiscal standard is employed, as expressed in White's formal model. However, the report is correct in arguing that there exists, ". . . a fiscal veil, that tends to obscure the other factors and issues influencing decisions on multifamily housing development."[85]

If it is the case that much of White's fiscal-squeeze transfer is actually a form of compensation rather than of fiscal exploitation, then state aid may simply replace such compensation currently exacted from multifamily development through zoning restrictions. The impact on exclusionary zoning practices may be limited, as is suggested by the New Jersey County and Municipal Government Study Commission report.

> If . . . policy makers trade off fiscal benefits against perceived social and visual disadvantages, changes in fiscal rules must provide clear and unequivocal advantages for the development of multifamily housing if

they are likely to influence local decisions and development patterns. . . . If, however, as we believe, local officials and their constitu-
encies perceive social as well as financial dangers in three and four
bedroom rental units, the removal of fiscal grounds for objection would
have only limited impact.[86]

Conclusion

In the landmark cases of *Mt. Laurel* and *Madison,* the New Jersey Supreme
Court accepted the validity of two related hypotheses about suburban zoning
practices. The exclusionary zoning hypothesis asserts that prevailing zoning
policies have significant allocative and distributional consequences. Exclusionary
zoning practices act indirectly through restrictions on the supply of building
sites to exclude low- and moderate-income households from suburban housing
opportunities. The possession of some degree of monopoly power over building
sites permits suburban communities to restrict the supply of apartment land and
to impose large minimum building requirements for single-family land. These
market restrictions discriminate against the poor because lower-cost housing is
undersupplied. At the same time, high-valued housing is oversupplied on
artificially low-valued land. The expected result of such land use restrictions
should be a significant degree of income segregation in metropolitan areas.
Moreover the price of available low-cost housing is presumably driven up by the
resulting housing shortage.

The fiscal zoning hypothesis asserts that suburban communities pursue such
restrictive policies for fiscal reasons arising largely from the prevailing system of
local property taxation. Suburban voters will seek to maintain some given level
of minimum house value (set by average service costs) in order to minimize their
property tax rates by preventing lower-value ratables from entering their
municipality. This fiscal strategy depends on the argument that certain zoning
practices widespread in suburban areas have specific fiscal effects under local
property taxation: (1) industrial promotion, involving excessive zoning for
commercial and industrial ratables, (2) exclusion of apartments, and (3) large
minimum building requirements in single-family zones.

The New Jersey Supreme Court has adopted two related strategies to
counter the effects of such exclusionary zoning policies. The Mt. Laurel strategy
forbids any zoning practices based on fiscal considerations. The fiscal implications of land use decisions must be disregarded by municipalities. They are
compelled under the recent *Madison* decision to practice least-cost zoning, by
which is meant the exact opposite of exclusionary zoning. They must make
vacant land available as cheaply as possible for the construction of low- and
moderate-income housing. The exact obligations of each municipality depend on
the regional housing market situation. The Robinson strategy seeks in part to

alleviate the fiscal incentives for noncompliance with the *Mt. Laurel* and *Madison* requirements by supplementing local property taxation for public education with substantial state aid (collected through an income tax). Hamilton is a strong proponent of this Robinson strategy. He is inclined to the view that fiscal reform is a superior instrument to zoning reform for alleviating exclusionary zoning practices by suburban communities.

Given the complexity of fiscal and nonfiscal factors involved in suburban land use decisions, there is little reason to believe that voters and local governments can readily compute the fiscal implications of alternative development proposals. These fiscal and nonfiscal considerations seem to reinforce each other. Suburban communities associate various problems with multifamily development. Nonfiscal considerations are also quite important: (1) negative externalities are expected from multifamily or high-density development (which may be a matter of tastes), (2) income and racial segregation may be practiced for their own sake, and (3) there is concern over the preservation of suburban life-style, including amenities, open space, and semirural environment.

It appears that White's pollution-compensating transfers absorb at least the scale effects of population growth and the loss of environmental amenities. There is little evidence that suburban public service costs are affected by population density, except as household characteristics are changed by the housing types constructed. Population growth, independent of housing type, may involve important scale diseconomies causing rising average costs, and lump-sum capital investments in facilities and infrastructure. Multifamily development brings these fiscal effects sooner and permits a much larger population, with consequent environmental and amenity effects. But the effects arise essentially from population, not from housing type. Cumulative single-family development should produce many of the same effects.

Suburban land use policies are adopted in this complicated environment. If zoning restrictions create a shortage of lower-value housing, they may also reduce the cost of land for single-family housing so that suburban homeowners can trade off commuting and structure costs against land costs. At the same time, suburban communities can more readily attract households desired on social as well as fiscal and environmental grounds. Excessive nonresidential and large-lot zoning serve to withhold vacant land from development and to reduce the density of permitted development. As we shall see in chapter 3, zoning restrictions are relaxed in nonresidential zones, implying that higher-density development occurs largely there, minimizing the negative externalities imposed on single-family neighborhoods.

Notes

1. Robert Schafer, *Conceptual and Empirical Problems in Measuring the Invisible Wall* (Cambridge, Mass.: Department of City and Regional Planning, Harvard University, February 1975), pp. 13-14.

2. U.S. National Commission on Urban Problems, *Building the American City* (Washington, D.C.: U.S. Government Printing Office, 1969), pp. 7-8.

3. See C.E. Elias, Jr., "Land Development and Local Public Finance," in *Essays in Urban Land Economics* (Los Angeles: Real Estate Research Program, University of California, 1966), pp. 263-272; Dick Netzer, *Economics of the Property Tax* (Washington, D.C.: Brookings Institution, 1966), "Fiscal Mercantilism," pp. 131-132; Seymour Sacks and Alan K. Campbell, "The Fiscal Zoning Game," *Municipal Finance* 36 (May 1964):140-149; Lynne B. Sagalyn and George Sternlieb, *Zoning and Housing Costs: The Impact of Land-Use Controls on Housing Price* (New Brunswick, N.J.: Center for Urban Policy Research, Rutgers University, 1972), chap. 1, "Exclusionary Development Controls: An Overview," pp. 1-19; William C. Smith, "Municipal Economy and Land Use Restrictions," *Law and Contemporary Problems* 20 (Summer 1955):481-492; Norman Williams, "The Three Systems of Land Use Control," *Rutgers Law Review* 25 (Fall 1970):80-101; Robert C. Wood, "The Local Government Response to the Urban Economy," in *City Politics and Public Policy*, ed. James Q. Wilson (New York: John Wiley, 1968), pp. 69-96.

4. Duane Windsor and Franklin J. James, "Breaking the Invisible Wall: Fiscal Reform and Municipal Land Use Regulation," in *Urban Problems and Public Policy*, ed. Robert L. Lineberry and Louis H. Masotti (Lexington, Mass.: Lexington Books, D.C. Heath and Co., 1975), chap. 9, pp. 87-105.

5. A distinction was drawn between developing and already developed municipalities. The latter are not obligated under *Mt. Laurel* and *Madison*. See Jerome G. Rose and Melvin R. Levin, "What Is a 'Developing Municipality' Within the Meaning of the *Mount Laurel* Decision?," *Real Estate Law Journal* 4 (Spring 1976):359-386.

6. Oakwood at Madison, Inc. v. Township of Madison, 283 A.2d 353,358 (1971).

7. N.J.S.A., 55:16-2 (Law of 1967, Chapter 112); cited in Madison, 283 A.2d 353,356 (1971).

8. Madison, 283 A.2d 353, 358 (1971).

9. Ibid., p. 357.

10. Ibid.

11. This regional standard is found in the original zoning case Village of Euclid v. Ambler Realty Co., 272 U.S. 365 (1926).

12. Madison, 283 A.2d 353, 357 (1971).

13. Madison, 320 A.2d 223,227 (1974).

14. Southern Burlington County N.A.A.C.P. v. Township of Mount Laurel, 336 A.2d 713, 725, n. 10 (1975).

15. Ibid., p. 730.

16. Ibid., p. 728.

17. Ibid., p. 723.

18. Ibid.

19. Ibid., p. 731.

20. Ibid., p. 731-732.

21. Madison, 371 A.2d 1192, 1200 (1977).

22. Ibid., p. 1208.

23. Robinson v. Cahill, 303 A.2d 273, 276 and 277 (1973).

24. Ibid., p. 276, citing 287 A.2d 187 (1972).

25. Robinson, 287 A.2d 187, 197, Tables I and II (1972). Data were originally taken from the New Jersey Education Association.

26. New Jersey Education Association, *Basic Statistical Data of New Jersey School Districts, 1973 Edition* (Trenton, N.J., July 1973), Bulletin A73-2; cited in David Listokin, "The Changing Framework: Educational Funding Alternatives," in *New Dimensions of Urban Planning: Growth Controls,* ed. James W. Hughes (New Brunswick, N.J.: Center for Urban Policy Research, Rutgers University, 1974), Exhibit 2, p. 127.

27. Julius Margolis, "On Municipal Land Policy for Fiscal Gains," *National Tax Journal* 9 (September 1956):247-257; "The Variation of Property Tax Rates Within a Metropolitan Region," *National Tax Journal* 9 (December 1956):326-330; "Municipal Fiscal Structure in a Metropolitan Region," *Journal of Political Economy* 65 (June 1957):226-236; "The Demand for Urban Public Services," in *Issues in Urban Economics,* ed. Harvey S. Perloff and Lowdon Wingo, Jr. (Baltimore, Md.: Johns Hopkins Press, 1968), pp. 527-565; Peter Mieszkowski, "Notes on the Economic Effects of Land-Use Regulation," in *Issues in Urban Public Finance* (Saarbrucken: Institut International de Finances Publiques, 1973), pp. 252-273; Edwin S. Mills and Wallace E. Oates, eds., *Fiscal Zoning and Land Use Controls: The Economic Issues* (Lexington, Mass.: Lexington Books, D.C. Heath and Co., 1975); Paul R. Portney, ed., *Economic Issues in Metropolitan Growth* (Baltimore, Md.: Johns Hopkins Press, 1976).

28. See Bruce W. Hamilton, Edwin S. Mills, and David Puryear, "The Tiebout Hypothesis and Residential Income Segregation," in *Fiscal Zoning and Land Use Controls,* chap. 4, pp. 101-118; James M. Buchanan and Charles J. Goetz, "Efficiency Limits of Fiscal Mobility: An Assessment of the Tiebout Model," *Journal of Public Economics* 1 (Spring 1972):25-43.

29. Charles M. Tiebout, "A Pure Theory of Local Public Expenditures," *Journal of Political Economy* 64 (October 1956):416-424.

30. Mills and Oates, "The Theory of Local Public Services and Finance: Its Relevance to Urban Fiscal and Zoning Behavior," in *Fiscal Zoning and Land Use Controls,* p. 5.

31. Bruce W. Hamilton, "Property Taxes and the Tiebout Hypothesis: Some Empirical Evidence," in *Fiscal Zoning and Land Use Controls,* chap. 2, pp. 13-30; "Zoning and Property Taxation in a System of Local Governments," *Urban Studies* 12 (June 1975):205-211; Werner Z. Hirsch, "The Efficiency of Restrictive Land Use Instruments," *Land Economics* 53 (May 1977):145-156; Takashi Negishi, "Public Expenditures Determined by Voting With One's Feet and Fiscal Profitability," *Swedish Journal of Economics* 74 (December

1972):452-458; Jon C. Sonstelie and Paul R. Portney, "Property Value Maximization as a Decision Criterion for Local Governments," in *Economic Issues in Metropolitan Growth,* ed. Paul R. Portney (Baltimore, Md.: Johns Hopkins Press, 1976), chap. 3, pp. 48-70.

32. Michelle J. White, "Fiscal Zoning in Fragmented Metropolitan Areas," in *Fiscal Zoning and Land Use Controls,* p. 31. Reprinted with permission.

33. Bruce W. Hamilton, "Property Taxation's Incentive to Fiscal Zoning," in *Property Tax Reform,* ed. George E. Peterson (Washington, D.C.: Urban Institute, 1973), p. 139. Reprinted with permission.

34. Ibid., p. 133.

35. White, "Fiscal Zoning in Fragmented Metropolitan Areas," p. 31, n.a.

36. Mills and Oates, "The Theory of Local Public Services," p. 4.

37. White, "Fiscal Zoning in Fragmented Metropolitan Areas," p. 85.

38. Ibid., pp. 80-83.

39. James C. Ohls, Richard C. Weisberg, and Michelle J. White, "The Effect of Zoning on Land Value," *Journal of Urban Economics* 1 (October 1974):428, 443; also see White, "Fiscal Zoning in Fragmented Metropolitan Areas," p. 81.

40. White, "Fiscal Zoning in Fragmented Metropolitan Areas," pp. 83-84.

41. Ohls, Weisberg, and White, "The Effect of Zoning on Land Value," pp. 432-435.

42. White, "Fiscal Zoning in Fragmented Metropolitan Areas," pp. 45-46.

43. Ibid., p. 98. Reprinted with permission.

44. Ibid.

45. Hamilton, "Property Taxation's Incentive to Fiscal Zoning," p. 138.

46. Ibid., p. 127.

47. Ibid., p. 138. Reprinted with permission.

48. For extensions to nonresidential zoning, see William A. Fischel, "Fiscal and Environmental Considerations in the Location of Firms in Suburban Communities," chap. 5, pp. 119-174, and Michelle J. White, "Firm Location in a Zoned Metropolitan Area," chap. 6, pp. 175-201, both in *Fiscal Zoning and Land Use Controls.*

49. See Richard F. Babcock, *The Zoning Game: Municipal Practices and Policies* (Madison, Wis.: University of Wisconsin Press, 1966); cited in Hamilton, "Property Taxation's Incentive to Fiscal Zoning," p. 126.

50. Eric J. Branfman, Benjamin I. Cohen, and David M. Trubek, "Measuring the Invisible Wall: Land Use Controls and the Residential Patterns of the Poor," *Yale Law Journal* 82 (January 1973):501-502.

51. New Jersey County and Municipal Government Study Commission, *Housing and Suburbs: Fiscal and Social Impact of Multifamily Development* (Trenton, N.J., October 1974), p. 8.

52. Ibid., p. 10; italics are in the original.

53. See Bernard J. Frieden, "Housing and National Urban Goals: Old Policies and New Realities," in *The Metropolitan Enigma: Inquiries into the*

Nature and Dimensions of America's "Urban Crisis," ed. James Q. Wilson (Cambridge, Mass.: Harvard University Press, 1968), chap. 6, pp. 159-204; William G. Grigsby, "Housing Markets and Public Policy," in *Urban Renewal: The Record and the Controversy,* ed. James Q. Wilson (Cambridge, Mass.: MIT Press, 1966), chap. 2, pp. 24-49; Ira S. Lowry, "Filtering and Housing Standards: A Conceptual Analysis," *Land Economics* 36 (November 1970):362-370.

54. Hamilton points out that his fiscal zoning model could be extended to include restrictions on the filtering process (that is, housing stock conversion). Hamilton, "Property Taxation's Incentive to Fiscal Zoning," p. 133. This issue is found in the recent controversy over the Belle Terre (Long Island) "anti-hippy" ordinance upheld by the U.S. Supreme Court in Village of Belle Terre v. Boraas, 416 U.S. 1 (1974).

55. New Jersey County and Municipal Government Study Commission, *Housing and Suburbs,* chap. 6, "Land Use Controls and Apartment Construction," pp. 101-115.

56. Schafer, *Conceptual and Empirical Problems,* p. 12; citing Larry Orr, "Municipal Governmental Policy and the Location of Population and Industry in a Metropolitan Area: An Econometric Study," Ph.D. diss., Massachusetts Institute of Technology, June 1967.

57. See John F. Kain, *Urban Form and the Costs of Urban Services* (Cambridge, Mass.: MIT-Harvard Joint Center for Urban Studies, Program on Regional and Urban Economics, May 1967, revised), pp. 71-72.

58. Criticism of cost-revenue methods can be found in the following: Ralph M. Barnes and George M. Raymond, "The Fiscal Approach to Land Use Planning: An Analysis of Current Surveys of the Relationship Between Various Land Use Types and the Local Tax Base," *Journal of the American Institute of Planners* 21 (Spring-Summer 1955):71-75; Laurence Dougharty et al., *Municipal Service Pricing: Impact on Fiscal Position* (Santa Monica, Calif.: Rand Corp., November 1975), chap. 2, "Cost/Revenue Analysis: A Review of Previous Research," pp. 5-11; Ruth L. Mace, *Municipal Cost-Revenue Research in the United States* (Chapel Hill, N.C.: Institute of Government, University of North Carolina, 1961), chaps. 1, 6; Thomas Muller, *Fiscal Impacts of Land Development: A Critique of Methods and Review of Issues* (Washington, D.C.: Urban Institute, 1975); William L.C. Wheaton, "Applications of Cost-Revenue Studies to Fringe Areas," *Journal of the American Institute of Planners* 25 (November 1959):170-174.

59. White, "Fiscal Zoning in Fragmented Metropolitan Areas," p. 32. Reprinted with permission.

60. New Jersey County and Municipal Government Study Commission, *Housing and Suburbs,* chap. 5, "Leadership Perceptions and Local Decisions," pp. 75-100.

61. White, "Fiscal Zoning in Fragmented Metropolitan Areas," p. 38.

62. See Mace, *Municipal Cost-Revenue Research,* chap. 1, "Background and Preview," pp. 1-27; George Sternlieb et al., *Housing Development and Municipal Costs* (New Brunswick, N.J.: Center for Urban Policy Research, Rutgers University, 1973), chap. 1, "Housing Development and Municipal Costs: A Summary," pp. 1-57.

63. This position is taken by the New Jersey County and Municipal Government Study Commission, *Housing and Suburbs;* Mace, *Municipal Cost-Revenue Research;* Sternlieb et al., *Housing Development and Municipal Costs;* Thomas Muller and Grace Dawson, *The Fiscal Impact of Residential and Commercial Development: A Case Study* (Washington, D.C.: Urban Institute, 1972).

64. Muller and Dawson, *The Fiscal Impact of Residential and Commercial Development,* p. 10; cited in New Jersey County and Municipal Government Study Commission, *Housing and Suburbs,* p. 7.

65. Muller, *Fiscal Impacts of Land Development,* pp. 19-20.

66. New Jersey County and Municipal Government Study Commission, *Housing and Suburbs,* chap. 2, "Forces and Factors Determining Municipal Expenditure Levels," pp. 13-29; Sternlieb et al., *Housing Development and Municipal Costs,* chaps. 4-6.

67. New Jersey County and Municipal Government Study Commission, *Housing and Suburbs,* pp. x-xi, 12; New Jersey County and Municipal Government Study Commission, *Housing and Suburbs: Fiscal and Social Impact of Multifamily Development. Summary of Findings, Conclusions and Recommendations* (Trenton, N.J., June 1974), pp. 4-6.

68. Mills and Oates, "The Theory of Local Public Services," pp. 7-8.

69. Real Estate Research Corporation, *The Costs of Sprawl: Environmental and Economic Costs of Alternative Residential Development Patterns at the Urban Fringe* (Washington, D.C.: U.S. Government Printing Office, 1974), 3 vols.

70. William L.C. Wheaton and Morton J. Schussheim, *The Cost of Municipal Services in Residential Areas* (Washington, D.C.: U.S. Government Printing Office, 1955); Massachusetts Department of Commerce and Massachusetts Institute of Technology, Urban and Regional Studies Section, *The Effect of Large Lot Size On Residential Development* (Washington, D.C.: Urban Land Institute, 1958).

71. Kain, *Urban Form.* Another principal study reviewed was Walter Isard and Robert E. Coughlin, *Municipal Costs and Revenues Resulting From Community Growth* (Wellesley, Mass.: Chandler-Davis, 1957).

72. Muller, *Fiscal Impacts of Land Development,* p. 22.

73. See Otto A. Davis, "Economic Elements in Municipal Zoning Decisions," *Land Economics* 39 (November 1963):375-386.

74. White, "Fiscal Zoning in Fragmented Metropolitan Areas," p. 32. Reprinted with permission.

75. Ibid., p. 33. Reprinted with permission.

76. Two recent empirical investigations, conducted with sample data from Pittsburgh census tracts, cast doubt on the existence of such negative externalities: John P. Crecine, Otto A. Davis, and John E. Jackson, "Urban Property Markets: Some Empirical Results and Their Implications for Municipal Zoning," *Journal of Law and Economics* 10 (October 1967):79-99; Frederick H. Rueter, "Externalities in Urban Property Markets: An Empirical Test of the Zoning Ordinance of Pittsburgh," *Journal of Law and Economics* 16 (October 1973):313-349. These studies suggest that a natural process of self-selection in locational decisions may remove interdependence from property markets without zoning. They also suggest that most externalities are a matter of taste, except for noise, smoke, and pollution from commercial and industrial activities.

77. Metropolitan Housing Development Corp. v. Village of Arlington Heights, 429 U.S. 252, 258 (1977).

78. White, "Fiscal Zoning in Fragmented Metropolitan Areas," p. 32. Reprinted with permission.

79. Ohls, Weisberg, and White, "Effect of Zoning on Land Value," p. 433, n. 7.

80. Hamilton, "Property Taxation's Incentive to Fiscal Zoning," p. 125. Reprinted with permission.

81. Schafer, *Conceptual and Empirical Problems,* p. 14; see Table 1, p. 16.

82. White, "Fiscal Zoning in Fragmented Metropolitan Areas," p. 42.

83. New Jersey County and Municipal Government Study Commission, *Housing and Suburbs,* pp. 10, 12.

84. See New Jersey County and Municipal Government Study Commission, *Summary of Findings, Conclusions and Recommendations,* pp. 6, 8.

85. New Jersey County and Municipal Government Study Commission, *Housing and Suburbs,* p. 12.

86. Ibid., pp. 9-10.

3 Exclusionary Zoning in Suburban Communities

This chapter reviews empirical evidence from New Jersey on the exclusionary zoning hypothesis. That hypothesis involves two conditions. First, exclusionary zoning practices must be sufficiently widespread to influence metropolitan housing markets and produce the predicted allocative and distributional effects. Second, local zoning restrictions must be binding on the one hand and not simply reflective of developer requirements on the other, so that the restrictions are actually effective in controlling community development and land use patterns. In other words, it is local zoning that regulates the supply of developable land. These two assumptions are minimum conditions even for the fiscal view of exclusionary zoning practices taken by the New Jersey Supreme Court.

In 1970 the New Jersey Department of Community Affairs surveyed and reported all current zoning ordinances in seventeen of the state's twenty-one counties.[1] The survey report contains information for each municipality in the seventeen counties on acres of vacant, developable land zoned for industrial, commercial, research and office, or residential use. In each county surveyed, municipalities that were 90 to 100 percent developed (including virtually all of Hudson County opposite New York City) were excluded from the survey report. Hudson contained only vacant industrial land.[2] In both residential and nonresidential categories there is a breakdown by number of acres zoned for single-family, multifamily, and mobile home uses. For single-family districts in all categories there is detailed information on provisions regulating minimum lot size, lot width (or frontage), and livable floor area (or building size).[3] This report provides information on the supply of vacant, developable land by municipality in the surveyed counties. Partial zoning reports are available for 1960 and 1967, so we can examine changes over time in nonresidential, multifamily, and lot size requirements.

We can also examine the demand for vacant, developable land in New Jersey through annual state reports on industrial or commercial construction plans and residential building permits. Although permits are issued by municipalities in New Jersey (which thus regulate both supply and demand), these reports give a rough idea of the relationship between supply and demand (in quantity of land). In addition, employment by county has been projected to 1980 for New Jersey by James and Hughes, so that we can also roughly gauge the likely growth pressures underlying the formation of demand for residential land.[4] *Mt. Laurel* and *Madison* tie zoning to employment as a standard for judging fair-share allocation plans on a regional basis.

This supply and demand information allows us to address three questions. First, what are the zoning patterns in New Jersey, as reported in the 1970 survey? Can we characterize the allocations of vacant land as likely to produce exclusionary effects (assuming that developers were willing to construct low- and moderate-income housing and leaving aside for the moment the filtering issue)? This position is taken by the New Jersey Supreme Court in *Mt. Laurel* and *Madison.* Second, what have been the historical trends in zoning policies since 1960? Has there been increased restrictiveness in suburban areas? Third, are these suburban zoning policies effective and binding? If zoning regulations have an effect on the supplies and prices of low- and moderate-income housing, then their removal should provide some degree of relief. We must consider the issues of developer preferences and housing stock filtering previously laid aside.

The principal land use policies may be classified into three main categories, which can be arranged hierarchically in terms of exclusionary effects.[5] This hierarchy is based on the model of price effects discussed in chapter 2. First, the breakdown between residential and nonresidential uses can have restrictive effects on the housing market, by reducing directly the amount of vacant land available for all residential uses. This device was an important consideration in the *Mt. Laurel* and *Madison* decisions. (The allocation of some, but rarely very much, nonresidential land to secondarily permitted residential uses may have a mitigating impact on these restrictive effects but hardly eliminates them.)

Second, the decision to exclude or restrict multifamily dwellings and mobile homes (and under what conditions) affects the supply of vacant land available for lower-cost housing types. Devices such as exclusion of, or quotas for, multifamily dwellings or mobile homes, as well as restrictions on number of bedrooms may be included here. Third, the controls imposed on the development of land in single-family districts have restrictive effects on the supply of vacant land available for lower-cost homes. Devices such as minimum building size, lot width, and lot size requirements may be included here. It is important to consider such devices together because they can interact in their restrictive effects. Larger lots typically (but not necessarily) are also wider and have large minimum building size requirements.[6]

1970 Zoning Patterns in New Jersey

Table 3-1 reports 1970 municipal zoning ordinances aggregated by county for the seventeen surveyed counties, using square-mile data which are converted into percentages in table 3-2. Industrial zoning in part of Hudson County is included. Of the 1,763,763 acres zoned for development in 1970, just under 19 percent was zoned for nonresidential uses (industrial, commercial, office and research).

Table 3-1
Zoning of Developable Land in New Jersey (1970)

County	Vacant Land in Square Miles	Residential Districts				Nonresidential Districts			
		Single Family	Multi-family	Mobile Homes	Subtotal	Commercial	Industrial	Office and Research	Subtotal
Atlantic		Not in survey				Not in survey			
Bergen	53.78	35.76	0.22		35.98	2.15	14.16	1.49	17.80
Burlington	395.64	308.54	21.09	0.44	330.07	19.54	45.77	0.26	65.57
Camden	95.69	41.29	28.12		69.41	3.69	22.49	0.10	26.28
Cape May		Not in survey				Not in survey			
Cumberland		Not in survey				Not in survey			
Essex	14.01	9.91	0.11		10.02	1.12	1.79	1.08	3.99
Gloucester	212.90	122.22	43.41	1.13	166.76	9.58	35.56	1.00	46.14
Hudson	5.97	No residential land					5.97		5.97
Hunterdon	287.89	262.85	0.67		263.52	7.65	13.91	2.81	24.37
Mercer	134.43	105.49	1.09	0.04	106.62	3.72	21.90	2.19	27.81
Middlesex	162.14	88.25	0.48		88.73	5.79	65.45	2.17	73.41
Monmouth	296.87	241.10	0.99		242.09	16.96	36.67	1.15	54.78
Morris	200.82	164.51	2.07		166.58	4.66	20.22	9.36	34.24
Ocean	288.46	226.39	17.11		243.50	8.03	36.62	0.31	44.96
Passaic	41.30	28.88	1.38		30.26	2.12	7.20	1.72	11.04
Salem		Not in survey				Not in survey			
Somerset	167.04	136.69			136.69	2.94	22.50	4.91	30.35
Sussex	202.97	170.93	12.98	0.06	183.97	4.65	13.91	0.44	19.00
Union	9.94	6.89	0.52		7.41	0.51	1.57	0.45	2.53
Warren	182.70	145.23	9.10		154.33	6.65	21.02	0.70	28.37
New Jersey	2752.55	2094.93	139.34	1.67	2235.94	99.76	386.71	30.14	516.61

Source: New Jersey Department of Community Affairs, "1970 Zoning Survey" (Trenton, N.J., 1971).

Note: Square mileage data are computed from acres and subject to minor rounding error.

Table 3-2
Percentage Table for Zoning of Developable Land in New Jersey (1970)

County	Vacant Land in Square Miles	Residential Districts				Commercial	Nonresidential Districts		
		Single Family	Multi-family	Mobile Homes	Subtotal		Industrial	Office and Research	Subtotal
Atlantic		Not in survey					Not in survey		
Bergen	100.0	66.5	0.4		66.9	4.0	26.3	2.8	33.1
Burlington	100.0	78.0	5.3	0.1	83.4	4.9	11.6	0.1	16.6
Camden	100.0	43.1	29.4		72.5	3.9	23.5	0.1	27.5
Cape May		Not in survey					Not in survey		
Cumberland		Not in survey					Not in survey		
Essex	100.0	70.7	0.8		71.5	8.0	12.8	7.7	28.5
Gloucester	100.0	57.4	20.4	0.5	78.3	4.5	16.7	0.5	21.7
Hudson	100.0	No residential land					100.0		100.0
Hunterdon	100.0	91.3	0.2		91.5	2.7	4.8	1.0	8.5
Mercer	100.0	78.5	0.8	a	79.3	2.8	16.3	1.6	20.7
Middlesex	100.0	54.4	0.3		54.7	3.6	40.4	1.3	45.3
Monmouth	100.0	81.2	0.3		81.5	5.7	12.4	0.4	18.5
Morris	100.0	81.9	1.0		82.9	2.3	10.1	4.7	17.1
Ocean	100.0	78.5	5.9		84.4	2.8	12.7	0.1	15.6
Passaic	100.0	69.9	3.3		73.2	5.1	17.4	4.2	26.7
Salem		Not in survey					Not in survey		
Somerset	100.0	81.8			81.8	1.8	13.5	2.9	18.2
Sussex	100.0	84.2	6.4	a	90.6	2.3	6.9	0.2	9.4
Union	100.0	69.3	5.2		74.5	5.1	15.8	4.5	25.4
Warren	100.0	79.5	5.0		84.5	3.6	11.5	0.4	15.5
New Jersey	100.0	76.1	5.1	0.1	81.3	3.6	14.0	1.1	18.7

Source: Table 3-1.

Note: All data are percentages and rounded to the nearest tenth.

aLess than 0.1 percent.

About 5.1 percent was zoned for multifamily and only 0.06 percent for mobile homes. About 76.1 percent was zoned single-family. However, exclusionary zoning is not indicated simply by such proportions. Rather land uses must be restricted vis-à-vis demand.

Excessive Commercial and Industrial Zoning

The first exclusionary device is excessive zoning for nonresidential purposes. About 332,784 acres were zoned for such uses in 1970. As table 3-3 reveals, the nonresidential zoning pattern varied greatly by region within New Jersey. The seventeen counties in the 1970 zoning survey have been grouped into four regions for greater ease of presentation in the analysis of zoning patterns. The principal purpose of this grouping is to permit comparison of the other regions with the six study counties that are used in chapter 5 for the fiscal evaluation of suburban zoning ordinances.

The study counties (Bergen, Middlesex, Monmouth, Morris, Ocean, and Somerset) cover the suburban center of New Jersey. The selection of this region was constrained largely by the availability of critical data on new single-family construction. The northeast region adjacent to New York City includes Essex, Hudson, Passaic, and Union. The northwest region includes Hunterdon, Sussex, and Warren. The southwest region adjacent to Philadelphia includes Burlington, Camden, Gloucester, and Mercer. The four excluded counties (Atlantic, Cape May, Cumberland, and Salem) form the southeast region.[7]

The northeast counties opposite New York City had the greatest proportion of nonresidential zoning at 36.1 percent, followed by the study counties at 21.9 percent and the southwest counties opposite Philadelphia at 19.8 percent. The northwest counties strongly emphasized residential zoning with only 10.6 percent nonresidential land. The use of county and regional aggregation raises the problem that the reported results may average different kinds of munici-

Table 3-3
Zoning of Vacant Nonresidential Land in New Jersey (1970)
(in acres and percentages)

Region	Total Area	Residential Uses		Nonresidential Uses	
Study counties	748,220	584,660	78.1%	163,560	21.9%
Northeast	47,729	30,520	63.9	17,209	36.1
Northwest	431,075	385,167	89.4	45,908	10.6
Southwest	536,739	430,632	80.2	106,107	19.8
Total	1,763,763	1,430,979	81.1	332,784	18.9

Source: New Jersey Department of Community Affairs, "1970 Zoning Survey" (Trenton, N.J., 1971).

palities. Most municipal ordinances follow these reported county and regional patterns.

These figures, while interesting, are somewhat deceptive, because they reflect only the supply side of zoning for vacant land. Supply must be compared with demand to determine whether restrictive effects are due to governmental regulation rather than to market forces. We may roughly estimate the magnitude of demand for nonresidential land by looking at commercial and industrial construction plans approved in New Jersey over the five-year period 1970 to 1974.[8]

These data are reported annually by the state of New Jersey as number of plans approved and square feet of floor area involved. Floor area is converted to estimated acres using the simple procedure of assuming that site requirements double required acreage.[9] In the seventeen counties a total of 5,360 acres (based on 116,769,000 square feet of floor area in 4,468 approved plans) would have been required during 1970 to 1974 or about 1.6 percent of the 332,784 acres zoned for nonresidential uses in 1970. This figure indicates that even if doubling were a gross underestimate of land requirements, relatively little land was being used annually. Within fairly wide limits, the weighting factor assumed for converting floor area to land acreage is probably unimportant.

The requirements were barely higher in the study counties, with 2,866 acres (based on 62,425,000 square feet in 2,002 plans) or 1.8 percent of the 163,560 nonresidential acres zoned. The northeast counties had the highest rate of land conversion, at 1,306 acres (28,436,000 square feet in 1,345 plans), which is 7.6 percent of the 17,209 acres zoned. The northwest and southwest had lower rates of land conversion. The southwest used 1,038 acres (22,623,000 square feet in 917 plans) or 1.0 percent of the 106,107 acres zoned. The northwest had very little commercial and industrial growth, using 150 acres (3,285,000 square feet in 204 plans), a mere 0.3 percent of the 45,908 acres zoned. (Based on 120,835,000 square feet in 264 plans, about 2,774 acres would have been used in the southeast counties, for which there are no zoning data.)

However, 37 percent of the 332,784 vacant nonresidential acres in the surveyed counties permitted some secondary residential uses in 1970 (making 123,116 acres available). This secondary allocation varied from 56.6 percent in the northeast (1,874 of 17,209 acres). The study counties allocated 28.5 percent of nonresidential land to secondary residential uses (46,642 of 163,560 acres). The northwest was slightly more flexible, allocating 31.7 percent (14,547 of 45,908 acres). Secondary residential uses must be permitted in nonresidential districts in New Jersey, under *Katobimar Realty Co. v. Webster.*[10]

Exclusion of Multifamily Dwellings
and Mobile Homes

The second exclusionary device is the restriction of multifamily structures and mobile homes in many suburban zoning ordinances. Data on the zoning of residential land into single-family, multifamily, and mobile home districts are reported in table 3-4, for both primary residential zones and secondary residential uses in nonresidential zones. In 1970 there were only 89,175 acres zoned multifamily (6.2 percent of 1,430,979 residential acres) and 1,072 acres zoned mobile home (0.07 percent). There were an additional 12,520 acres (10.2 percent of the 123,116 nonresidential acres permitting secondary residential uses) of multifamily and 184 acres (0.1 percent) of mobile home land permitted as secondary uses. Hence there was a total of 101,695 acres available for multifamily (6.5 percent of 1,554,095 residential acres) and 1,256 acres for mobile home (0.1 percent) purposes.

This pattern did not vary particularly by region of the state, except in the southwest which was zoned more heavily multifamily (13.9 percent of residential districts). The study counties were the most restrictive in their residential zoning patterns, with only 2.3 percent (13,354 acres) of primary residential land zoned multifamily and none mobile home. This restrictive pattern was generally relaxed in all regions in nonresidential districts. The study counties zoned 9.5 percent of the nonresidential land permitting residential uses multifamily (4,419

Table 3-4
Zoning of Vacant Residential Land in New Jersey (1970)

Region	Number of Acres				Percentage Distribution			
	Total Area in Acres	Single Family	Multi-family	Mobile Homes	Total Area in Acres	Single Family	Multi-family	Mobile Homes
	Residential districts							
Study counties	584,660	571,306	13,354	–	100.0	97.7	2.3	–
Northeast	30,520	29,234	1,286	–	100.0	95.8	4.2	–
Northwest	385,167	370,567	14,562	38	100.0	96.2	3.8	a
Southwest	430,632	369,625	59,973	1,034	100.0	85.8	13.9	0.2
Total	1,430,979	1,340,732	89,175	1,072	100.0	93.7	6.2	0.1
	Residential uses in nonresidential districts							
Study counties	46,642	42,103	4,419	120	100.0	90.3	9.5	0.3
Northeast	1,874	1,343	531	–	100.0	71.7	28.3	–
Northwest	14,547	13,003	1,544	–	100.0	89.4	10.6	–
Southwest	60,053	53,963	6,026	64	100.0	89.9	10.0	0.1
Total	123,116	110,412	12,520	184	100.0	89.7	10.2	0.1
	Total residential land							
Study counties	631,302	613,409	17,773	120	100.0	97.2	2.8	a
Northeast	32,394	30,577	1,817	–	100.0	94.4	5.6	–
Northwest	399,714	383,570	16,106	38	100.0	96.0	4.0	a
Southwest	490,685	423,588	65,999	1,098	100.0	86.3	13.5	0.2
Total	1,554,095	1,451,144	101,695	1,256	100.0	93.4	6.5	0.1

Source: New Jersey Department of Community Affairs, "1970 Zoning Survey" (Trenton, N.J., 1971).
aLess than 0.1 percent.

acres) and 0.3 percent mobile home (120 acres). The northeast counties zoned 28.3 percent of such land multifamily.

As in the case of nonresidential land uses, we can evaluate restrictions on the supply of vacant land for residential uses only by reference to the expected demand for such land. We may do so by looking at residential construction authorized by building permits over the five-year period 1970 to 1974. It is necessary to convert these building permit data into estimates of required acreage.[11] However, we require only a rough measure of the acreage being used for residential development. Regional summaries of estimated acreage required by authorized building permits (1970 to 1974) are reported in table 3-5.[12] An estimated 140,792 acres were required by the building permits issued over the five-year period 1970 to 1974. Of that amount, 95.3 percent was for single-

Table 3-5
Estimated Residential Land Required by Authorized Building Permits in New Jersey (1970-1974)

	Number of Acres			Percentage Distribution		
Region	Total	Single Family	Multi-family	Total	Single Family	Multi-family
	Estimated acreage required by building permits					
Study counties	84,441	81,424	3,017	100.0	96.4	3.6
Northeast	7,912	6,669	1,243	100.0	84.3	15.7
Northwest	17,602	17,317	285	100.0	98.4	1.6
Southwest	30,837	28,747	2,090	100.0	93.2	6.8
Total	140,792	134,157	6,635	100.0	95.3	4.7
	Housing capacity of primary residential districts					
Study counties	584,660	571,306	13,354	100.0	97.7	2.3
Northeast	30,520	29,234	1,286	100.0	95.8	4.2
Northwest	385,129	370,567	14,562	100.0	96.2	3.8
Southwest	429,598	369,625	59,973	100.0	86.0	14.0
Total	1,429,907	1,340,732	89,175	100.0	93.8	6.2
	Housing capacity including secondary residential uses					
Study counties	631,182	613,409	17,773	100.0	97.2	2.8
Northeast	32,394	30,577	1,817	100.0	94.4	5.6
Northwest	399,676	383,570	16,106	100.0	96.0	4.0
Southwest	489,587	423,588	65,999	100.0	86.5	13.5
Total	1,552,839	1,451,144	101,695	100.0	93.5	6.5

Sources: Dwelling unit estimates are taken from New Jersey Department of Labor and Industry, *New Jersey Residential Building Permits: 1974 Annual Summary* (Trenton, N.J., 1974). These are converted to estimated acreage using platting coefficients from Franklin J. James and James W. Hughes, *Modeling State Growth: New Jersey 1980* (New Brunswick, N.J.: Center for Urban Policy Research, Rutgers University, 1973), p. 92. Zoning data are taken from table 3-4.

Note: Platting coefficients are 14 garden apartments; quarter-acre lots 2.42; half-acre lots 1.80; acre lots 1.01; larger lots 0.43 units per acre.

family uses, and 4.7 percent was for multifamily uses. Roughly the same pattern was followed in all regions except the northeast, where 15.7 percent of the required land was for multifamily uses.

If we look at the supply of vacant land (measured as either zoned residential capacity in primary residential districts or total residential capacity including residential uses permitted in nonresidential districts), the distribution of total available supply between single-family and multifamily uses appears to match roughly the distribution of demand for vacant land (as estimated by conversion from building permits). However, considerable regional imbalances are evident. In the northeast the zoning patterns strongly emphasized single-family uses (with only 4 percent to 6 percent multifamily in either zoned or total residential capacity), even though 15.7 percent of required residential land was going to multifamily uses. On the other hand, in the southwest much more land was zoned for multifamily use (about 14 percent), even though only 6.8 percent of required acreage was multifamily.

Single-Family Zoning Controls

The third exclusionary device consists of various controls on single-family uses, especially minimum requirements for lot size, lot width, and building size. These requirements can (but do not necessarily) match one another and interact. Table 3-6 compares these three sets of requirements for each region using percentage distributions based on number of acres. The data include both primary residential districts and secondary-use possibilities in nonresidential districts.

Primary Residential Districts. In the study counties almost three-quarters of vacant single-family land was zoned for one acre or greater lots (with 8.1 percent over three acres). Only 12 percent was zoned under a half-acre. The northwest counties had almost 80 percent large lot zoning (with 17.6 percent over three acres) and only 3.8 percent under a half-acre. There was, however, a strong emphasis on small lot sizes under a half-acre in the northeast (44.2 percent), with only 33.2 percent zoned over an acre. The next closest region was the southwest, with 27.1 percent zoned under a half-acre and 45.8 percent over an acre. This pattern is probably consistent with that region's stronger emphasis on multifamily housing.

There is similarly a strong emphasis on wide lots in the study counties (62.2 percent over 150 feet, including 37.6 percent over 200 feet). Only 10.1 percent of the land was zoned under 99 feet. The northwest also emphasized wide lots (85.9 percent over 150 feet, including 49.8 percent over 200 feet), with little scope for narrow lots (only 4.9 percent was under 99 feet). The northeast (80.6 percent) and southwest (59.1 percent) emphasized lot widths under 150 feet, principally between 100 and 149 feet. All regions, however, strongly emphasized

Table 3-6
Comparison of Single-Family Zoning Controls in New Jersey (1970)

Region	Total Acres		Minimum Lot Size (in acres)				
			0-0.24	0.25-0.49	0.50-0.99	1-2.99	3 or More
Study counties	613,409	100.0%	33,341 5.4%	40,353 6.6%	93,511 15.2%	396,387 64.6%	49,817 8.1%
Northeast	30,577	100.0	3,514 11.5	10,001 32.7	6,894 22.5	6,276 20.5	3,892 12.7
Northwest	383,570	100.0	3,358 0.9	11,202 2.9	65,222 17.0	236,301 61.6	67,487 17.6
Southwest	423,588	100.0	34,709 8.2	79,996 18.9	115,136 27.2	141,387 33.4	52,360 12.4
Total	1,451,144	100.0	74,922 5.2	141,552 9.8	280,763 19.3	780,351 53.8	173,556 12.0

Region	Total Acres[a]		Minimum Lot Width (in feet)				
			0-49	50-99	100-149	150-199	200 or More
Study counties	613,383	100.0%	15,832 2.6%	45,846 7.5%	170,134 27.7%	151,046 24.6%	230,525 37.6
Northeast	30,577	100.0	3,578 11.7	5,407 17.7	15,652 51.2	2,879 9.4	3,061 10.0
Northwest	383,570	100.0	6,476 1.7	12,224 3.2	35,509 9.3	138,404 36.1	190,957 49.8
Southwest	423,588	100.0	935 0.2	74,612 17.6	174,794 41.3	65,995 15.6	107,252 25.3
Total	1,451,118	100.0	26,821 1.8	138,089 9.5	396,089 27.3	358,324 24.7	531,795 36.6

Region	Total Acres[a]		Minimum Building Size (in square feet)				
			None	0-699	700-999	1,000-1,599	1,600 or More
Study counties	613,383	100.0%	6,827 1.1%	17,515 2.9%	129,330 21.1%	396,667 64.7%	63,044 10.3%
Northeast	30,577	100.0	4,227 13.8	96 0.3	4,006 13.1	21,507 70.3	741 2.4
Northwest	383,570	100.0	44,013 11.5	1,619 0.4	132,568 34.6	204,711 53.4	659 0.2
Southwest	423,588	100.0	61,040 14.4	18,932 4.5	78,188 18.5	251,381 59.3	14,047 3.3
Total	1,451,118	100.0	116,107 8.0	38,162 2.6	344,092 23.7	874,266 60.2	78,491 5.4

Source: New Jersey Department of Community Affairs, "1970 Zoning Survey" (Trenton, N.J., 1971).
[a]Lot width and building size requirements were not reported for twenty-six acres in one municipality in the study counties.

buildings of at least 1,000 square feet, especially the study counties (75 percent) and the northeast (72.7 percent), with the northwest and southwest both over 50 percent. Very little land was zoned for residences under 700 square feet in the study counties (4 percent), with 12 percent to 19 percent so zoned in other regions. The study and northwest counties were characterized by large lot sizes, lot widths, and building sizes. The requirements were more relaxed in the northeast and southwest, except for lot size.

Relaxation of Zoning Controls in Nonresidential Districts. The data just analyzed combined residential and nonresidential districts. Zoning controls over single-family uses are widely relaxed in the nonresidential districts, as was the case with multifamily and mobile home controls. Lot width and building size requirements were reported in the New Jersey survey only for total vacant land. However lot size requirements were reported separately for residential and nonresidential districts. We may use these lot size data, presented in table 3-7, to examine the extent of relaxation in zoning controls.

In the seventeen counties overall 67.1 percent of single-family land (899,302 acres) was zoned over an acre in residential districts, with 14.1 percent (188,663 acres) zoned under a half-acre. In contrast only 49.4 percent of single-family land (54,605 acres) was zoned over an acre in nonresidential districts, and 25.2 percent (27,811 acres) was zoned under a half-acre. These figures indicate a clear relaxation in lot size requirements between the two types of districts. The degree of relaxation varies considerably by region. In the study counties 74.7 percent was zoned over an acre in residential districts (and 11.4 percent under a half-acre), with 46.2 percent over an acre in nonresidential districts (and 33.8 percent between a half-acre and an acre).

Historical Zoning Patterns (1960-1970)

There is some evidence available on the change over time in zoning patterns by county in New Jersey. For eight counties (including all the study counties except Ocean), the Regional Plan Association (RPA) published certain zoning data for 1960.[13] We can thus compare zoning patterns in these eight counties (Hudson has been dropped) between 1960 and 1970. These data are reported in table 3-8. In each year total vacant land, reported in thousands of acres, has been divided into nonresidential, multifamily, and single-family uses. The residential acreages reported here are for primary residential districts only.

In 1960 there were 733,800 acres of nonresidential, multifamily, and single-family land available for development in the study counties (excluding Ocean); by 1970 this figure had declined to 557,100 acres. The declines occurred in the multifamily (from 4,200 to 2,300 acres) and single-family (from 638,300 to 426,500 acres) categories. Nonresidential zoning rose from 91,300 to

Table 3-7
Minimum Lot Size Requirements in New Jersey (1970)

Region	Total Acres	0-0.24 Acre	0.25-0.49 Acre	0.50-0.99 Acre	1-2.99 Acre	3 or More Acres
		Number of Acres				
Single-family districts						
Study Counties	571,306	30,398	34,866	79,289	380,738	46,015
Northeast	29,234	3,392	8,780	6,894	6,276	3,892
Northwest	370,567	3,147	8,866	63,141	232,464	62,949
Southwest	369,625	30,892	68,322	103,443	114,896	52,072
Total	1,340,732	67,829	120,834	252,767	734,374	164,928
Nonresidential districts						
Study Counties	42,103	2,943	5,487	14,222	15,649	3,802
Northeast	1,343	122	1,221			
Northwest	13,003	211	2,336	2,081	3,837	4,538
Southwest	53,963	3,817	11,674	11,693	26,491	288
Total	110,412	7,093	20,718	27,996	45,977	8,628
		Percentage Distribution				
Single-family districts						
Study Counties	100.0	5.3	6.1	13.9	66.6	8.1
Northeast	100.0	11.6	30.0	23.6	21.5	13.3
Northwest	100.0	0.8	2.4	17.0	62.7	17.0
Southwest	100.0	8.4	18.5	28.0	31.1	14.1
Total	100.0	5.1	9.0	18.9	54.8	12.3
Nonresidential districts						
Study Counties	100.0	7.0	13.0	33.8	37.2	9.0
Northeast	100.0	9.1	90.9			
Northwest	100.0	1.6	18.0	16.0	29.5	34.9
Southwest	100.0	7.1	21.6	21.7	49.1	0.5
Total	100.0	6.4	18.8	25.4	41.6	7.8

Source: New Jersey Department of Community Affairs, "1970 Zoning Survey" (Trenton, N.J., 1971).

128,300 acres. Thus while residential land declined by 213,700 acres, nonresidential land rose by 37,000 acres, even though such land was being used for development. The proportion of land zoned nonresidential was nearly doubled (from 12.4 percent to 23.0 percent), while the proportions zoned residential dropped from 0.6 percent to 0.4 percent for multifamily and from 87 percent to 76.6 percent for single-family.

In the northeast (excluding Hudson) nonresidential zoning dropped slightly from 14,600 to 11,300 acres. There was a large decline in single-family land from 63,900 to 29,200 acres, with a fall in multifamily zoning of 4,300 acres. Vacant land fell by more than half over the decade, with the decline concentrated in residential land. As a result, the proportion of nonresidential land rose from 17.4 percent to 25.2 percent, while the proportion of multifamily land was cut by more than half from 6.6 percent to 3.2 percent.

Table 3-8
Change in Zoning Patterns in New Jersey (1960-1970)

County	Total	1960 Non-residential	Multi-family	Single Family	Total	1970 Non-residential	Multi-family	Single Family
				Thousands of Acres				
Bergen	63.0	9.9	1.5	51.6	27.9	4.9	0.1	22.9
Middlesex	127.0	34.0	2.0	91.0	103.8	47.0	0.3	56.5
Monmouth	209.4	14.6	0.1	194.7	190.0	35.1	0.6	154.3
Morris	192.4	22.5	0.4	169.5	128.5	21.9	1.3	105.3
Somerset	142.0	10.3	0.2	131.5	106.9	19.4	–	87.5
Study counties	733.8	91.3	4.2	638.3	557.1	128.3	2.3	426.5
Essex	22.2	2.9	0.2	19.1	9.0	2.6	0.1	6.3
Passaic	41.0	5.9	0.3	34.8	26.5	7.1	0.9	18.5
Union	20.9	5.8	5.1	10.0	6.3	1.6	0.3	4.4
Northeast	84.1	14.6	5.6	63.9	41.8	11.3	1.3	29.2
Total	817.9	105.9	9.8	702.2	598.9	139.6	3.6	455.7
				Percentage Distribution				
Bergen	100.0	15.7	2.4	81.9	100.0	17.6	0.4	82.1
Middlesex	100.0	26.8	1.6	71.7	100.0	45.3	0.3	54.4
Monmouth	100.0	7.0	a	93.0	100.0	18.5	0.3	81.2
Morris	100.0	11.7	0.2	88.1	100.0	17.0	1.0	81.9
Somerset	100.0	7.3	0.1	92.6	100.0	18.1	–	81.9
Study counties	100.0	12.4	0.6	87.0	100.0	23.0	0.4	76.6
Essex	100.0	13.1	0.9	86.0	100.0	20.0	1.2	78.8
Passaic	100.0	14.4	0.7	84.9	100.0	26.8	3.4	69.8
Union	100.0	27.8	24.4	47.8	100.0	25.4	4.8	69.8
Northeast	100.0	17.4	6.6	76.0	100.0	25.2	3.2	71.6
Total	100.0	12.9	1.2	85.9	100.0	23.3	0.6	76.1

Sources: 1960 data are taken from Regional Plan Association, *Spread City* (New York, 1962), Bulletin 100, table 10, p. 40, reprinted with permission; 1970 data from New Jersey Department of Community Affairs, "1970 Zoning Survey" (Trenton, N.J., 1971).
aLess than 0.1 percent.

Changes in Nonresidential Zoning

We can compare the changes in nonresidential zoning between 1960 and 1970 in these eight counties to an estimate of requirements for commercial and industrial land over the period 1960 to 1969. In the eight counties, while vacant land declined by 219,000 acres (from 817,900 to 598,900), nonresidential zoning rose by 33,700 acres (from 105,900 to 139,600). Multifamily land declined from 9,800 to 3,600 acres; single-family land declined from 702,200 to 455,700 acres. In 1970 the five study counties contained roughly 20,803 acres of commercial, 12,215 acres of office and research, and 95,308 acres of industrial vacant land. The three northeast counties contained about 2,401 acres of commercial, 2,081 acres of office and research, and 6,756 acres of industrial vacant land.

Using the doubling assumption invoked earlier, only about 5,100 acres are estimated for both commercial and industrial development in the eight counties during the period 1960 to 1969. Perhaps 38,800 acres of new nonresidential zoning was added over the decade, with only about 13.1 percent probably being used. The study counties added 37,000 acres of nonresidential land and required about 3,400 acres. The northeast counties lost about 3,300 acres of nonresidential land net and required an estimated 1,700 acres.

Land required for industrial and commercial plans (1960-1969) has been computed using the same procedure and data source as in the section Excessive Commercial and Industrial Zoning. Bergen required 1,200 acres, based on 26,136,000 square feet in 1,473 approved plans. Middlesex required 1,200 acres in 1,084 plans. Figures for the other study counties are as follows: Monmouth, 300 acres based on 6,534,000 square feet in 278 plans; Morris, 500 acres based on 10,890,000 square feet in 583 plans; Somerset, 200 acres based on 4,356,000 square feet in 256 plans. Figures for the northeast counties are as follows: Essex, 600 acres based on 13,068,000 square feet in 901 plans; Passaic, 400 acres based on 8,712,000 square feet in 651 plans; Union, 700 acres based on 15,246,000 square feet in 1,106 plans.

We can compare requirements for industrial and commercial plans on a regional basis. Adding Ocean to the study counties, about 3,570 acres were required, based on 77,759,000 square feet in 3,797 plans during 1960 to 1969. With Hudson added to the northeast, the figures were 2,222 acres from 48,410,000 square feet in 3,182 plans. The southwest region opposite Philadelphia had much lower requirements of 830 acres from 18,073,000 square feet in 1,354 plans. The northwest counties reported only 380 plans of 4,067,000 square feet requiring about 186 acres. In the southeast (the region for which 1970 zoning data is missing) about 261 acres were required, based on 5,677,000 square feet in 455 plans.

Changes in Residential Zoning

In 1960 the five study counties included in the RPA report had zoned 642,500 acres for residential purposes, of which fully 99.3 percent (638,300 acres) was single-family. There were only 4,200 acres zoned multifamily. The three northeast counties had zoned 91.9 percent of residential land single-family (63,900 acres), with only 5,600 acres zoned multifamily. Over half of the total 9,800 multifamily acres in both regions were located in Union County alone. By 1970 as shown in table 3-8, residential capacity had shrunk by one-third from 642,500 to 428,800 acres in the five study counties. In the three northeast counties the decline in residential capacity was over one-half, falling from 69,500 to 30,500 acres. The decline in single-family acreage was about one-third (211,800 acres) in the study counties and one-half (34,700 acres) in the northeast. The proportional decline in multifamily acreage was much greater in the northeast (4,300 of 5,600 acres) than in the study counties (1,900 of 4,200 acres).

We may compare this change to residential construction authorized by building permits over the period 1960 to 1969 by region. In table 3-9 permits have been converted to required acres by using essentially the same procedure as for table 3-5. (Duplexes and multifamily structures of three or four dwelling units have been excluded for ease of computation using 1960-1969 data, which must be taken from separate annual reports. Neither housing type seems to have been very important during that period.) It will be seen that the decline in residential capacity between 1960 and 1970 reported in table 3-8 roughly matches the estimated acreage required between 1960 and 1969 in both the study and northeast counties, allowing for possible errors in the estimation procedure. In the study counties about 192,792 acres were required for single-family uses (compared with a decline of 211,800 acres excluding Ocean) and 5,803 acres for multifamily uses (compared to a decline of 1,900 acres excluding Ocean). In the northeast counties about 23,364 acres were required for single-family uses (compared with a decline of 34,700 acres excluding Hudson) and 3,501 acres for multifamily uses (compared with a decline of 4,300 acres excluding Hudson).

Lot Size Requirements. Using the RPA data, we can also compare minimum lot size requirements for 1960 and 1970 in the same eight counties. This comparison yields some insight into changes in lot size requirements over time in suburban New Jersey. These data are presented in table 3-10 as a percentage distribution based on number of acres. The minimum requirements appear to have increased substantially over the decade in the five study counties included in the RPA report. In 1960, 13.3 percent of the land was zoned under a half-acre and 56.7 percent over an acre. In 1970 only 6.2 percent (half as much) was zoned under a half-acre and 76.7 percent (almost half as much again) over an acre. The situation in the three northeast counties was the reverse. There 34.7 percent was zoned under a half-acre in 1960 and 41.6 percent in 1970, versus 34.4 percent and 34.8 percent over an acre. Large lot zoning was held constant, with an increase in small lot zoning.

In terms of individual counties, Somerset remained stable at about 85 percent over an acre. Monmouth and Morris showed large lot zoning sharply increased to percentiles in the low eighties. Bergen and Middlesex showed moderate increases in large lot zoning. In the northeast Passaic remained stable with percentiles in the low forties, while Union showed a moderate increase. Essex showed a sharp decrease from 30.4 percent to 15.1 percent in zoning over an acre, with a sharp increase in zoning under a half-acre from 30.4 percent to 46.3 percent.

There is other evidence of increases in minimum lot sizes during the 1960s.

Table 3-9
Estimated Residential Land Required by Authorized Building Permits in New Jersey (1960-1969)

Region	Building Permits Authorized			Acres Required		
	Total	Single-Family	Multifamily	Total	Single-Family	Multifamily
Study counties	219,802	138,556 63.0%	81,246 37.0%	198,595	192,792 97.1%	5,803 2.9%
Northeast	79,397	30,396 38.3	49,001 61.7	26,865	23,364 87.0	3,501 13.0
Northwest	18,941	15,209 80.3	3,732 19.7	26,847	26,580 99.0	267 1.0
Southwest	93,250	56,695 60.8	36,555 39.2	56,199	53,659 95.5	2,540 4.5
Total	411,390	240,856 58.7	170,534 41.3	308,506	296,395 96.1	12,111 3.9

Source: New Jersey Department of Labor and Industry, Division of Planning and Research, *New Jersey Residential Building Permits* (Trenton, N.J.: 1960-1969), annual summaries.

Note: For ease of computation, duplexes and multifamily structures containing three or four units were not included. The 1970 annual summary reported 19,571 single-family (50 percent), 2,102 duplex (5.4 percent), 713 three- or four-family (1.8 percent), and 16,789 five (or-more)-family units (42.8 percent) authorized.

Table 3-10
Change in Minimum Lot Size Requirements in New Jersey (1960-1970)
(in acres and percentages)

County	Total Acres		0-0.24 Acre		0.25-0.49 Acre		0.50-0.99 Acre		1 or More Acres	
1960										
Bergen	51,600	100.0	4,500	8.7	8,700	16.9	14,700	28.5	23,700	45.9
Middlesex	91,000	100.0	20,000	22.0	9,500	10.4	40,200	44.2	21,300	23.4
Monmouth	194,700	100.0	6,000	3.1	14,200	7.3	83,400	42.8	91,100	46.8
Morris	169,500	100.0	4,700	2.8	15,600	9.2	35,000	20.6	114,200	67.4
Somerset	131,500	100.0	300	0.2	1,100	0.8	18,500	14.1	111,600	84.9
Study counties	638,300	100.0	35,500	5.6	49,100	7.7	191,800	30.0	361,900	56.7
Essex	19,100	100.0	2,000	10.5	3,800	19.9	7,500	39.3	5,800	30.4
Passaic	34,800	100.0	1,900	5.5	7,900	22.7	10,600	30.5	14,400	41.4
Union	10,000	100.0	3,400	34.0	3,200	32.0	1,600	16.0	1,800	18.0
Northeast	63,900	100.0	7,300	11.4	14,900	23.3	19,700	30.8	22,000	34.4
Total	702,200	100.0	42,800	6.1	64,000	9.1	211,500	30.1	383,900	54.7
1970										
Bergen	22,885	100.0	1,011	4.4	4,364	19.1	4,909	21.5	12,601	55.1
Middlesex	56,477	100.0	2,783	4.9	5,183	9.2	26,630	47.2	21,881	38.7
Monmouth	154,290	100.0	1,600	1.0	6,033	3.9	16,097	10.4	130,560	84.6
Morris	105,287	100.0	359	0.3	4,464	4.3	13,241	12.6	87,223	82.8
Somerset	87,479	100.0	218	0.2	359	0.4	12,140	13.9	74,762	85.5
Study counties	426,418	100.0	5,971	1.4	20,403	4.8	73,017	17.1	327,027	76.7
Essex	6,343	100.0	307	4.8	2,630	41.5	2,448	38.6	958	15.1
Passaic	18,482	100.0	1,702	9.2	4,512	24.4	4,120	22.3	8,148	44.1
Union	4,409	100.0	1,383	31.4	1,638	37.2	326	7.4	1,062	24.1
Northeast	29,234	100.0	3,392	11.6	8,780	30.0	6,894	23.6	10,168	34.8
Total	455,652	100.0	9,363	2.1	29,183	6.4	79,911	17.5	337,195	74.0

Sources: Data for 1960 are taken from Regional Plan Association, *Spread City* (New York, 1962), Bulletin 100, table 11, p. 40, reprinted with permission; 1970 data from New Jersey Department of Community Affairs, "1970 Zoning Survey" (Trenton, N.J., 1971).

The New Jersey Department of Community Affairs surveyed municipal zoning ordinances in 1960 and 1967, as well as in 1970. Table 3-11 compares the minimum lot size requirement for single-family construction in 1960 and 1967. These data indicate a clear upward drift in the minimum lot sizes. In the study counties 88 of 241 municipalities (36.5 percent) had lot sizes under 5,000 square feet in 1960; in 1967 only 52 municipalities (21.6 percent) had such small lot sizes. There were some increases in the proportion zoned in each of the larger lot size categories. Similar shifts upward are observable in all regions of the state.

Possible Sources of Lot Size Changes. There are, however, two possible explanations for the observed shifts in lot size requirements between 1960 and

Table 3-11
Change in Minimum Lot Size Requirements by Municipality in New Jersey (1960-1967)

Region	Year	None	Less than 5,000 Square Feet	4,000- 9,999	10,000- 19,999	20,000- 39,999	40,000 or More	Total
			Number of Municipalities					
Study counties	1960	60	28	97	43	10	3	241
	1967	27	25	118	45	19	7	241
Northeast	1960	30	9	23	9	–	–	71
	1967	17	12	30	12	–	–	71
Northwest	1960	65	–	3	2	2	–	72
	1967	29	2	11	11	13	7	73
Southwest	1960	45	16	30	18	3	2	114
	1967	17	17	52	22	4	2	114
Southeast	1960	40	8	16	3	–	–	67
	1967	17	9	17	14	10	1	68
New Jersey	1960	240	61	169	75	15	5	565
	1967	107	65	228	104	46	17	567
			Percentage Distribution					
Study counties	1960	24.9	11.6	40.2	17.8	4.1	1.2	100.0
	1967	11.2	10.4	49.0	18.7	7.9	2.9	100.0
Northeast	1960	42.3	12.7	32.4	12.7	–	–	100.0
	1967	23.9	16.9	42.3	16.9	–	–	100.0
Northwest	1960	90.3	–	4.2	2.8	2.8	–	100.0
	1967	39.7	2.7	15.1	15.1	17.8	9.6	100.0
Southwest	1960	39.5	14.0	26.3	15.8	2.6	1.8	100.0
	1967	14.9	14.9	45.6	19.3	3.5	1.8	100.0
Southeast	1960	59.7	11.9	23.9	4.5	–	–	100.0
	1967	25.0	13.2	25.0	20.6	14.7	1.5	100.0
New Jersey	1960	42.5	10.8	29.9	13.3	2.7	0.9	100.0
	1967	18.9	11.5	40.2	18.3	8.1	3.0	100.0

Sources: New Jersey Department of Community Affairs, *Zoning in New Jersey: 1960* (Trenton, N.J., 1961); *Zoning in New Jersey: 1967* (Trenton, N.J., 1968).

1970. The first explanation, of course, is that lot size requirements have been progressively increased to slow the pace of suburban development. The second explanation is that while lot size requirements have been left largely unchanged, the smaller lot sizes have been used up first by developers, altering the proportional distributions over time. Both factors may actually be at work.

The total amount of vacant single-family land in the study counties dropped from 638,300 to 426,418 acres, as reported in table 3-10. The drop was even more dramatic in the northeast counties, from 63,900 to 29,234 acres. In the study counties there was only a slight drop in acreage zoned greater than an acre, from 361,900 to 327,027 acres. But there were large drops in smaller lot sizes: from 35,500 to 5,971 acres under a quarter-acre; from 49,100 to 20,403 acres under a half-acre; and from 191,800 to 73,017 acres under an acre. These figures indicate a rapid use of smaller lot sizes, with developers avoiding lots over an acre. The implication is that large lot zoning may tend to retard land development. In contrast to the study counties, the northeast showed heavy use of all lot size categories, which all had large drops (from 22,000 to 10,168 acres over an acre); but there was only a tenth as much vacant land as in the study counties.

Sagalyn and Sternlieb assembled a nonrandom sample of 529 newly constructed single-family units from 153 subdivisions in suburban New Jersey and analyzed the various cost components using multiple-regression procedures.[14] Their sample data provide some evidence that developers tend to choose construction at the smallest lot size and frontage requirements.[15] I have tabulated distribution of the Sagalyn and Sternlieb sample in terms of lot size, lot width, and building size. These distributions are compared in table 3-12 with distributions under zoning requirements in the seventeen surveyed counties.

In the case of lot size and width, it is clear that developers were building at minimal levels. In single-family and nonresidential districts combined, 65.7 percent of land was zoned over an acre (67 percent in single-family districts) and only 15 percent under a half-acre (14.1 percent in single-family districts). In contrast, 52.9 percent of the sample was constructed on lot sizes under a half-acre, 34.6 percent between a half-acre and an acre, and only 12.5 percent over an acre. A similar pattern was evident for lot width. About 61.4 percent of all residential land was zoned for over 150 feet, with only 11.4 percent under 100 feet. But 24.2 percent of the sample was constructed on lots under 100 feet and only 16.7 percent on lots over 150 feet. In fact 59.2 percent of the sample was built on intermediate lots between 100 and 150 feet, versus 27.3 percent of all residential land.

Building size is a very different matter. Generally the sample was larger than the minimum requirements. About 34.3 percent of all land was zoned for floor areas under 1,000 square feet. But only 3.6 percent of the sample (all over 700 square feet) was constructed for such small dimensions. Almost two-thirds (60.3 percent) of all land was zoned between 1,000 and 1,600 square feet, but only

Table 3-12
Distribution of Single-Family Sample by Zoning Requirements in New Jersey (1970)

| | Distribution by Lot Size (in acres) | | | | | |
	0-0.24	0.25-0.49	0.50-0.99	1-2.99	3 or More	Total
Single-family sample (units)						
Number		193	183	63	3	529
Percent		36.5	34.6	11.9	0.6	100.0
Total zoning requirements (thousands of acres)						
Number	75	142	281	780	174	1,452
Percent	5.2	9.8	19.4	53.7	12.0	100.0
Single-family districts (thousands of acres)						
Number	68	121	253	734	165	1,341
Percent	5.1	9.0	18.9	54.7	12.3	100.0

| | Distribution by Lot Width (in feet) | | | | | |
	0-49	50-99	100-149	150-199	200 or More	Total
Single-family sample (units)						
Number	–	128	313	48	40	529
Percent	–	24.2	59.2	9.1	7.6	100.0
Total zoning requirements (thousands of acres)						
Number	27	138	396	358	532	1,451
Percent	1.9	9.5	27.3	24.7	36.7	100.0

| | Distribution by Building Size (in square feet) | | | | | |
	None	1-699	700-999	1000-1599	1600 or More	Total
Single-family sample (units)						
Number	–	–	19	66	444	529
Percent	–	–	3.6	12.5	83.9	100.0
Total zoning requirements (thousands of acres)						
Number	116	38	344	874	78	1,450
Percent	8.0	2.6	23.7	60.3	5.4	100.0

Sources: Sample data were computed by the author from the original survey results on computer tape employed by Lynne B. Sagalyn and George Sternlieb for *Zoning and Housing Costs: The Impact of Land-Use Controls on Housing Price* (New Brunswick, N.J.: Center for Urban Policy Research, Rutgers University, 1972); zoning data were computed from New Jersey Department of Community Affairs, "1970 Zoning Survey" (Trenton, N.J., 1971).

Note: Zoning data are rounded to the nearest thousand, producing some variance in the total acres reported in each category.

12.5 percent of the sample was so constructed. A full 83.9 percent of the sample consisted of units with at least 1,600 square feet, versus 5.4 percent of the land so zoned. The implication is, of course, that developers are building large houses on small lots (in terms of size and width). The explanation is straightforward in terms of an economic calculus. Maximum subdivision of land combined with construction of large houses on small lots is probably the most profitable procedure for developers.

Price Effects of Housing Supply Restrictions

It is not possible to project the 1970-1974 data used in this chapter for either nonresidential or residential construction plans, except as a meaningless linear trend. However, James and Hughes have done a projection (based on shift-and-share techniques) of new employed households (net of all population movements) to be expected by county in New Jersey over the decade 1970 to 1980. Their projections are presented in the first data column of table 3-13. The seventeen surveyed counties were forecasted to receive 261,831 net job-related households over 1970 to 1980, of which 186,642 (over half) would be in the study counties and 58,123 in the southwest. Only 2,112 households were expected in the northeast (due to anticipated losses of 13,826 in Essex and 13,692 in Hudson) and 14,954 in the northwest. Bergen was expected to receive the largest number of new households (60,434), followed after a large gap by Middlesex (38,538), Monmouth (30,764), and Morris (22,724).

Following the approach of James and Hughes, I have estimated from the data presented in table 3-4 on zoned residential capacity, the numbers of dwelling units (multifamily and single-family) permitted by 1970 zoning ordinances. The procedure of table 3-5 has been employed. These data are included in table 3-13 for comparison and permit a projection of relative supply and demand in terms of dwelling units by county over the decade 1970 to 1980. About 2,855,380 dwelling units can be constructed at currently zoned densities. (New job-related households cannot be converted directly into acres, as the division into housing types and lot sizes cannot be projected in any reasonable fashion.) In each of the regions the total residential capacity (including both residential and nonresidential districts) is more than sufficient to handle the expected new households. The same is true of every individual county except Bergen and Union (both on the suburban fringes of New York City). The study counties most strongly emphasized single-family housing in their 1970 zoning regulations.

It is not the supply of housing in general, however, but the supply of lower-cost housing in particular that is important. As table 3-13 demonstrates, the higher the expected growth rate by county (in terms of new job-related households forecasted over the decade 1970 to 1980), the smaller the proportion of permitted multifamily housing. This pattern is particularly evident in rapidly growing Bergen, Middlesex, Morris, and Somerset counties. In the seventeen surveyed counties 71.3 percent of the new households are projected to live in the six study counties and 22.2 percent in the southwest. The 1970 zoning patterns placed 30.6 percent of permitted multifamily housing and 65.8 percent of permitted single-family housing in the southwest. The study counties

Table 3-13
Housing Demand and Housing Supply in New Jersey (1970-1980)

County	New Job-Related Households (1970-1980)	Total Units	Permitted Housing Supply (1970)			
			Residential Districts		Nonresidential Districts	
			Multi-family	Single Family	Single Family	Multi-family
County summaries						
Study counties	186,642	690,254	186,956	399,906	41,526	61,866
Northeast	2,112	63,279	18,004	35,348	2,493	7,434
Northwest	14,954	750,276	203,868	514,373	10,419	21,616
Southwest	58,123	1,351,571	839,622	374,011	53,574	84,364
Total	261,831	2,855,380	1,248,450	1,323,638	108,012	175,280
Study counties						
Bergen	60,434	27,245	1,974	20,678	1,289	3,304
Middlesex	38,538	92,869	4,298	52,369	9,420	26,782
Monmouth	30,764	124,377	8,862	87,130	15,015	13,370
Morris	22,724	87,653	18,508	59,783	5,190	4,172
Ocean	16,026	309,325	153,314	134,363	8,306	13,342
Somerset	18,156	48,785	—	45,583	2,306	896
Northeast						
Essex	−13,826	10,309	952	8,361	632	364
Hudson	−13,692	4,746	—	—	—	4,746
Passaic	10,044	35,845	12,404	19,906	1,827	1,708
Union	19,586	12,379	4,648	7,081	34	616
Northwest						
Hunterdon	3,507	87,835	6,006	76,289	5,358	182
Sussex	5,505	192,426	116,298	74,005	331	1,792
Warren	5,942	470,015	81,564	364,079	4,730	19,642
Southwest						
Burlington	21,303	449,016	188,958	199,732	38,304	22,022
Camden	22,383	350,807	251,944	35,950	1,019	61,894
Gloucester	4,482	483,111	388,948	81,720	11,995	448
Mercer	9,955	68,637	9,772	56,609	2,256	—

Sources: Household estimates are taken from Franklin J. James and James W. Hughes, *Modeling State Growth: New Jersey 1980* (New Brunswick, N.J.: Center for Urban Policy Research, Rutgers University, 1973), Exhibit 4-8, p. 59, reprinted with permission. Housing estimates are developed from table 3-4 using platting coefficients from James and Hughes, p. 92.

contained 30.8 percent of permitted multifamily and 16.8 percent of permitted single-family housing. The northwest contained 35.8 percent of permitted multifamily and 15.8 percent of permitted single-family housing. Relatively little of the permitted housing supply was located in the northeast (2.9 percent of multifamily and 1.5 percent of single-family). Little of the employment growth was expected in the northeast (0.8 percent) or in the northwest (5.7 percent).

This distribution of permitted housing supply can be compared with the distribution of vacant land reported in table 3-4. The study counties contained 24.3 percent of total permitted units but 40.6 percent of vacant residential land (in both residential and nonresidential districts) and 40.9 percent of residential districts. The northwest had a similarly restrictive pattern—25.7 percent of vacant residential land (26.9 percent in residential districts), reduced to 26.3 percent of permitted housing supply. In contrast, the southwest had 47.3 percent of total units but only 31.6 percent of vacant residential land (30.1 percent of residential districts). The northeast was essentially balanced at 2.1 percent of vacant residential land (the same in residential districts) and 2.2 percent of permitted housing supply.

The combination of commercial and industrial zoning beyond requirements, restrictions on multifamily use, and large lot zoning within single-family districts may result in raising housing costs over market-determined values for multi-family and smaller lot size uses. Table 3-14 gives average estimated market values by county for newly constructed multifamily housing in New Jersey during 1973. For the six study counties average market values by lot size have been estimated in table 3-15 for newly constructed single-family housing in 1970. These values are highest in precisely those counties that have the most restrictive zoning practices and the highest expected employment growth.

The critical issue in the exclusionary zoning hypothesis is the effects of land use restrictions on housing supplies and prices. We have found in New Jersey that the higher the expected employment rate in a county, the smaller the proportion of permitted multifamily housing. At the same time, market values are relatively higher in the same counties for new multifamily and single-family housing. But we cannot readily determine whether such evidence supports the

Table 3-14
Estimated Market Value for Apartments in New Jersey (1970)

County	Market Value	County	Market Value
Atlantic	$13,536	Middlesex	$14,832
Bergen	21,024	Monmouth	14,040
Burlington	13,752	Morris	16,056
Camden	14,904	Ocean	13,464
Cape May	11,736	Passaic	17,856
Cumberland	13,104	Salem	10,440
Essex	16,344	Somerset	13,392
Gloucester	12,312	Sussex	13,680
Hudson	13,968	Union	18,432
Hunterdon	14,184	Warren	11,880
Mercer	15,480	New Jersey	15,192

Source: New Jersey Department of Community Affairs, *New Multi-Family Dwellings in New Jersey: 1970* (Trenton, N.J., n.d.), p. 5.
Note: Market value is computed as 72 times average monthly rent per apartment (12 months times a factor of 6). This procedure is a typical assessment method in New Jersey.

Table 3-15
Estimated Market Value for Single-Family Homes in the Study
Counties by Lot Size (1970)

County	0.25 Acre or Less	0.25-0.49 Acre	0.50-0.99 Acre	1.00 or More Acres
Bergen	$51,667	$60,217	$72,333	$91,667
Middlesex	40,556	48,824	46,667	52,172
Monmouth	31,280	37,222	42,222	58,636
Morris	29,918	40,600	50,972	80,588
Ocean	28,023	31,957	35,000	41,329
Somerset	30,000	40,000	66,667	60,652

Source: Lynne B. Sagalyn and George Sternlieb, *Zoning and Housing Costs: The Impact of Land-Use Controls on Housing Price* (New Brunswick, N.J.: Center for Urban Policy Research, Rutgers University, 1972). Data computed by author.

exclusionary hypothesis. Demand factors (employment growth) and supply restrictions (exclusionary zoning) will force up market values. We cannot easily disentangle these demand and supply forces at such an aggregate level. Indeed a study by James suggests that there may be very little evidence of imbalance between housing supply and demand by income level on a regional basis in New Jersey.[16]

Suburban Strategies for Regulating Multifamily Development

Despite the severe restrictions on multifamily zoning, much of the housing construction in New Jersey has been multifamily. As table 3-9 showed, during 1960 to 1969 there were authorized 240,856 single-family (58.7 percent) and 170,534 multifamily (41.3 percent) units. These data agree with the general trends in suburban construction of multifamily housing reported by Schafer. In 1967 private multifamily housing constituted 42 percent of all housing starts (excluding mobile homes) and had been increasing since 1957.[17] Over the period 1962 to 1970 private multifamily starts in the suburban rings of 63 Standard Metropolitan Statistical Areas (SMSAs) analyzed by Schafer rose from 40.3 to 57.3 percent (averaging 52.1 percent over the period). Multifamily starts were even higher in the older SMSAs of the northeast and midwest sections of the nation. These starts averaged eighteen dwelling units per structure. Schafer concluded that demand for suburban apartments generated by suburbanization of employment is reflected in new construction.[18] He attributed demand for various housing types to family life cycle. Large households with children demand homes; small households without children demand apartments or townhouses.[19]

The New Jersey County and Municipal Government Study Commission report examined case studies of multifamily approvals in twenty-seven communities (including the twenty-one communities approving the most multifamily construction in New Jersey), which demonstrate the widespread existence of two suburban strategies for regulating multifamily development.[20] The first strategy is the use of variances for the approval of such development. The considerable multifamily construction occurs largely through an informal process for allocating vacant land.[21] There is rarely large-scale multifamily zoning, due to the hostile political environment. However officials often perceive multifamily development to be fiscally profitable. At the same time, an informal process permits more control over the specific characteristics (structural, fiscal, and social) of development proposals that are approved. It also permits the enforcement of additional compensation for the approval of multifamily proposals.[22] Multifamily developments that do not greatly violate community social and visual standards but are fiscally advantageous will be given such variances.[23] The report found that most zoning amendments in the twenty-seven municipalities studied were to incorporate into the zoning ordinance already existing multifamily areas created through the previous use of variances.

The second strategy is to employ bedroom and other restrictions when multifamily districts are created or variances granted. There is a widespread fiscal rule in suburban New Jersey that has required (formally or informally) that apartment developments have roughly 80 percent one-bedroom and 20 percent two-bedroom units. The commission report found that apartment construction in New Jersey closely approximates this 80:20 rule, especially in the New York metropolitan region where development pressure is strongest. During 1968 to 1971, 79.6 percent of apartment units constructed in the New York ring (for New Jersey counties with over 1,000 apartment units constructed) were efficiency or one-bedroom; only 1 percent were three-bedroom. In the Philadelphia ring 71.2 percent were efficiency or one-bedroom, and only 2.7 percent were three-bedroom.[24]

In the seventeen surveyed counties (Hudson had no residential land), 59 percent of the multifamily land permitted only one-bedroom or efficiency apartments, 20.5 percent permitted two-bedroom apartments, and only 20.4 percent permitted larger units. Bedroom restrictions were very high in both the study counties (69.6 percent one-bedroom or efficiency, 17.5 percent two-bedroom, and only 12.9 percent larger units) and the southwest (62.4 percent one-bedroom or efficiency, 22.1 percent two-bedroom, and 15.5 percent larger units). They were relatively low in the northeast (37.3 percent, 11.1 percent, and 51.5 percent respectively). The northwest fell in between with 34 percent of multifamily land permitting units of three or more bedrooms (with 45.5 percent one-bedroom or efficiency and 20.5 percent two-bedroom). The results in the study and southwest counties were particularly dominated by Burlington (71.1 percent one-bedroom or efficiency), Middlesex (73.9 percent), Monmouth (64.9

percent), and Morris (81.2 percent). Bergen permitted units of three or more bedrooms on 51.1 percent of multifamily land, Camden on 66.4 percent, Gloucester on 86.5 percent, and Somerset on 100 percent. However, relatively little multifamily land is zoned in Bergen or Somerset.[25]

We can also examine multifamily construction patterns in these counties.[26] Over the period 1970 to 1973 there were 108 private multifamily developments containing 6,024 apartments constructed in Bergen. Of these apartments 55.2 percent (3,327) were one-bedroom or efficiency, 38.7 percent were two-bedroom, and only 6 percent (364) were three-bedroom or larger. A similar pattern is found in Camden and Gloucester, with a stronger emphasis on two-bedroom units. In Camden there were 65 developments with 9,869 apartments, of which 55.6 percent (5,491) were two-bedroom, 38.5 percent (3,795) were smaller, and 5.9 percent (583) were larger. In Gloucester of 2,323 units in 22 developments, 45.9 percent (1,066) were two-bedroom, with 49.6 percent (1,153) being smaller and 4.5 percent (104) larger. Somerset, which had no bedroom restrictions, had 56.7 percent two-bedroom (835), 43.1 percent one-bedroom or efficiency, and only two units three-bedroom or larger, in 13 developments containing 1,472 apartments. Passaic had the highest proportion of three-or-more-bedroom apartments, 12.1 percent (125) of 1,033 units in 23 developments. Small units composed 65.9 percent (681) and two-bedroom units 22 percent (227).

The general assumption has been that the principal purpose of these bedroom requirements (and other cost-raising zoning or subdivision restrictions) is to reduce the number of school-age children permitted in multifamily developments, as well as to drive up taxable valuation per unit on the argument that smaller units will cost more per square foot. The apartment data used in chapter 5 are largely restricted to efficiency, one-bedroom, and two-bedroom units, because of the existing construction patterns. Nevertheless there is no evidence presented in the report of the New Jersey County and Municipal Government Study Commission which shows that, without present zoning restrictions, substantial numbers of three-bedroom or larger apartment units would be constructed by developers.[27] The issue is whether developers would build such apartments if zoning restrictions were removed. If smaller units do cost more per square foot, developers would presumably maximize profit per acre of developable land by squeezing as many units as feasible onto each acre. Developers may avoid large apartments, just as they appear to build large homes on small lots, as the result of their own economic calculus.

As we shall see in chapter 5, apartments do not necessarily impose worse fiscal impacts than single-family homes. The report of the New Jersey County and Municipal Government Study Commission concluded that even developments with 10 percent three-bedroom units would probably not impose fiscal deficits (in a pattern of 40 percent one-bedroom and 50 percent two-bedroom units).[28] Multifamily development does involve much larger population for a given amount of land to be developed. The variance process and the 80:20 rule permit much finer control over such population growth and the resulting loss of semirural character, open space, and environmental amenities.

The Theory of Least-Cost Zoning

The *Mt. Laurel* doctrine has been modified by the New Jersey Supreme Court in its recent *Madison* decision to incorporate a requirement for least-cost zoning. In their study of 1970 New Jersey zoning ordinances, Williams and Norman conclude that the removal of large lot requirements will not necessarily reduce housing costs.[29] The authors suggest that two factors are more important than lot size. The first is building size, which is widely regulated in zoning ordinances, both as to minimum and maximum (via coverage limitations) floor area.[30] The second is site improvements, which are related to lot width (or frontage) and setback rather than lot size.[31] Site improvements are typically controlled by subdivision regulations rather than by zoning ordinances. Neither building size nor lot width may be particularly related to lot size.[32]

The implication is that a reduction of minimum lot size requirements might have little effect on building size and hence on housing costs. (Hamilton emphasizes that quite large lot sizes must be used as a substitute for a direct capital-consumption requirement.) Developers would presumably prefer to build larger houses on smaller lots, in order to maximize profit per acre of developable land.[33] It is conceivable that lot size requirements are enacted in part to counteract this market tendency by controlling population density. Indeed, such density control is one of the two classic functions of the zoning ordinance (the other being control of land use).[34] Williams and Norman conclude that it is unlikely that large lot zoning is a major factor in preventing lower-cost housing. They expect (precisely as White predicted) that smaller lots will be more expensive than larger lots, after site improvements are included.[35] The authors argue that a principal motive for large lot zoning is simply that it functions as a holding device to delay development.[36] Hence litigation to break large lot requirements may not have much benefit in terms of lower-cost single-family housing.

Maisel found that the cost of developed lots ready for single-family construction in the San Francisco Bay Area should be attributed at least 50 percent to the price of raw land, 28 percent to the cost of site improvements, and only 20 percent to 25 percent to the density of land use permitted by required lot sizes.[37] Sagalyn and Sternlieb reported that floor area was the most important factor (over 57 percent of variation) explaining selling price.[38] The second most important factor was the existing single-family housing value in a municipality, used by the authors as an index of socioeconomic status.[39] However, the cumulative effect of lot size and lot frontage was significant, with a correlation of 0.61 between lot size and selling price.[40] Williams and Norman argue that lot frontage is actually the operative factor. In the sample used by Sagalyn and Sternlieb, lot size was correlated 0.43 with floor area (building costs) and 0.50 with lot frontage (site improvement costs).[41] Setback requirements were inconsequential.[42] It is important to note that subdivision improvements were so uniform at a high level in the sample that the cost effect could not be measured statistically.[43]

The *Warth v. Seldin* decision brings this entire problem to light. The opinion relied on the technical argument that no evidence had been presented to demonstrate that the Penfield, New York, zoning ordinance actually excluded the plaintiffs, even though housing costs may have been substantially increased. Although the ordinance might have an exclusionary motive, no evidence was presented that altering the ordinance would provide any effective relief to low- and moderate-income households. On the contrary, the opinion suggests that market forces (income distribution and housing costs) would have excluded the plaintiffs in any case independent of the exclusionary effects of the zoning ordinance.

Since removing the zoning restrictions was not shown to provide relief, there was no point to the complaint, and the plaintiffs had no standing to sue. The issues of income distribution and housing costs were beyond the U.S. Supreme Court's ability to handle competently. The opinion's technical analysis of relief ultimately rests on certain assumptions about the effects of zoning ordinances on housing supplies and costs. (Properly speaking, the opinion relies on the lack of any evidence demonstrating that relief could be provided judicially.) These assumptions are contrary to those made implicitly by the New Jersey Supreme Court in its policy of least-cost zoning.

Even least-cost zoning to place multifamily housing on inexpensive land might not be sufficient to insure the construction of low- and moderate-income housing.[44] On the contrary, in addition to zoning, substantial housing subsidies and developer incentives (such as density bonuses) may be required. *Mt. Laurel* correctly observed that municipalities do not build housing. Moreover, housing subsidy is essentially a federal and state problem, especially given the undisguised criticism of local taxation made by the New Jersey Supreme Court in both *Robinson* and *Mt. Laurel*. The principal problem is that low- and moderate-income households cannot afford privately financed suburban housing. Federal and state housing programs are limited. Indeed, there have been recent freezes on federal housing programs and a shift to limited demand subsidies under Section 8 of the 1974 Housing and Community Development Act.[45] The test of the *Madison* doctrine of least-cost zoning will lie in the future activities of private developers and the effect on the filtering process.

Conclusion

We can establish the widespread existence of exclusionary zoning practices in suburban New Jersey as defined by the New Jersey Supreme Court. Suburban ordinances are characterized by excessive commercial and industrial zoning, exclusion of multifamily uses, and large minimum requirements in single-family zones. There may be some evidence that housing supplies and costs in New Jersey are affected by these practices. Multifamily zoning is most restricted, and market values appear to be highest, in precisely those counties that have the most restrictive zoning practices.

There are, however, several reservations to be noted about this evidence. First, it appears that the demand for residential land roughly matches the supply in terms of zoned capacity. Although building permits are issued by the same local governments that hold zoning authority, permits are probably a rough measure of demand. Nearly half of permitted construction is multifamily. Zoning itself is not necessarily binding. Informal practices may be more important. Much of the multifamily construction may occur informally through variances granted outside the formal zoning process.

Second, while large lot and nonresidential zoning became more prevalent over the decade 1960 to 1970, there is some indication that the former may have resulted, in part, from developer preferences. Developers appear to construct large homes on smaller lots. While municipalities often constrain apartment structures to the 80:20 rule, there is little evidence that developers may prefer to build above two bedrooms or that the actual market varies much from that rule, even in the case of low- and moderate-income housing. Third, high market values may result as much from demand factors (in terms of growth pressures) as from supply restrictions; demand as well as supply affects market prices. The very counties with the most restrictive practices and highest market values also have the highest expected employment growth.

An unresolved controversy is whether removing suburban zoning restrictions will in fact promote the construction of suitably priced housing for low- and moderate-income households. Much developer litigation may simply seek to increase profit ratios by permitting construction of high-cost housing at higher densities (single-family or multifamily). If so, the benefit to low- and moderate-income households of least-cost zoning may be minimal. This conclusion must be tempered somewhat by the consideration that most low- and moderate-income housing may be provided through the filtering process. The effects of least-cost zoning on filtering of the housing stock are not known. The issue is an empirical one. Will least-cost zoning sufficiently increase the supply of new suburban housing so as to influence significantly the filtering process in regional housing markets?

Notes

1. These municipal data were recorded by the New Jersey Department of Community Affairs on large rolled sheets with information aggregated by county for each municipality. All data used in this study from that survey were computed by the author from the original sheets. The data were collected under

the direction of Norman Williams and Thomas Norman, who made a preliminary report on some of the data in "Exclusionary Land Use Controls: The Case of North-Eastern New Jersey," *Syracuse Law Review* 22 (1971):475-507. The survey design and procedure is discussed there in a short methodological appendix. The 1970 zoning survey results are also partly reported in these other works: Franklin J. James and James W. Hughes, *Modeling State Growth: New Jersey 1980* (New Brunswick, N.J.: Center for Urban Policy Research, Rutgers University, 1973); New Jersey Department of Community Affairs, Division of State and Regional Planning, *Land Use Regulation: The Residential Land Supply* (Trenton, N.J., April 1972); Lynne B. Sagalyn and George Sternlieb, *Zoning and Housing Costs: The Impact of Land-Use Controls on Housing Price* (New Brunswick, N.J.: Center for Urban Policy Research, Rutgers University, 1972).

2. The four counties in the southeastern section of the state (Atlantic, Cape May, Cumberland, and Salem) were excluded from the survey due to their largely rural and less developed character. Little pressure for urban land conversion was anticipated in those counties. Hudson County in the northeast is essentially developed and urbanized, with the exception of four municipalities located in the Hackensack Meadowlands District. Only those four municipalities were included in the survey. As a result, other reports refer to sixteen rather than seventeen surveyed counties.

3. Within the residential use category, there is a breakdown by number of acres into single-family, multifamily, and mobile home uses. The multifamily designation includes garden apartments, high-rise structures, and all residential dwellings providing for three or more families. The single-family designation includes duplexes (two-family dwellings) but not townhouses (attached single-family dwellings) which are a multifamily use. The nonresidential zoning categories (industrial, commercial, office and research) are primary land uses. Typically municipal zoning ordinances in New Jersey permit some residential development in nonresidential districts as secondary uses. Hence nonresidential categories also sometimes contain secondary residential uses, broken down as before (in the residential category) into single-family, multifamily, and mobile home uses by number of acres. For areas zoned as primary single-family districts or designated as secondary single-family districts, there is detailed information on provisions regulating minimum lot size, lot width (or frontage), and livable floor area (or building size). These provisions are reported in number of acres. Minimum lot size requirements are reported separately for primary and secondary districts. But the minimum requirements for lot width and building size are reported only for the primary and secondary districts lumped together without distinction. Minimum lot size provisions were reported in both primary and secondary districts as under a quarter-acre, a quarter-acre to just under a half-acre, a half-acre to just under an acre, one to just under three acres, and three or more acres. No municipal zoning ordinance failed to have minimum lot size requirements in single-family districts. Minimum lot width provisions were reported as none, 1-49 feet, 50-99 feet, 100-149 feet, 150-199 feet, and 200 or

more feet. Minimum floor area provisions were reported as none, less than 700 square feet, 700-799 square feet, 800-899 square feet, 900-999 square feet, 1,000-1,199 square feet, 1,200-1,399 square feet, 1,400-1,599 square feet, and 1,600 or more square feet.

4. James and Hughes, *Modeling State Growth*, Exhibit 4-8, p. 59.

5. For a different sixfold classification, see Williams and Norman, "Exclusionary Land Use Controls." I have regrouped their six types into multifamily and single-family controls and added nonresidential zoning.

6. Ibid., pp. 484, n. 17; 489; 492.

7. A previous study has concluded that these regions constitute socioeconomic units. For an ecological analysis of the regions, see George Sternlieb et al., *Housing Development and Municipal Costs* (New Brunswick, N.J.: Center for Urban Policy Research, Rutgers University, 1973), "Selection of Sampling Areas," pp. 317-324.

8. This technique was suggested by Williams and Norman, "Exclusionary Land Use Controls."

9. New Jersey Department of Labor and Industry, Division of Planning and Research, *Commercial and Industrial Construction Plans Approved: 1974 Annual Summary* (Trenton, N.J., 1974). One acre equals 43,560 square feet. The data include both new buildings and additions to existing buildings. There is no way of estimating directly the amount of vacant land consumed. Additions may involve acquisition of adjacent land, use of land on the existing structure site, or demolition of existing buildings either on or off the site.

10. 20 N.J. 114, 118 A.2d 824 (1955).

11. The data series employed here reports the number of building permits for single-family, two-family (duplex), three- or four-family, five-family or more, and public housing units. Unfortunately it does not clearly distinguish between new construction and additions or alterations to existing buildings. Moreover some dwelling units were also demolished, opening up already developed land not covered in the zoning survey. These problems make it difficult to convert building permits directly to new acreage. During 1974 about 77 percent of the dollar volume of residential construction was for new buildings according to the annual summary. There were 25,878 building permits issued and 4,293 dwelling units demolished (of which 2,279 were single-family). There are two additional caveats in using this data series. First, "Building permit data reflect *planned* construction and not construction actually put in place. However, studies have indicated that construction is actually undertaken in the majority of cases." Second, "Since only the number of permits and the estimated costs of construction are collected in the case of additions and alterations, no information is available concerning the change in number of dwelling units that might result from conversions." New Jersey Department of Labor and Industry, Division of Planning and Research, *New Jersey Residential Building Permits: 1974 Summary* (Trenton, N.J., 1974), p. 6.

12. Dwelling units were converted to estimated acreage using average

platting coefficients calculated for suburban New Jersey by James and Hughes, *Modeling State Growth*, p. 92, based on data reported in Regional Plan Association, *Spread City* (New York, 1962), RPA Bulletin 100, p. 42. A platting coefficient is the ratio of dwelling units to acres (the average number of units that can be constructed per gross acre of land, including streets and other subtractions from vacant land). Multifamily units were converted using a plat of 14 for garden apartments, duplexes (typically found on lots under a quarter-acre per unit) using the plat of 2.42 for such lot sizes. Single-family units were converted (since lot size is unknown here) using an average plat estimated from the minimum lot size patterns in each county, as developed by the author from the 1970 zoning survey. These average plats were calculated using the RPA estimates of 2.42 for less than a quarter-acre and 0.43 for lot sizes of an acre or more. Following the pattern adopted in the 1970 zoning survey, duplexes were then combined with single-family units; three- or four-family units were combined with units of five families or more as multifamily. In the official state data series on building permits, however, the category single family may include both detached and attached (townhouse) units. Land required for multifamily construction is probably overestimated, since no distinction is made between high-rise and garden apartments.

13. Regional Plan Association, *Spread City*. These eight counties are the portion of New Jersey that falls within the New York Metropolitan Region defined by RPA. They constitute most of the study and northeast regions. Ocean is not included in the RPA study. Hudson was included as a ninth county but has been dropped here due to lack of data in the 1970 zoning survey. The RPA data are also available in Sagalyn and Sternlieb, *Zoning and Housing Costs*, Exhibit 1-3, p. 18; Neil N. Gold and Paul Davidoff, "The Supply and Availability of Land for Housing for Low- and Moderate-Income Families," in *The Report of the President's Committee on Urban Housing*, 2 vols. (Washington, D.C.: U.S. Government Printing Office, 1968), vol. 2: *Technical Studies*, pp. 340-346.

14. Sagalyn and Sternlieb, *Zoning and Housing Costs*, especially appendix A, "Sampling Procedures and Sample Characteristics," pp. 71-80. The original data set from this survey was made available to the author on computer tape. This sample is used in chapter 5 to estimate market value and household characteristics for single-family homes in the study counties.

15. Ibid., p. 69.

16. Franklin J. James, "Can Suburbs House Suburban Workers in New Jersey?" in *New Jersey Trends*, ed. Thomas P. Norman (New Brunswick, N.J.: Institute for Environmental Studies, 1974), chap. 26, pp. 332-352.

17. Robert Schafer, *The Suburbanization of Multifamily Housing* (Lexington, Mass.: Lexington Books, D.C. Heath and Co., 1974), chap. 1, "Multifamily Housing: An Historical Perspective," pp. 1-12.

18. Ibid., chap. 2, "The Suburban Housing Market," pp. 13-30.

19. Ibid., chap. 3, "The Demand for Multifamily Housing in Metropolitan Areas," pp. 31-58.

20. See New Jersey County and Municipal Government Study Commission, *Housing and Suburbs: Fiscal and Social Impact of Multifamily Development* (Trenton, N.J., October 1974), chap. 6, "Land Use Controls and Apartment Construction," pp. 101-115.

21. New Jersey County and Municipal Government Study Commission, *Housing and Suburbs: Fiscal and Social Impact of Multifamily Development. Summary of Findings, Conclusions and Recommendations* (Trenton, N.J., June 1974), p. 13.

22. Ibid., p. 15.

23. New Jersey County and Municipal Government Study Commission, *Housing and Suburbs*, chap. 5, "Leadership Perceptions and Local Decisions," pp. 75-100.

24. Ibid., table 6-4, p. 109.

25. New Jersey Department of Community Affairs, Division of State and Regional Planning, *Land Use Regulation: The Residential Land Supply*, table VI, "Multi-Dwelling Bedroom Restrictions for Three-or-More-Unit Dwellings in Residential and Non-Residential Zones, by County," p. 11A. Bedroom restrictions by municipality, as a proportion of units rather than land, is reported in J. Gary Cruzan, "Home Rule versus Housing Production in New Jersey: A Report Prepared for the Governor's Task Force on Housing" (Trenton, N.J., November 1971), Exhibit 6, "Municipalities with Multi-Family Zoning on Vacant Land in 16 County Study Area," pp. 11A-20A.

26. These data are computed from New Jersey Department of Community Affairs, Division of Housing and Urban Renewal, *New Multi-Family Dwellings in New Jersey* (Trenton, N.J.), annual reports for 1970-1973. These reports do not contain number of bedrooms, only number of rooms. I have treated anything above 5½ rooms as a three-bedroom unit, anything above 3½ rooms as a two-bedroom unit. This procedure is supported by the relationship between bedroom and room counts for apartments found in the 1970 census data for New Jersey, as reported in Duane Windsor and Franklin J. James, "Statewide Multipliers for Municipal Cost-Revenue Analysis," paper presented at the national conference of the American Institute of Planners, Denver, Colo. (October 1974).

27. The study argues that zoning considerably alters bedroom sizes from what the marketplace would produce. New Jersey County and Municipal Government Study Commission, *Housing and Suburbs*, p. 109.

28. Ibid., p. 44.

29. Williams and Norman, "Exclusionary Land Use Controls," pp. 476, n. 4; 484.

30. Ibid., p. 481.

31. Ibid., p. 484.

32. Ibid., p. 484, n. 17. The relationship of these factors is analyzed in New Jersey Department of Community Affairs, *Land Use Regulation*, "Correlation Among Minimum Lot Size, Frontage and Building Size Requirements," pp. 20-24.

33. Williams and Norman, "Exclusionary Land Use Controls," p. 497, n. 47.

34. Stephen Sussna, "Residential Densities or a Fool's Paradise," *Land Economics* 49 (February 1973):1-2.

35. Williams and Norman, "Exclusionary Land Use Controls," p. 496.

36. Ibid., p. 495.

37. Sherman J. Maisel, "Background Information on Costs of Land, Single Family Housing," in *Appendix to the Report on Housing in California* (Sacramento, Calif.: Governor's Advisory Commission on Housing Problems, April 1963), pp. 221-282; cited in Sagalyn and Sternlieb, *Zoning and Housing Costs*, p. 28.

38. Sagalyn and Sternlieb, *Zoning and Housing Costs*, p. 54.

39. Ibid., p. 52.

40. Ibid., p. 66.

41. Ibid.

42. Ibid., p. 56.

43. Ibid., p. 52.

44. Jerome G. Rose, "*Mt. Laurel*: Is it Based on Wishful Thinking?" *Land Use Law and Zoning Digest* 27 (1975):18-21; Peter L. Abeles, "Madison Township: Twenty Years Too Late," in *New Dimensions in Urban Planning: Growth Controls*, ed. James W. Hughes (New Brunswick, N.J.: Center for Urban Policy Research, Rutgers University, 1974), chap. 11, pp. 160-164.

45. See Peter R. Morris, *State Housing Finance Agencies: An Entrepreneurial Approach* (Lexington, Mass.: Lexington Books, D.C. Heath and Co., 1974).

4

Fiscal Stakes of Suburban Growth Management

The zoning practices cited in chapter 3 indicate that suburban municipalities in New Jersey typically exclude apartments and zone for large lot homes, often in connection with excessive commercial and industrial zoning. This situation may be partly mitigated by informal practices focused on the variance process. It is not entirely clear that local zoning requirements are binding on developers. The fiscal motive theory assumes that a direct fiscal strategy is involved. However, the fiscal implications of suburban land use and growth management policies are complicated, as this chapter will show. The specific fiscal mechanism analyzed by Hamilton and White may be relatively weak in its empirical effects. Evidence from New Jersey cited in this chapter indicates that only a few communities have successfully used such fiscal strategies.

At root, the Hamilton and White formulations must assume that single-family housing will maximize taxable valuation per household. It is true that the market value per dwelling unit is higher for such housing. As chapter 5 will show, however, it is not necessarily true that the direct fiscal impact of single-family housing is better than that of apartments; the contrary is often the case in suburban New Jersey. Hamilton and White neglect the relationship between house value on the one hand and demography (especially household size and age composition) on the other. It is that relationship which determines cost-revenue balances. This relationship does not necessarily favor single-family housing.

Exclusionary zoning practices may be aimed, not at the fiscal zoning mechanism described by Hamilton and White, but at avoiding the scale effects and opportunity costs of population growth. In other words, the real fiscal strategy may not be one of maximizing tax base through high-value residential ratables supplemented by commercial or industrial ratables but rather one of minimizing property tax rates by withholding land from development or restricting population densities. Current zoning policies in New Jersey are fully consistent with such a fiscal strategy. The fiscal stakes of suburban growth management are probably much more important in local decision making than the cost-revenue balances imposed by particular housing types. This fiscal strategy is reinforced by several nonfiscal considerations that are important in suburban growth management but are overlooked by the fiscal motive theory.

The implication of this argument is that the fiscal zoning practiced by suburban communities is a very different proposition from the simple cost-revenue strategy assumed in the fiscal motive theory. It is true that exclusionary zoning practices will raise housing costs through supply restrictions (which is the starting point for the allocative and distributional effects analyzed by Hamilton and White). However, as chapter 3 concluded, there is little evidence at present to indicate that the removal of such supply restrictions would do very much to provide suburban housing opportunities for low- and moderate-income households. It may be the case that such restrictions simply reinforce the basic market forces underlying income segregation. The restrictions probably impose higher costs on middle-income households moving into suburban communities. Low- and moderate-income households may not be affected directly at all, except through the filtering process about which we know relatively little.

The Empirical Evidence on Fiscal Zoning

The evidence cited in support of the fiscal motive theory is surprisingly thin. Hamilton asserts the fiscal stakes of zoning decisions to taxpayers. For example, with a tax rate of 2.5 percent ($2.50 per $100), a house assessed at $40,000 is subject to an annual tax liability of $1,000. Doubling the taxable valuation per household (without any increase in average public service costs!) would cut that tax liability in half.[1] The empirical issue, of course, is whether valuation can be increased to such an extent while holding service costs and tax rates constant.

White's principal evidence for fiscal zoning is the widespread existence of exclusionary practices. The Ohls, Weisberg, and White article emphasizes the exclusion of multifamily dwellings and the allocation of residential land to single-family uses.[2] The same evidentiary importance is assigned by White to suburban reliance on only one or two lot sizes in single-family districts. "In a sample of about 300 New Jersey communities in the New York metropolitan area, about three-quarters of the communities zoned 75 percent or more of their land for development in a single lot size. Most of the remainder divided their vacant land into regions set aside for two different, but similar lot sizes."[3] This approach argues, but cannot demonstrate, that exclusionary and fiscal zoning are synonymous.

There is some statistical evidence concerning the influence of fiscal incentives on exclusionary zoning practices. The theory of fiscal zoning has two implications. First, local fiscal variables should influence patterns of income segregation in metropolitan areas. Second, household location decisions should be affected by the same fiscal considerations. Studies have been conducted recently into both problems. Hamilton comments that "there is only slender statistical evidence on the effects that local fiscal considerations have on residential location patterns."[4]

Two Tests of Fiscal Zoning

Hamilton cites two recent studies by economists that present evidence relating local fiscal considerations to exclusionary zoning practices. Both studies attempt to measure the degree of income segregation in metropolitan areas and identify the related causal factors. "In conclusion, I find that the two studies cited here lend considerable, though far from overwhelming, support to the notion that local fiscal incentives intensify income clustering."[5] However, as Hamilton himself indicates, the two studies cited are in substantial disagreement with each other over the nature of the fiscal considerations involved and the proper conclusions to be drawn about fiscal reform.

Hamilton, Mills, and Puryear Study. The first study cited by Hamilton was conducted by himself with Mills and Puryear.[6] They correlated a set of explanatory variables (presumed to be related to local fiscal incentives) with the degree of income segregation (measured as the Gini coefficient of household income calculated from 1970 census data) in census tracts taken from nineteen Standard Metropolitan Statistical Areas (SMSAs). In each SMSA, suburban and central city tracts (selected to be relatively homogeneous) were compared. Put simply, the authors attempted to measure the degree of segregation of households (using family income as a crucial determinant of demand for public services) as a function of the local fiscal environment (looking at public education as the dominant local service). Their hypothesis was that income homogeneity by census tract should rise with the number of school districts in metropolitan areas. A positive and significant correlation was found.

They also tested the hypothesis that the level of state and federal aid to local school districts should be negatively correlated with income homogeneity. The implication of this hypothesis is that the fiscal advantage to current residents of fiscal zoning to protect the local tax base would be lessened by such external aid. The authors tested for the effects of both flat aid (which is completely unrelated to any variable under local control except number of pupils) and compensatory aid (based on the number of poor households or inversely related to the local tax base). Matching aid provisions typically had ceilings low enough to be treated as essentially flat grants.[7] The authors again found their predicted results. On the average, changes in compensatory aid brought about twice the reduction in the segregation index as did changes in flat aid. (The regression coefficient of the former was somewhat more significant statistically.)

There are three difficulties in this analysis. The first is that the Gini index used for income segregation is difficult to interpret. The index indicates direction but not magnitude of change. It does not measure the degree or strength of the relationship.[8] We know only that the variables tested increase income segregation. Second, the relationship failed to hold when tested using house value in place of income. The Hamilton and White models deal with fiscal zoning to control minimum house values. Since house value and income are closely correlated, households are segregated by demand for public services (income) and by house value.[9] Therefore the Gini coefficient for house value by census tract (defined in census data only for owner-occupied, single-family dwellings, attached and detached) was regressed on the same explanatory variables. The results were strongly opposed to those just discussed for income. Higher aid to school districts increased segregation measured by housing value. Hamilton and his colleagues professed themselves at a loss to explain such wholly anomalous results, since income and house value are highly correlated. They suggest that whereas income includes all families, house value excludes rental property, which results in a biased sample of households.[10]

Third, this approach employs fragmentation of local government (measured as number of school districts in an SMSA) as a local fiscal variable. External aid is measured directly but local fiscal impacts are not. The authors have found that metropolitan fragmentation is correlated positively with income segregation (but negatively with housing value). It is important to stress in this connection that these two studies involve a difficult methodological problem pointed out by Schafer. They do not determine whether income segregation is a result of exclusionary land use controls, or vice versa. In other words, income segregation could have preceded the adoption of exclusionary practices.[11] These studies deal simply with the correlation of the two phenomena, not their causal relationship. The critical issue is whether number of school districts in a metropolitan area can be properly interpreted as a fiscal variable.

I am not surprised by the anomalies in Hamilton's evidence. I see no reason to assume that the fragmentation of local government should be regarded as a fiscal measure. This assumption rests on the view that fragmentation must be prompted by fiscal considerations. Hamilton cites similar evidence elsewhere in support of his contention. He correlated by state the average number of suburban school districts per capita and the percent of local school expenditure financed by the state. He found that state aid explained 35 percent of the variation in number of school districts. From this result, he concludes that a high level of state aid reduces the fiscal incentive to form a fragmented system of local governments and that such fragmentation is a fiscal phenomenon.[12] I see no reason why this result makes fragmentation a fiscal measure. On the contrary I would simply expect high levels of state aid to be associated with strong state pressures for school district consolidation (which is not the same thing).

Branfman, Cohen, and Trubek Study. This second study reached different conclusions regarding the relationship between fiscal variables and income segregation.[13] The authors analyzed a sample of thirty SMSAs using 1970 census data. The specific purpose of their analysis was to assess the relative importance of discriminatory and fiscal motives in observed zoning practices. They found considerable evidence of income clustering related to public land use controls (for example, the greater the number of zoning authorities in an SMSA, the greater the degree of segregation) but little evidence of fiscal zoning for a number of fiscal variables examined. These fiscal variables included the proportion of the school budget financed locally, local property tax payments as a proportion of personal income, local property tax payments as a proportion of local revenue, and an index for state educational aid.

They concluded that changes in state aid formulas or the local proportion of school budgets had only a weak effect on income segregation. They found that the number of local zoning authorities (per million population) in an SMSA was the most important variable explaining income segregation. Unlike Hamilton and his colleagues, the authors specifically decline to interpret number of zoning authorities as a fiscal measure. As a result, they conclude that land use controls are either not fiscally motivated or, regardless of motivation, have little effect on income segregation.[14] This difference in interpretation is critical, as Hamilton points out.[15] (Schafer suggests that the specific clustering index used in the study—calculated using municipalities rather than census tracts—is misspecified and overstates the influence of public land use controls on income segregation, because the index is by definition related to the number of municipalities in an SMSA).[16]

Two Tests of the Tiebout Hypothesis

The basic assumption of the fiscal motive theory is that income segregation results from exclusionary zoning practices and governmental fragmentation in metropolitan areas (an assumption not clearly demonstrated in the two statistical studies cited). On the contrary, however, it is not necessary to fall back on the Tiebout mechanism to explain income clustering. The Tiebout model is based on highly artificial conditions. Tiebout assumed a simple world of retired households, living on dividend incomes, who thus have no workplace constraints and can migrate without cost. The Tiebout model neglects both workplace location and transportation costs. In doing so, the model disregards crucial considerations in residential location decisions. It is reasonable to believe that income, commuting costs, and demand for housing services can account for the segregation of high- and low-income households in suburbs and central cities without considering public expenditures, taxes, and land use controls.[17]

Methodologically, in order to assess the effects of the public sector on metropolitan housing markets, we must first evaluate the effects of the factors underlying supply and demand.[18] The Tiebout model does not deal solely with the public sector, but it ignores employment and transportation considerations. In the same vein, as was discussed in chapter 3, even if land use controls are fiscally motivated, we must still show that such controls affect housing supplies and prices to low- and moderate-income households. The public sector may well, of course, reinforce the effects of supply and demand in creating income segregation in metropolitan housing markets. If demand for public services is related to income, there should be a tendency toward income segregation. Fiscal zoning might tend to be employed to exclude free riders from wealthier communities.[19] The empirical question is how powerful these tendencies are, compared with the market forces also operating.

There is no single accepted theory of residential location that will explain how and why some households locate in central cities and others in suburbs.[20] There is agreement that location is determined by a cost-benefit calculus in which household income and tastes are the principal factors. The disagreement arises over the specific costs and benefits that various types of households take into account and the effects of constraints such as workplace, income, and discrimination. Among the factors considered may be various characteristics of residences and neighborhoods; accessibility to employment, shopping, and other activities; housing and land costs; commuting costs; local public services and taxes. Local zoning practices may affect residential characteristics, accessibility, and housing or land costs. The fiscal zoning hypothesis argues that local public services and taxes are manipulated as well.

Mayo suggests that a principal distinction between such theories is precisely their treatment of the local public sector.[21] The most widely accepted theory (the private sector theory of Alonso, Kain, and Muth) argues that households trade off commuting costs and residential space (with consideration for the quality as well as quantity of housing services).[22] The local public sector is not included in this theory. However exclusionary zoning would presumably affect the price of residential space. On the other hand, the Tiebout hypothesis (or public sector theory) argues that public services and taxes are important determinants of residential location choices by households. In neither case are residential location choices and local budgetary decisions integrated into a single simultaneous theory.

Two recent studies have addressed this problem. Both reached largely the same conclusion that fiscal considerations play only a minor role in household location decisions. Both housing stock and population characteristics had more impact on residential location decisions than did fiscal conditions and on fiscal conditions themselves than vice versa. There was evidence of some influence on residential location decisions by fiscal characteristics, but this influence was not particularly important and was restricted to high-income households with school-age children.

Bloom, Brown, and Jackson Study. The authors of this study argue that the essence of the private sector theory is the relationship between workplace accessibility and land availability.[23] The essence of the public sector theory is the relationship between neighborhood characteristics and local fiscal variables. In principle the two theories may be linked by recognizing that the private sector model partly determines the population characteristics and tax base for the public sector, while the public sector model partly determines land availability and housing costs in the private sector (through land use controls), as well as the availability and cost of public services. If demand for public services is strongly correlated with demographic and economic characteristics, then we would expect relatively homogeneous communities and the income stratification of metropolitan areas through self-selection without the fiscal zoning of the Hamilton and White models.

In an attempt to link the private sector and public sector theories, the authors create three separate submodels explaining the fiscal, population, and housing characteristics of suburban communities. Population characteristics are defined in terms of income, education, and school-age children. The model is tested using data from a sample of sixty-five suburban communities in the Boston metropolitan area. Data observations were taken from 1960 and 1970 for fiscal, census, land use, employment, and accessibility measures. Fiscal characteristics are defined as school expenditures per household, equalized property tax rates, and state aid. Using observations weighted by 1970 population, the model is tested using two-stage least-squares multiple regression (to handle the simultaneous relationships). The relationships are measured over a ten-year period with highly aggregated (municipal) and collinear data in a specific geographic area.[24]

The authors concluded that fiscal considerations were relatively unimportant in residential location decisions and that income segregation in metropolitan areas results largely from supply and demand forces. They indicate, however, that fiscal considerations could not be entirely ignored.[25] Housing stock and population characteristics were more important than, and affected, fiscal conditions. Hamilton's fiscal zoning mechanism does appear to be at work. Municipalities with high school expenditures attracted families with school-age children; communities with low tax rates attracted other households.[26] The question is how strong, in the adoption of local zoning policies, the house value (or cost-revenue) factor will be in comparison with the scale effects and opportunity costs of population growth, discrimination, and negative externalities.

Mayo Study. Mayo reaches much the same conclusions as the authors of the first study, but his analysis shows somewhat more responsiveness of locational decisions to school expenditures. The housing characteristics of the first study (like most studies of residential location) are defined in terms of highly aggregated hedonic price indexes (the average market value of all owner-occupied units and the average rent of all rental units). Mayo examines the effects of various explanatory variables on several categories of households, defined in terms of household characteristics and workplace location. His principal measure is the probability of a particular category (or submarket) of households locating at a site, given household characteristics and workplace. This probability is simply the proportion of the group actually locating at that site. Mayo includes travel time from workplace to residential site, housing and neighborhood characteristics, accessibility to shops, local public services and tax levels, land use, and topography as explanatory variables. He tests this model using data taken from a 1963 household interview survey of some 17,000 households (about a 3 percent sample) conducted in and around the Milwaukee SMSA (with 10,000 households located within the SMSA). The sample is stratified by income, race, household size, sex of head of household, and number of persons contributing to family income. Mayo also stratified the sample by residential census tract (the actual observation unit he employs) and four workplace zones in the Milwaukee SMSA (containing about 80 percent of all SMSA employment). A representative workplace district was taken from each zone, and the residential locations of all employees (by census tract) in those districts were analyzed. The model was tested using least-squares regression for each category of household.

The private sector model of residential location was again found to have the greatest influence; local public services and tax differentials were not found to be major determinants of residential location. However, the model results varied widely among the household categories. The effects of the public sector model seemed to matter (though not markedly) for higher-income groups but not for lower-income groups. The influence of housing- and transportation-cost constraints declined with income, leaving more scope for housing quality, neighborhood characteristics, and public services in residential location.[27] However Jackson suggests that Mayo's results may be biased by the spatial distribution of the sample households. Low- and middle-income households tend to reside in Milwaukee, high-income households in its suburbs. As a result, tax and service levels do not vary except for high-income households.[28]

Fiscal Stakes of Population Growth

Better evidence of a fiscal motivation for suburban exclusionary zoning can be found. Table 4-1 categorizes the 567 municipalities in New Jersey by equalized valuation per capita (in increments of $2,500 up to $15,000, with a final category of $20,000 or more).[29] About half of the communities (284) were in the range of $5,000-9,999 valuation per capita. About 108 had valuations under $5,000; 42 had valuations over $20,000. Total tax rates are four times higher in the poorest communities. The average school tax rate in 1970 ($2.09 for all municipalities) declined steadily from $4.55 in the below $2,500 group (12 municipalities to $0.84 in the above $20,000 group (42 municipalities). The average municipal tax rate ($0.66 for all municipalities) also steadily declined from $1.35 to $0.64 in 1970. After an initial drop expenditures rise steadily with equalized valuation. There is a tremendous jump above $20,000 valuation. Median house value rises on average with valuation, but the pattern shows unusually high house value in the poorest communities (under $2,500 valuation) and lower house value in the wealthiest communities (over $20,000 valuation).

There are two problems with this demonstration. First, the exclusionary effect of fiscal zoning has nothing to do with property taxation per se. Rather it results from local taxation combined with the local power of exclusion through land use controls. Assume, for example, that local revenues are raised solely by an income tax. If average household income is $10,000 and local expenditures

Table 4-1
Fiscal Disparities in Local Public Services in New Jersey (1970)

Equalized Valuation per Capita	Equalized School Tax Rate	Equalized Municipal Tax Rate	Local Tax Expenditure per Capita	Median House Value	Number of Municipalities	Percent of Municipalities
Less than $2,500	$4.55	$1.35	$191	$19,153	12	2.1
$2,500-4,999	2.51	0.91	179	13,792	96	17.0
$5,000-7,499	2.22	0.65	230	19,635	156	27.6
$7,500-9,999	2.16	0.59	291	25,312	128	22.6
$10,000-12,499	1.99	0.51	341	29,493	70	12.4
$12,500-14,999	1.56	0.47	344	31,812	35	6.2
$15,000-19,999	1.50	0.45	404	33,239	28	4.9
$20,000 or more[a]	0.84	0.64	496	25,355	41	7.2
Total	2.09	0.66	284	22,981	566	100.0

Sources: Fiscal data are taken from New Jersey Department of Community Affairs, *Thirty-Third Annual Report of the Division of Local Government Services, 1970: Statements of Financial Condition of Counties and Municipalities* (Trenton, N.J., 1971); median house value from 1970 Census of Population and Housing.

Notes: All data are on a municipality basis. All data are the average value for cases in the category. Valuation and tax data are equalized for 100 percent assessment. Local tax expenditures include both school and municipal functions.

[a]An industrial enclave has been removed from this category, with valuation of $3,917,772 and expenditures of $28,016 per capita.

per household are $1,000, a proportional tax rate will be 10 percent. A household earning $20,000 will pay $2,000 in local income tax. A household earning $5,000 will pay only $500 and thus will not cover the marginal cost of its public services. The richer household will have a fiscal incentive to exclude any additional poorer households on this evidence in order to keep its tax rate from rising. It would rather admit a household earning $30,000 and paying $3,000 in taxes. If only two households reside in the community, at $1,000 in service costs per household (assuming that the richer household does not have higher demand for public services and moves to the community for $1,000 worth of services), the tax rate can be reduced to only 4 percent (to raise $2,000 in revenue from $50,000 aggregate community income), and the $20,000-income household pays $800 rather than $1,000. The local income tax must be regressive to avoid this problem. The same illustration can be applied to a sales tax based on household consumption.

The exclusionary effect arises under property taxation because present residents can regulate the tax payments of new residents indirectly by setting minimum house value through local land use controls. House value is related to income, which in turn will affect consumption or sales. The apparent solution must be to separate tax revenues and expenditures from land use (state aid might accomplish this separation), not simply to change tax base (even at the state level). The real question to investigate is how strongly voters are influenced by such fiscal considerations in the adoption of community land use policies and how particular fiscal reforms will affect those considerations. The real issue at stake is a distributional one among taxpayers of different incomes (and different preferences for public services and tax rates): Who should bear the burden of tax expenditures (present residents, new residents, or all equally) and how?

Second, chapter 2 suggested that population size and growth rate are more important fiscal considerations than the immediate cash-flow implications of particular development proposals. These fiscal considerations depend on housing type only in the sense of the population density and pupils permitted per acre. The scale effects and opportunity costs of development may be induced more rapidly when land is zoned for denser development because of larger populations, even though density per se may not particularly affect public service costs. These scale effects and opportunity costs are different from the cost-revenue implications of housing type.

Land Development and Population Growth

Table 4-2 examines the fiscal consequences of differences in population size (using 1960 as a base for 1960-1970 population growth) and growth rate (1960-1970). Three local fiscal measures are used: (1) 1970 property tax rates (school and municipal combined), (2) local expenditures per capita (school and municipal combined), which is to say average service costs, and (3) equalized valuation per capita (average tax base). Cross-sectional data are employed in this analysis. (Muller points out that time series data might impound rising average service costs together with growth effects. He suggests that cross-sectional data permit a better comparison of different growth patterns.)[30] Tax rates, expenditures, and valuations are reported as averages for the cases in each table cell.

Local property tax rates (combining municipal and school functions together) rise steadily with population size from $2.62 to $3.95 per $100. This same pattern, though broken on occasion, holds fairly well regardless of growth rate, except in declining communities. The highest tax rates (about $5.00) are found in declining cities under 2,500 or over 50,000 population. There is a tendency for tax rates first to fall with population growth in smaller cities and then to rise with growth in medium-sized cities. There is some rise again above 100 percent growth rates in all cities over 2,500 population.

Per capita expenditures (again combining municipal and school functions) rise with growth rate. Expenditures are highest in communities under 2,500 population (at $321) but otherwise are very close overall, varying from $262 to $273. Declining communities often have somewhat lower expenditures than growing communities of similar size. Per capita equalized valuation falls steadily with population size. In general the valuation pattern is constant between 20 percent and 200 percent growth, declining both above and below those limits. Hence we should expect tax rates to rise and average valuation to fall with community development. Expenditures per capita are less affected. In general the categories with the highest increases in tax rate also had the highest valuations. However large cities with high increases had very low valuations, under $7,000 per resident.[31]

Population Implications of
Zoning Controls

The fiscal considerations ultimately involved in suburban growth management are given more substance when we examine the likely population implications of zoning regulations in New Jersey. Table 4-3 estimates the housing units, population, and pupils permitted by the 1970 zoning ordinances in the six study counties (for 176 municipalities with vacant, developable land). The housing unit estimates were computed following the method of table 3-13 using the platting coefficient and acres of vacant land for each land use category. Population and pupils were computed from estimates of household characteristics by household type (apartments and single-family lot size categories). These characteristics, taken from 1970 census data for New Jersey, are explained in chapter 5. The estimates were done separately for primary residential districts and nonresidential districts where secondary residential uses were partially

Table 4-2
Fiscal Stakes of Population Size and Growth in New Jersey (1970)

Population (1960)	Growth Rate, 1960-1970 (percent)						
	Declining	0-19.9	20-49.9	50-99.9	100-199.9	200 or More	Total
Municipal and School Property Tax Rates							
Less than 2,500	4.80a	2.51	2.20	2.45	2.31	2.28	2.62
2,500-4,999	2.99	2.72	2.58	2.61	2.67	2.77	2.69
5,000-9,999	3.19	2.66	2.73	2.76	3.08	3.91	2.77
10,000-24,999	2.97	2.70	2.68	2.74	3.05	3.95	2.77
25,000-49,999	3.70	2.95	2.90	2.38	2.85	–	3.03
50,000 or more	5.08	3.39	2.27	–	–	–	3.95
Total	3.73	2.70	2.51	2.60	2.64	2.88	2.75
Municipal and School Local Expenditure per Capita							
Less than 2,500	230a	269	353	395	358	254	321
2,500-4,999	231	244	254	281	345	189	262
5,000-9,999	222	267	283	267	295	254	270
10,000-24,999	265	266	268	278	253	208	267
25,000-49,999	256	287	242	303	262	–	273
50,000 or more	310	248	220	–	–	–	270
Total	247	269	297	316	330	224	283
Equalized Valuation per Capita							
Less than 2,500	9,983a	11,762	15,819	19,181	14,156	9,521	14,319
2,500-4,999	6,984	9,009	8,703	9,592	12,226	5,044	9,055
5,000-9,999	5,966	8,508	9,337	8,251	8,409	6,180	8,509
10,000-24,999	6,987	8,552	8,527	7,906	7,396	4,935	8,137
25,000-49,999	5,296	7,961	6,909	11,721	8,297	–	7,500
50,000 or more	4,377	6,474	6,810	–	–	–	5,650
Total	7,240	9,294	11,253	12,268	11,733	6,851	10,277

Number of Municipalities

Less than 2,500	18a	51	56	29	14	3	171
2,500-4,999	16	37	31	25	14	3	126
5,000-9,999	9	46	37	19	5	1	117
10,000-24,999	16	42	26	13	4	1	102
25,000-49,999	5	19	6	1	2	–	33
50,000 or more	7	8	2	–	–	–	17
Total	71	203	158	87	39	8	566

Sources: Fiscal data are taken from New Jersey Department of Community Affairs, *Thirty-Third Annual Report of the Division of Local Government Services, 1970: Statements of Financial Condition of Counties and Municipalities* (Trenton, N.J., 1971); population data from 1960 and 1970 Censuses of Population and Housing.

aAn industrial enclave has been removed from this category, with tax rate of $0.23, expenditures of $28,016 per capita, valuation of $3,917,772 per capita, and population of 22.

Table 4-3
Population Implications of 1970 Zoning Ordinances in the Study Counties (1970)

County	Least-Cost Residential Zones	1970 Zoning Ordinances			Least-Cost Commercial and Industrial Zones	1970 Zoning Ordinances		
		Total	Multi-family	Single Family		Total	Multi-family	Single Family
Housing Units								
Bergen	322,381	21,576	1,974	19,602	588,406	4,646	3,486	1,160
Middlesex	795,021	51,725	4,298	47,427	657,748	36,734	27,314	9,420
Monmouth	1,492,557	95,992	8,862	87,130	306,796	26,586	13,370	13,216
Morris	2,240,806	78,089	17,528	60,561	490,826	6,264	4,172	2,092
Ocean	2,181,760	288,768	153,314	135,454	402,836	21,648	13,342	8,306
Somerset	1,224,742	45,586	—	45,586	271,936	3,202	896	2,306
Total	8,257,267	581,736	185,976	395,760	2,718,548	99,080	62,580	36,500
Population								
Bergen	834,967	78,275	4,781	73,494	1,523,972	13,912	8,361	5,551
Middlesex	1,929,516	251,588	9,273	242,315	1,596,354	107,226	61,783	45,443
Monmouth	3,814,976	416,274	56,655	359,619	784,171	91,741	32,905	58,836
Morris	5,552,717	319,463	41,174	278,289	1,216,267	11,474	4,663	6,811
Ocean	5,397,674	900,669	363,273	537,396	996,616	63,601	31,473	32,128
Somerset	3,066,754	205,880	—	205,880	680,928	12,410	2,155	10,255
Total	20,596,604	2,172,149	475,156	1,696,993	6,798,308	300,364	141,340	159,024
Schoolchildren								
Bergen	89,622	33,158	608	32,550	163,577	2,799	1,080	1,719
Middlesex	137,539	88,407	804	87,603	113,790	21,019	5,107	15,912
Monmouth	367,169	139,211	2,465	136,746	75,472	24,546	3,718	20,828
Morris	445,920	106,212	3,768	102,444	97,674	4,236	897	3,339
Ocean	427,625	202,608	33,269	169,339	78,956	12,513	2,895	9,618
Somerset	273,117	72,695	—	72,695	60,642	3,811	229	3,582
Total	1,740,992	642,291	40,914	601,377	590,111	68,924	13,926	54,998

Sources: Housing unit and population estimates are developed from zoning data in New Jersey Department of Community Affairs, "1970 Zoning Survey" (Trenton, N.J., 1971), using household characteristics reported in table 5-1 and plating coefficients taken from Franklin J. James and James W. Hughes, *Modeling State Growth: New Jersey 1980* (New Brunswick, N.J.: Center for Urban Policy Research, Rutgers University, 1973), p. 92.

permitted. For comparison, housing units, population, and pupils were also calculated on the *Madison* assumption of least-cost zoning, with all vacant land developed for garden apartments at a density of fourteen units per gross acre.

In 1970 residential zones over eight million garden apartments could have been constructed on the vacant land available. The potential population capacity of that land was over 20.5 million persons, including 1.7 million pupils. As actually zoned in 1970, the capacity was cut to 2.2 million persons and 642,000 schoolchildren. A similar reduction in capacity occurs in nonresidential zones. The potential population capacity was 6.8 million persons, including 590,000 schoolchildren. As zoned in 1970, capacity was cut to 300,000 persons and 69,000 children. We can see at a glance that the combination of multifamily exclusion, lot size restrictions, and holding of vacant land in commercial or industrial districts has tremendous population—and ultimately fiscal— implications.

The Fiscal Zoning Mechanism

The fiscal motive theory is essentially the argument that housing value per dwelling unit and industrial promotion are the obvious keys to fiscal balance in suburban communities. If so there must be at least a demonstration that housing value, housing-stock composition, and tax-base composition will significantly affect local fiscal variables. Moreover these effects must be sufficiently wide-spread among suburban communities to influence metropolitan housing markets. Chapter 5 will demonstrate that housing value per se is not a reliable guide to fiscal impact. The actual criterion should be taxable valuation per household. Hamilton and White are well aware of that criterion. Their mistake lies in assuming that taxable valuation per household is necessarily higher for single-family than for multifamily housing.

In this section we examine the effect for the 567 New Jersey municipalities of housing value, housing-stock composition, and tax-base composition on the three local fiscal variables: property tax rates, expenditures per capita, and equalized valuation per capita. In general tax rates decline with housing value and household income, rise with the proportion of multifamily housing, and decline with the proportion of tax base composed of commercial and industrial ratables. These results form the foundation of Hamilton and White's fiscal zoning mechanism. But a review of this evidence indicates that marked effects may be restricted to a few communities. Moreover the effects seem to vary significantly by population size and growth rate. Most important, these effects must still be disentangled from the scale and nonfiscal considerations discussed in chapter 2. The rise of tax rates with the multifamily proportion of the tax base is not necessarily attributable to cost-revenue deficits imposed by such housing (chapter 5 will demonstrate otherwise), but rather to the scale effects of larger populations permitted by higher housing densities.

Chapter 3 concluded that there was substantial evidence of excessive nonresidential zoning in suburban New Jersey, in addition to restrictive residential controls. It is generally assumed that commercial and industrial development is fiscally profitable for communities due to the nature of local property taxation (at least up to the point at which undesirable environmental impacts may offset desirable tax-base effects). Communities with a large proportion of nonresidential ratables are expected to have lower property tax rates for the same per capita expenditures, because the average tax base will be higher for a given population. The general theory is that from the fiscal viewpoint communities will attempt to maximize the nonresidential share of the tax base in order to reduce residential taxes.

This policy will presumably make residential zoning more restrictive, both to preserve vacant land for nonresidential ratables and to force new residential construction toward housing values equal to the existing average tax base (which now includes nonresidential ratables). Chapter 2 suggested, however, that nonresidential zoning may not be directed at such a fiscal purpose. On the contrary it may serve as a technique to withhold vacant land from development. Even if the purpose is fiscal, such zoning may not be successful. Zoning may prevent industrial development (if binding), but it is unlikely to attract such development when most communities pursue the same policy of industrial promotion.

Fiscal Implications of Housing Value

As a rough check on the empirical validity of the Hamilton and White formulations, we can examine the relationship of house value to the three fiscal measures already introduced. Table 4-4 reports the fiscal implications of 1970 median house value and median household income in New Jersey municipalities. The average tax rate declines from $3.03 to $1.89 as median house value rises over $50,000, and local expenditures per capita rise steadily from $234 to $444. Taxable valuation per capita rises from $8,261 to $25,262, but the phenomenon is confined to a relative handful of communities. The 304 communities between $20,000 and $50,000 median house value show roughly constant tax rates (averaging between $2.51 and $2.60). The Hamilton effect is largely restricted to 12 very wealthy communities over $50,000 median house value.

Median household income bears a straightforward relationship to the three fiscal measures. Tax rates decline while expenditures and valuation rise with income. Table 4-4 indicates that relatively poor communities will have high tax rates, low expenditures, and low taxable valuation. However it is hardly clear that restricting entrance to high-income households will confer distinct fiscal advantages on poorer communities (in contrast to the exclusion of poorer households by high-income communities). The marked rise in valuation occurs only above $15,000 median income and is confined to eighty communities.

Table 4-4
Fiscal Implications of Median House Value and Median Household Income in New Jersey (1970)

Median Value	Property Tax Rate	Local Expenditure per Capita	Equalized Valuation per Capita	Number of Municipalities
Single-family housing				
$0-19,999a	$3.03	$234	$ 8,261	250
$20,000-29,999	2.56	295	10,523	201
$30,000-39,999	2.60	352	12,971	79
$40,000-49,999	2.51	387	12,873	24
$50,000 or more	1.89	444	25,262	12
Total	2.75	283	10,277	566
Household income				
$5,000-9,999	$2.93	$270	$ 9,494	163
$10,000-14,999	2.71	268	9,740	323
$15,000-19,999	2.66	359	12,749	65
$20,000 or morea	2.19	376	15,353	15
Total	2.75	283	10,277	566

Sources: Fiscal data are taken from New Jersey Department of Community Affairs, *Thirty-Third Annual Report of the Division of Local Government Services, 1970: Statements of Financial Condition of Counties and Municipalities* (Trenton, N.J., 1971); median household value and income from 1970 Census of Population and Housing.

aAn industrial enclave has been removed from this category, with tax rate of $0.23, expenditures of $28,016 per capita, and valuation of $3,917,772 per capita.

The previous section emphasized the fiscal implications of population size and growth rate. Now let us control the house-value relationships of table 4-4 for the influence of these factors. Table 4-5 presents median house value and the three fiscal variables controlled for population size (using 1960 as a base for 1960-1970 growth). Whereas average tax rates decline with median house value, they rise with population size. In other words two contradictory factors are at work. The tendency for tax rates to decline with house value is largely confined to municipalities with population below 25,000. In the category between 25,000 and 50,000, an initial drop is followed by rising tax rates. However this trend is not marked. It is caused by a jump in per capita expenditures, despite rising valuation in those municipalities. Tax rates rise with population size regardless of house value.

Per capita expenditures rise on average with house value after an initial decline. However they are roughly constant (between $262 and $273) with population size following a substantial drop. While expenditures in general rise with house value, the pattern is U-shaped in the 171 small communities with populations under 2,500. A similar pattern holds for valuation, which is U-shaped with regard to house value (especially in communities under 2,500 population) but declines with population.

Table 4-6 controls the relationship between house value and the three fiscal

Table 4-5
Fiscal Implications of Median House Value in New Jersey
Controlled for Population Size (1970)

Population (1960)	Median Value of Single-Family Housing					Total
	$0-19,999	$20,000-29,999	$30,000-39,999	$40,000-49,999	$50,000-59,999	
	Municipal and School Property Tax Rates					
Less than 2,500	$2.97[a]	$2.24	$2.05	$2.26	$1.54	$2.61
2,500-4,999	2.81	2.66	2.46	2.61	2.18	2.69
5,000-9,999	2.93	2.61	2.90	2.50	–	2.77
10,000-24,999	2.98	2.75	2.63	2.37	2.06	2.77
25,000-49,999	4.07	2.57	2.96	3.36	–	3.03
50,000 or more	4.85	2.67	–	–	–	3.95
Total	3.03	2.56	2.60	2.51	1.89	2.75
	Municipal and School Expenditure per Capita					
Less than 2,500	$261[a]	$401	$369	$424	$488	$321
2,500-4,999	206	277	363	388	409	262
5,000-9,999	212	258	347	384	–	270
10,000-24,999	221	259	334	350	420	267
25,000-49,999	237	257	344	433	–	273
50,000 or more	286	248	–	–	–	270
Total	234	295	352	387	444	283
	Equalized Valuation per Capita					
Less than 2,500	$11,402[a]	$17,472	$19,464	$16,059	$35,510	$14,663
2,500-4,999	7,025	8,912	13,126	12,655	18,249	9,055
5,000-9,999	6,016	8,515	10,927	13,354	–	8,509
10,000-24,999	5,650	8,215	10,905	10,270	17,172	8,137
25,000-49,999	4,930	7,454	10,316	12,003	–	7,500
50,000 or more	4,298	7,582	–	–	–	5,650
Total	9,265	10,523	12,971	12,873	25,262	10,277
	Number of Municipalities					
Less than 2,500	98[a]	49	15	4	5	171
2,500-4,999	69	27	17	8	5	126
5,000-9,999	37	48	26	6	–	117
10,000-24,999	28	52	15	5	2	102
25,000-49,999	8	18	6	1	–	33
50,000 or more	10	7	–	–	–	17
Total	250	201	79	24	12	566

Sources: Fiscal data are taken from New Jersey Department of Community Affairs, *Thirty-Third Annual Report of the Division of Local Government Services, 1970: Statements of Financial Condition of Counties and Municipalities* (Trenton, N.J., 1971); median house value from 1970 Census of Population and Housing; population data from 1960 Census of Population and Housing.

[a]An industrial enclave has been removed from this category, with tax rate of $0.23, expenditures of $28,016 per capita, and valuation of $3,917,772 per capita.

Table 4-6
Fiscal Implications of Median House Value in New Jersey
Controlled for Growth Rate (1960-1970)

Growth Rate (1960-1970)	Median Value of Single-Family Housing					
	$0-19,999	$20,000-29,999	$30,000-39,999	$40,000-49,999	$50,000-59,999	Total
	Municipal and School Property Tax Rates					
Declining	$4.30a	$2.40	$2.17	$2.36	–	$3.73
0-19.9 percent	2.82	2.57	2.66	2.62	$2.09	2.70
20-49.9 percent	2.59	2.43	2.75	2.19	1.55	2.51
50-99.9 percent	2.73	2.63	2.47	2.78	0.60	2.60
100-199.9 percent	2.60	2.75	2.52	–	2.35	2.64
200 percent or more	1.89	3.54	3.16	–	–	2.88
Total	3.03	2.56	2.60	2.51	1.89	2.75
	Municipal and School Expenditure per Capita					
Declining	$232a	$259	$345	$371	–	$247
0-19.9 percent	233	258	344	393	$438	264
20-49.9 percent	236	320	361	393	408	297
50-99.9 percent	241	332	346	373	718	316
100-199.9 percent	241	335	410	–	420	330
200 percent or more	169	245	304	–	–	224
Total	234	295	352	387	444	283
	Equalized Valuation per Capita					
Declining	$ 5,450a	$ 8,023	$25,081	$12,846	–	$ 7,240
0-19.9 percent	9,390	8,493	11,873	12,001	$17,701	9,584
20-49.9 percent	8,229	12,681	12,252	15,982	23,145	11,253
50-99.9 percent	7,912	13,470	12,673	10,040	93,141	12,268
100-199.9 percent	12,801	9,456	14,610	–	16,403	11,733
200 percent or more	7,195	6,393	7,653	–	–	6,851
Total	8,261	10,523	12,971	12,873	25,262	10,277
	Number of Municipalities					
Declining	50a	16	4	1	–	71
0-19.9 percent	97	70	25	9	2	203
20-49.9 percent	64	61	21	8	4	158
50-99.9 percent	26	30	24	6	1	87
100-199.9 percent	10	20	4	–	5	39
200 percent or more	3	4	1	–	–	8
Total	250	201	79	24	12	566

Sources: Fiscal data are taken from New Jersey Department of Community Affairs, *Thirty-Third Annual Report of the Division of Local Government Services, 1970: Statements of Financial Condition of Counties and Municipalities* (Trenton, N.J., 1971); median house value and growth rates from 1970 Census of Population and Housing.

aAn industrial enclave has been removed from this category, with tax rate of $0.23, expenditures of $28,016 per capita, and valuation of $3,917,772 per capita.

variables for growth rate. Average tax rates decline at first with population growth but then appear to rise again in a U-shaped function. Tax rates are highest in declining ($3.73) and very rapidly growing communities above 200 percent growth ($2.88). High tax rates for declining communities are concentrated in those with median house value below $20,000. In general, tax rates fall with growth rate in that category. There is some tendency for tax rates to rise with growth rate in other categories. Tax rates generally decline with median value regardless of growth rate, but the pattern is very uneven. Tax rates rise in the communities growing faster than 200 percent.

Per capita expenditures show a strong tendency to rise with growth rate but are very low in communities growing faster than 200 percent. The average is lower than in declining communities. This drop occurs in all housing-value categories as higher growth rates are achieved. In general expenditures rise with growth rate regardless of house value, and vice versa. Equalized valuation rises and then falls with growth rate, whereas it rises with house value. The rise of valuation with house value is largely independent of growth rate, but there is little variation in the rapidly growing communities over 200 percent. A U-shaped function is exhibited in communities with growth rates between 50 percent and 100 percent.

Fiscal Implications of Housing-Stock Composition

We may similarly examine the fiscal implications of housing-stock composition to determine the influence of housing type on the three local fiscal measures. Table 4-7 reports the fiscal implications of the proportion of housing stock in single-family and multifamily types. As the proportion of multifamily housing rises, so do average tax rates. But this increase is marked only in the 87 municipalities where the proportion rises above 25 percent. Otherwise the tax rate varies between $2.50 and $2.78; it varies between only $2.70 and $2.78 in the 244 municipalities between 10 percent and 25 percent. The 236 municipalities with less than 5 percent of multifamily housing do have slightly lower tax rates (which may be related to smaller population sizes and growth rates). Correspondingly, tax rates tend to decline as the proportion of single-family housing rises. The decrease is again marked only in proportions above 50 percent (in 92 municipalities).

Only at extreme proportions are tax rates affected strongly; these extremes are likely to be associated with population and growth characteristics. The specific population patterns of fewer than one hundred municipalities are probably the critical considerations rather than housing stock per se. Tax rates, expenditures, and valuation are higher where the proportion of single-family housing is below 50 percent (which includes, however, the seventeen largest cities in New Jersey). When we look at the eighty-seven municipalities with 25

Table 4-7
Fiscal Implications of Housing-Stock Composition in New Jersey (1970)

Proportion of Housing Stock	Property Tax Rate	Local Expenditure per Capita	Equalized Valuation per Capita	Number of Municipalities
Single-family (detached)				
0-49.9 percent	$3.37	$558	$50,993	92
50-59.9 percent	2.73	287	10,081	39
60-69.9 percent	2.86	245	7,683	55
70-79.9 percent	2.68	262	9,945	103
80-89.9 percent	2.53	301	10,606	134
90 percent or more	2.59	312	12,379	144
Total	2.75	332	17,169	567
Multifamily				
0-4.9 percent	$2.50	$426	$28,992	236
5-9.9 percent	2.73	274	9,147	84
10-14.9 percent	2.70	263	10,092	68
15-19.9 percent	2.73	275	8,354	55
20-24.9 percent	2.78	252	8,956	37
25 percent or more	3.50	257	7,440	87
Total	2.75	332	17,169	567

Sources: Fiscal data are taken from New Jersey Department of Community Affairs, *Thirty-Third Annual Report of the Division of Local Government Services, 1970: Statements of Financial Condition of Counties and Municipalities* (Trenton, N.J., 1971); housing stock data from 1970 Census of Population and Housing.

Note: Municipal and school functions are combined.

percent or more multifamily housing, tax rates are high but expenditures and valuation are low.

Fiscal Implications of
Tax-Base Composition

In *Mt. Laurel* and *Madison* the New Jersey Supreme Court criticizes excessive zoning for commercial and industrial ratables as restricting residential development. However, following Justice Furman in the lower *Madison* decisions, *Mt. Laurel* approved nonresidential zoning to attract tax base. These cases distinguish between two forms of fiscal zoning. Level of the property tax rate is not an acceptable consideration in the control of residential growth, but tax revenues from industrial development are acceptable within limits.[32] Nonresidential zoning for tax revenues is approved only within the context of least-cost zoning for residential land with specific provision required for the households employed by firms located within the municipality.

Provision of housing needs overrides any fiscal considerations: "We have no hesitancy in now saying, and do so emphatically, that, considering the basic importance of the opportunity for appropriate housing for all classes of our citizenry, no municipality may exclude or limit categories of housing for that reason or purpose."[33] Industrial zoning implies a direct responsibility to permit housing for employees: "... when a municipality zones for industry and commerce for local tax benefit purposes, it without question must zone to permit adequate housing within the means of the employees involved in such uses."[34] The amount of commercial and industrial zoning must be justified by such responsibility. "The amount of land removed from residential use by allocation to industrial and commercial purposes must be reasonably related to the present and future potential for such purposes. . . . [S]uch municipalities must zone primarily for the living welfare of people and not for the benefit of the local tax rate."[35]

In part, approval of some nonresidential zoning may have been intended to provide a degree of fiscal compensation to suburban communities for fair-share responsibilities. As chapter 2 pointed out, nonresidential zoning can be used to control population growth rather than, or in addition to, direct employment as a fiscal tool. Every acre of land devoted to commercial or industrial purposes necessarily reduces additional housing opportunities, with possible effects on housing supplies and prices.

Table 4-8 examines the fiscal implications of tax-base composition, com-

Table 4-8
Fiscal Implications of Tax-Base Composition in New Jersey (1970)

Proportion of Tax Base	Property Tax Rate	Local Tax Expenditure per Capita	Equalized Valuation per Capita	Number of Municipalities
Commercial and industrial ratables				
0-19.9 percent	$2.79	$285	$10,683	342
20-39.9 percent	2.75	270	8,755	175
40-59.9 percent	2.81	301	9,910	34
60-79.9 percent	2.18	339	12,539	11
80 percent or more[a]	1.41	404	39,115	4
Total	2.75	283	10,277	566
Residential and apartment ratables				
0-19.9 percent	$2.07	$309	$23,796	9
20-39.9 percent	2.17	296	10,720	23
40-59.9 percent	2.58	284	10,152	120
60-79.9 percent	2.74	271	9,298	246
80 percent or more	3.02	297	11,017	168
Total	2.75	283	10,277	566

Source: New Jersey Department of Community Affairs, *Thirty-Third Annual Report of the Division of Local Government Services, 1970: Statements of Financial Condition of Counties and Municipalities* (Trenton, N.J., 1971).

Note: Municipal and school functions are combined.

[a]An industrial enclave has been removed from this category with tax rate of $0.23, expenditures of $28,016 per capita, and valuation of $3,917,772 per capita.

paring the proportion consisting of commercial or industrial ratables to that of residential or apartment ratables. Nonresidential ratables are associated with lower tax rates, residential and apartment ratables with higher tax rates. As commercial and industrial ratables dominate the tax base on a proportional basis, average tax rates steadily decline, from $2.79 (under 20 percent) to $1.41 (over 80 percent in industrial enclaves). However average tax rates are roughly constant (between $2.75 and $2.81) for the 551 municipalities with less than 60 percent of such ratables. An extraordinary emphasis on commercial and industrial ratables (over 60 percent) is required to produce a marked decline. Only 16 municipalities fall into these categories. As residential and apartment ratables dominate the tax base, property tax rates steadily rise after declining at first.

Local expenditures and equalized valuation show a mixed picture. There is a tendency for both to rise with commercial and industrial tax base. There is a decline at first, and the rise is marked only above 60 percent (in sixteen municipalities). The relationship is even weaker for residential and apartment ratables. The only marked rise occurs below 20 percent of the tax base (in nine communities), where results are distorted by industrial enclaves. It would appear that marked effects of fiscal zoning strategies are restricted to a small handful of municipalities and that expenditures may rise with industrialization. Moreover the table results are dramatically affected by industrial enclaves, which produce the extremely low tax rates and extremely high expenditures or valuations.

As before, we now control these relationships for population size and growth rate. Table 4-9 controls the fiscal implications of tax-base composition (in terms of the proportion of commercial and industrial ratables) for population size. Tax rates rise with population but are constant at about $2.77 in the 219 communities between 5,000 and 25,000 population. Controlled for population size, commercial and industrial ratables do cause tax rates to fall in communities of less than 25,000. However the fall is marked in only 15 smaller communities with over 60 percent of such ratables. Commercial and industrial ratables are associated with rising tax rates in the seventeen large cities over 50,000 population. Controlled for population size, commercial and industrial ratables seem to produce rising expenditures, although the relationship is U-shaped in communities below 50,000 population. Going from 20 percent to 40 percent of such ratables is associated with a drop in expenditures, except in the seventeen large cities. Equalized valuation per capita declines with population size. Controlled for population, valuation seems to rise above 60 percent of tax base. This phenomenon is a restricted one, occurring in 15 communities.

Table 4-10 controls the fiscal implications of tax-base composition for population growth. Analysis of the fiscal implications of growth is more difficult, because the provision of public services may lag behind community development. The highest tax rates ($3.68) are found in the seventy-two declining communities. (Their expenditure and valuation figures are distorted by two industrial enclaves. In general declining communities have high tax rates but

Table 4-9
Fiscal Implications of Tax-Base Composition in New Jersey
Controlled for Population Size (1970)

Population (1960)	Commercial and Industrial Ratables					Total
	0-19.9 Percent	20-39.9 Percent	40-59.9 Percent	60-79.9 Percent	80 percent Or More	
	Municipal and School Property Tax Rates					
Less than 2,500	$2.69	$2.57	$2.56	$1.67	$1.26a	$2.61
2,500-4,999	2.77	2.76	1.84	1.31	1.83	2.69
5,000-9,999	2.87	2.66	2.54	1.10	–	2.77
10,000-24,999	2.88	2.78	1.95	1.60	–	2.77
25,000-49,999	3.16	3.04	2.48	3.28	–	3.03
50,000 or more	2.53	3.22	5.38	4.14	–	3.95
Total	2.79	2.75	2.81	2.18	1.41	2.75
	Municipal and School Local Expenditure per Capita					
Less than 2,500	$321	$311	$279	$447	$428a	$321
2,500-4,999	246	270	441	266	329	262
5,000-9,999	282	244	296	252	–	270
10,000-24,999	264	261	311	396	–	267
25,000-49,999	302	265	205	310	–	273
50,000 or more	214	261	269	461	–	270
Total	285	270	301	339	404	283
	Equalized Valuation per Capita					
Less than 2,500	$14,649	$12,688	$ 9,558	$18,986	$47,241a	$14,663
2,500-4,999	8,367	8,527	20,365	13,088	14,715	9,055
5,000-9,999	8,688	7,648	10,669	18,338	–	8,509
10,000-24,999	8,248	7,563	10,367	8,084	–	8,137
25,000-49,999	8,567	7,069	5,243	9,250	–	7,500
50,000 or more	5,715	7,099	3,552	6,519	–	5,650
Total	10,683	8,755	9,910	12,539	39,108	10,277
	Number of Municipalities					
Less than 2,500	124	35	7	2	3a	171
2,500-4,999	78	39	5	3	1	126
5,000-9,999	72	39	5	1	–	117
10,000-24,999	56	38	7	1	–	102
25,000-49,999	10	16	4	3	–	33
50,000 or more	2	8	6	1	–	17
Total	342	175	34	11	4	566

Sources: Fiscal data are taken from New Jersey Department of Community Affairs, *Thirty-Third Annual Report of the Division of Local Government Services, 1970: Statements of Financial Condition of Counties and Municipalities* (Trenton, N.J., 1971); population data from 1960 Census of Population and Housing.

aAn "industrial enclave" has been removed from this category, with tax rate of $0.23, expenditures of $28,016 per capita, and valuation of $3,917,772 per capita.

Table 4-10
Fiscal Implications of Tax-Base Composition in New Jersey
Controlled for Growth Rate (1960-1970)

Growth Rate, 1960-1970	Commercial and Industrial Ratables					
	0-19.9 Percent	20-39.9 Percent	40-59.9 Percent	60-79.9 Percent	80 Percent or More	Total
	Municipal and School Property Tax Rates					
Declining	$4.28	$3.30	$3.96	$3.29	$0.21	$3.68
0-19.9 percent	2.74	2.70	2.80	1.70	–	2.70
20-49.9 percent	2.57	2.56	1.83	1.15	1.81	2.51
50-99.9 percent	2.65	2.48	2.45	–	–	2.60
100-199.9 percent	2.67	3.01	1.77	–	–	2.64
200 percent or more	3.11	2.49	–	–	–	2.88
Total	2.79	2.75	2.81	2.18	1.17	2.75
	Municipal and School Local Expenditure per Capita					
Declining	$224	$266	$235	$282	$14,153	$632
0-19.9 percent	261	257	298	381	–	264
20-49.9 percent	290	302	307	348	441	297
50-99.9 percent	324	288	328	–	–	316
100-199.9 percent	325	270	477	–	–	330
200 percent or more	257	169	–	–	–	224
Total	285	270	301	339	5,926	332
	Equalized Valuation per Capita					
Declining	$ 6,732	$ 6,626	$ 3,703	$ 8,389	a	$61,553
0-19.9 percent	10,560	8,225	9,610	12,157	–	9,584
20-49.9 percent	10,314	11,940	11,611	21,794	$ 29,968	11,253
50-99.9 percent	13,055	9,256	14,298	–	–	12,268
100-199.9 percent	11,427	7,444	22,036	–	–	11,733
200 percent or more	8,074	4,814	–	–	–	6,851
Total	10,683	8,755	9,910	12,539	814,842	17,169
	Number of Municipalities					
Declining	28	29	9	4	2	72
0-19.9 percent	102	83	13	5	–	203
20-49.9 percent	111	36	6	2	3	158
50-99.9 percent	65	19	3	–	–	87
100-199.9 percent	31	5	3	–	–	39
200 percent or more	5	3	–	–	–	8
Total	342	175	34	11	5	567

Sources: Fiscal data are taken from New Jersey Department of Community Affairs, *Thirty-Third Annual Report of the Division of Local Government Services, 1970: Statements of Financial Condition of Counties and Municipalities* (Trenton, N.J., 1971); growth rates from 1970 Census of Population and Housing.

aTwo industrial enclaves of $3,917,722 and $66,533 for an average valuation of $1,992,253.

quite low expenditures and valuation in New Jersey.) Tax rates first decline with
growth and then rise again above 100 percent growth. Real declines occur only
above 60 percent of tax base in the sixteen highly industrialized communities.

Regardless of growth rate, expenditures tend to rise with commercial and
industrial ratables. This pattern is fairly marked, although there is a decline in
several categories at 20 percent to 40 percent of tax base. Since the same pattern
was found by population size, it appears that industrialization may be associated
with rising expenditures per capita. Equalized valuation also shows an unsteady
reaction to population growth. Generally valuation tends to rise with commercial and industrial tax base, regardless of growth rate. But the pattern is typically
U-shaped, with a decline from 20 percent to 40 percent (in 175 communities)
and a rise only above 40 percent (in 50 communities).

The distribution of commercial and industrial ratables among municipalities
may be an important consideration. Table 4-11 relates median house value and
median household income to tax-base composition, using proportion of tax base
in commercial and industrial ratables. Most of the municipalities in New Jersey
(517) have less than 40 percent of nonresidential ratables (with 342 or 60
percent having less than 20 percent of such ratables). Communities with higher
median house value tend to have a more heavily residential tax base. As the
median house value rises, so does the proportion of municipalities falling into
the category of less than 20 percent nonresidential ratables. A similar pattern is
evident for median household income, although the relationship is weaker.
Commercial and industrial ratables (measured in proportional, not dollar terms)
are found in poorer communities.

Both Hamilton and White expect commercial and industrial zoning to be
found in poorer communities, because wealthier communities will demand
higher compensation for the external effects of industrial development. Poorer
communities are more willing to accept these effects in return for fiscal
benefits.[36] Hamilton, however, argues that—in the absence of such externalities—wealthier communities would also be expected to zone for nonresidential
ratables.[37] He bases this conclusion on findings by Fischel, who uses a sample of
fifty-four (of seventy) municipalities in Bergen County (one of the study
counties). Fischel computes a fiscal dividend (or net revenue) per capita in
dollars resulting from additional commercial and industrial tax ratables per
capita.

Using a multiple-regression procedure, Fischel finds this fiscal dividend to be
positively related to nonresidential ratables per capita and negatively related to
income per capita, indicating that poorer communities are more willing to
foresake environmental quality for tax revenues. The mean school and municipal
property tax rate in Fischel's sample of municipalities was 2.4 percent. In other
words, $1,000 of ratables produces $24 of tax revenue. Fischel concluded that
of every $24 of such tax payments, about $8.60 (36 percent) of commercial and
$10.40 (43 percent) of industrial tax payments are used to reduce local

residential taxes. About $8.10 (34 percent) of commercial and $2.15 (9 percent) of industrial tax payments go to additional school expenditures. The rest of the $24 in tax revenue is not accounted for.[38]

The alleged fiscal benefits of commercial and industrial ratables were challenged by Margolis in a widely referenced trilogy of articles.[39] He analyzed

Table 4-11
Relationship of Median House Value and Median Household Income to Tax-Base Composition in New Jersey (1970)

| Median Value | Commercial and Industrial Ratables | | | | | |
	0-19.9 Percent	20-39.9 Percent	40-59.9 Percent	60-79.9 Percent	80 Percent or More	Total
Single-family housing						
		Percentage distribution				
$0-19,999	58.2	32.3	6.8	1.6	1.2	44.3
$20,000-29,999	55.7	35.3	5.0	3.5	0.5	35.4
$30,000-39,999	69.6	21.5	7.6	–	1.3	13.9
$40,000-49,999	75.0	25.0	–	–	–	4.2
$50,000-59,999	91.7	–	8.3	–	–	2.1
Total	60.3	30.9	6.0	1.9	0.9	100.0
		Number of municipalities				
$0-19,999	146	81	17	4	3	251
$20,000-29,999	112	71	10	7	1	201
$30,000-39,999	55	17	6	–	1	79
$40,000-49,999	18	6	–	–	–	24
$50,000-59,999	11	–	1	–	–	12
Total	342	175	34	11	5	567
Household income						
		Percentage distribution				
$ 5,000-9,999	60.7	28.2	8.6	2.5	–	28.7
$10,000-14,999	55.7	36.8	4.6	2.2	0.6	57.0
$15,000-19,999	78.5	13.8	6.2	–	1.5	11.5
$20,000 or more	75.0	6.3	6.3	–	12.5	2.8
Total	60.3	30.9	6.0	1.9	0.9	100.0
		Number of municipalities				
$ 5,000-9,999	99	46	14	4	–	163
$10,000-14,999	180	119	15	7	2	323
$15,000-19,999	51	9	4	–	1	65
$20,000 or more	12	1	1	–	2	16
Total	342	175	34	11	5	567

Sources: Fiscal data are taken from New Jersey Department of Community Affairs, *Thirty-Third Annual Report of the Division of Local Government Services, 1970: Statements of Financial Condition of Counties and Municipalities* (Trenton, N.J., 1971); median house value and median household income from 1970 Census of Population and Housing.

property tax rates for municipal (noneducational) services in the San Francisco Bay Area, using a sample of fifty-five cities (including San Francisco and Oakland). He found that the presence of industrial and commercial property tax ratables increased the municipal tax costs per dollar of property tax valuation in that metropolitan region. He reported that higher property tax rates were found in cities with a larger ratio of jobs to residents. He also found that such "business" cities actually had lower per capita valuation in taxable property than "dormitory" cities despite far greater industrial and commercial ratables per capita. The basic reason was that in addition to higher residential property tax ratables per capita, dormitory cities had lower population densities and higher household incomes.

For this particular sample Margolis found not a simple fiscal formula for commercial and industrial development but rather a complicated relationship among property tax-base composition, population density, average household income, and property tax rates. The specific conclusion of his study was that commercial and industrial development would increase property tax rates per dollar of property valuation due to lower value of residential property tax ratables and higher population density (both associated in turn with lower average household income). This conclusion contradicts the conventional fiscal wisdom. Only in three industrial enclaves did Margolis find lower tax rates (one community levied no property tax at all). The explanation here was that such communities contained little or no residential population.

One serious problem with the Margolis findings is that while school costs are a large component of suburban expenditures, municipal services are more important in central city expenditures. However Muller found in a national study much the same pattern that Margolis found in the San Francisco Bay Area. Muller found that property valuation per housing unit is higher in growing than in declining cities. Declining cities (which had higher expenditures, wages, and debt in the public sector) had proportionately stronger commercial and industrial tax bases. In 1971 declining cities had 40 percent of their property tax base in commercial and industrial ratables while growing cities had 27 percent.[40]

Conclusion

The fiscal implications of housing value, housing-stock composition, and tax-base composition seem to be relatively limited. The effects of these factors may be restricted to a small number of municipalities in New Jersey. Large increases in nonresidential and high-valued residential ratables are necessary to produce marked fiscal effects on tax rates, expenditures, and valuation. For most communities it is dubious that fiscal zoning practices will be productive in the face of widespread regional competition. The question is whether we are willing to believe that many of these communities have failed to learn this lesson when it appears that the same zoning practices will have other consequences (both fiscal and nonfiscal) which communities may be able to control.

The fiscal stakes of suburban communities are largely tied up with population growth itself. Important fiscal, environmental, and externality effects may be involved in the control of growth. Nonresidential zoning, multifamily exclusion, and large minimum requirements are growth management techniques as much as—or more than—fiscal zoning devices (in the strict cost-revenue sense). The fiscal and nonfiscal implications of growth management are apt to be more powerful incentives than fiscal zoning. If so, it is a mistake to lump these various forces (cost-revenue, growth, environmental, and externality implications) together as fiscal zoning simply because they all have fiscal consequences. These fiscal effects are different in character.

Notes

1. Bruce W. Hamilton, "Property Taxation's Incentive to Fiscal Zoning," in *Property Tax Reform*, ed. George E. Peterson (Washington, D.C.: Urban Institute, 1973), p. 126.

2. James C. Ohls, Richard C. Weisberg, and Michelle J. White, "The Effect of Zoning on Land Value," *Journal of Urban Economics* 1 (October 1974):433.

3. Michelle J. White, "Fiscal Zoning in Fragmented Metropolitan Areas," in *Fiscal Zoning and Land Use Controls: The Economic Issues*, ed. Edwin S. Mills and Wallace E. Oates (Lexington, Mass.: Lexington Books, D.C. Heath and Co., 1975), p. 46, n. n. Reprinted with permission.

4. Hamilton, "Property Taxation's Incentive to Fiscal Zoning," p. 127. Reprinted with permission.

5. Ibid., p. 130.

6. Bruce W. Hamilton, Edwin S. Mills, and David Puryear, "The Tiebout Hypothesis and Residential Income Segregation," in *Fiscal Zoning and Land Use Controls*, chap. 4, pp. 101-118; see also Bruce W. Hamilton, "Property Taxes and the Tiebout Hypothesis: Some Empirical Evidence," in *Fiscal Zoning and Land Use Controls*, chap. 2, pp. 13-30.

7. Hamilton, Mills, and Puryear, "Property Taxes and the Tiebout Hypothesis," p. 109.

8. Hamilton, "Property Taxation's Incentive to Fiscal Zoning," p. 129.

9. Hamilton, Mills, and Puryear, "Property Taxes and the Tiebout Hypothesis," p. 113.

10. Ibid.

11. Robert Schafer, *Conceptual and Empirical Problems in Measuring the Invisible Wall* (Cambridge, Mass.: Department of City and Regional Planning, Harvard University, February 1975), p. 7, n. *.

12. Hamilton, "Property Taxation's Incentive to Fiscal Zoning," p. 129;

citing Bruce W. Hamilton, "The Impact of Zoning and Property Taxes on Urban Structure and Housing Markets," Ph.D. diss., Princeton University, 1972.

13. Eric J. Branfman, Benjamin I. Cohen, and David M. Trubek, "Measuring the Invisible Wall: Land Use Controls and the Residential Patterns of the Poor," *Yale Law Journal* 82 (January 1973):483-508.

14. Ibid., pp. 501-502.

15. Hamilton, "Property Taxation's Incentive to Fiscal Zoning," p. 129.

16. Schafer, *Conceptual and Empirical Problems*, p. 5.

17. Mills and Oates, "The Theory of Local Public Services and Finance: Its Relevance to Urban Fiscal and Zoning Behavior," in *Fiscal Zoning and Land Use Controls*, p. 10.

18. See Schafer, *Conceptual and Empirical Problems*, pp. 7-8.

19. Mills and Oates, "The Theory of Local Public Services," p. 5.

20. Stephen K. Mayo, "Local Public Goods and Residential Location: An Empirical Test of the Tiebout Hypothesis," in *Public Needs and Private Behavior in Metropolitan Areas*, ed. John E. Jackson (Cambridge, Mass.: Ballinger, 1975), chap. 2, pp. 31-72. See commentary by John E. Jackson, "Public Needs, Private Behavior, and Metropolitan Governance: A Summary Essay," in *Public Needs and Private Behavior*, chap. 1, pp. 1-30.

21. Mayo cites in this connection Michael J. Ball, "Recent Empirical Work on the Determinants of Relative Housing Prices," *Urban Studies* 10 (June 1973):213-233.

22. See William Alonso, *Location and Land Use: Toward a General Theory of Land Rent* (Cambridge, Mass.: Harvard University Press, 1964); John F. Kain, "The Journey-to-Work as a Determinant of Residential Location," *Regional Science Association Papers and Proceedings* 9 (1962):137-160; Richard F. Muth, *Cities and Housing: The Spatial Pattern of Urban Residential Land Use* (Chicago: University of Chicago Press, 1969).

23. Howard S. Bloom, H. James Brown, and John E. Jackson, "Residential Location and Local Public Services," in *Public Needs and Private Behavior*, chap. 3, pp. 73-98.

24. Jackson, "Public Needs," p. 13.

25. Bloom, Brown, and Jackson, "Residential Location," pp. 96-98.

26. Ibid., p. 96.

27. Mayo, "Local Public Goods and Residential Location," p. 64.

28. Jackson, "Public Needs," pp. 10-12.

29. Data per capita for fiscal year 1970 (January-December 31, 1970) used in this study are taken from New Jersey Department of Community Affairs, *Thirty-Third Annual Report of the Division of Local Government Services, 1970: Statements of Financial Condition of Counties and Municipalities* (Trenton, N.J., 1971). These data were available on computer tape, together with similar data for fiscal year 1960 and data from the 1960 and 1970 Censuses of Population and Housing, for all 567 municipalities in New Jersey. The tape was

assembled and made available to the author by Patrick Beaton, a former colleague at the Center for Urban Policy Research of Rutgers University. The tape was employed for George Sternlieb et al., *Housing Development and Municipal Costs* (New Brunswick, N.J.: Center for Urban Policy Research, Rutgers University, 1973), chaps. 4-6. Valuation and tax rates are equalized for 100 percent assessment. All data are on a municipality basis.

30. Thomas Muller, *Fiscal Impacts of Land Development: A Critique of Methods and Review of Issues* (Washington, D.C.: Urban Institute, 1975), p. 25. See analysis of the relationship between service costs and population size, density, and growth in chap. 4, "Fiscal Impact Analysis: Major Issues," pp. 19-33. Also see Thomas Muller, *Growing and Declining Urban Areas: A Fiscal Comparison* (Washington, D.C.: Urban Institute, 1975); Sternlieb et al., *Housing Development and Municipal Costs*, chaps. 4-6.

31. This same result for large cities in a national sample is reported in George E. Peterson and Arthur P. Solomon, "Property Taxes and Populist Reform," *The Public Interest*, no. 30 (Winter 1973):60-75.

32. Michael LaFontaine, "The Limits of Permissible Exclusion in Fiscal Zoning," *Boston University Law Review* 53 (March 1973):460.

33. Southern Burlington County N.A.A.C.P. v. Township of Mount Laurel, 336 A.2d 713, 731 (1975).

34. Ibid., p. 732.

35. Ibid.

36. Michelle J. White, "Firm Location in a Zoned Metropolitan Area," in *Fiscal Zoning and Land Use Controls*, pp. 198-199.

37. Hamilton, "Property Taxation's Incentive to Fiscal Zoning," pp. 130-132.

38. William A. Fischel, "Fiscal and Environmental Considerations in the Location of Firms in Suburban Communities," in *Fiscal Zoning and Land Use Controls*, pp. 153, 155.

39. Julius Margolis, "On Municipal Land Policy for Fiscal Gains," *National Tax Journal* 9 (September 1956):247-257; "The Variation of Property Tax Rates Within a Metropolitan Region," *National Tax Journal* 9 (December 1956):326-330; "Municipal Fiscal Structure in a Metropolitan Region," *Journal of Political Economy* 65 (June 1957):226-236.

40. Muller, *Growing and Declining Urban Areas*, p. 65.

5

Fiscal Evaluation of Suburban Zoning Policies

The fundamental assumption of the fiscal motive theory is that under the prevailing system of local property taxation, single-family homes are fiscally superior to multifamily dwellings. Empirical evidence from New Jersey reported in this chapter indicates that in cost-revenue terms, multifamily construction is often not only fiscally advantageous in suburban communities but generally more profitable than all but the most expensive single-family housing.[1]

Critics of the conventional wisdom have long suspected that small apartments at least (having up to two bedrooms) may be a valuable fiscal asset to communities, precisely because of the demographic profile of apartment residents. (The apartment data used in this chapter reflect existing construction patterns, which largely exclude units with more than two bedrooms. However there is little evidence that such units would be built under least-cost zoning ordinances.) A survey conducted for the New Jersey County and Municipal Government Study Commission found this favorable attitude to be common among local officials in New Jersey. (Citizens surveyed had a very different attitude.)[2] The empirical evidence reported in this chapter lends support to this position.

The widespread view that multifamily development is fiscally unfavorable rests on three methodological errors characteristic of typical cost-revenue studies. First, that view is generally based on fiscal-impact results computed per dwelling unit. Such results ignore the possible effects of housing density. Per acre data often reverse per unit conclusions. Second, that view is based on specific case studies, which Kain has criticized as not being generalizable or transferable.[3] Third, that view assumes that market value rises more rapidly than public service costs as housing density per acre decreases.

This chapter will demonstrate considerable variation in the fiscal impact of housing types among counties and municipalities in suburban New Jersey. Hence no general conclusions can be readily drawn about the relative fiscal impacts of single-family and multifamily development. Either, both, or neither housing type may be fiscally advantageous, depending on several important community characteristics. As a result considerable uncertainty exists over the fiscal implications of particular development alternatives. This uncertainty is a principal consideration underlying municipal land use policies. Rather than computing their tax bills, as Hamilton and White suppose, voters are confronted with fiscal uncertainty, favor single-family housing on nonfiscal grounds, and anticipate externalities and opportunity costs from multifamily development that are not included in standard cost-revenue computations. These problems may explain in part the disagreement between local officials and citizens over the anticipated fiscal impacts of multifamily development reported by the New Jersey County and Municipal Government Study Commission. Voters may demand additional compensation for approval of multifamily housing, with local officials employing variance procedures, in part, to enforce payment of such compensation.

Multifamily development implies scale effects and opportunity costs from substantial population growth, with fiscal implications that are difficult to forecast. If so, zoning devices may be widely employed as growth management techniques—not because of the alleged fiscal benefits of restrictive single-family requirements—but rather to serve as holding devices controlling the development of vacant land, both in terms of timing and population density. It is possible, therefore, that excessive zoning for commercial and industrial land uses may have the same growth management objective rather than some fiscal purpose of attracting tax ratables. While it is true that growth management strategies have fiscal implications, these effects are different from what is traditionally meant by fiscal zoning in the strict cost-revenue sense.

A Simple Cost-Revenue Model

This chapter employs a simple cost-revenue model to forecast the fiscal impact of residential development. The model is specifically designed to estimate fiscal impact in New Jersey, where county and municipal finance was heavily dependent on local property taxation prior to adoption of the Robinson strategy. This model, based on an average-cost methodology, is widely used in cost-revenue studies.[4] It is generally applicable to any state in which there is primary local reliance on property taxation. Such a model may be used to measure and evaluate the fiscal efficiency of suburban zoning ordinances. The model is incorporated into White's formula as the term $(R - C) Q_A$.

Typical cost-revenue studies are based on this fiscal impact model in which costs and revenues to local government of residential development are compared. In this model estimates of household size per dwelling unit are used in conjunction with average (per capita) service costs to project the expected tax cost of municipal services. Estimates of schoolchildren per dwelling unit who attend public schools are used in conjunction with average (per pupil) service costs to project the expected tax cost of public education. In this study school-age children are used to approximate schoolchildren attending public schools. The difference between the two figures is not particularly large in suburban New Jersey. An approximation should be sufficient for the problem under investigation here.[5] Tax revenues are obtained by multiplying market value per dwelling unit against the municipal and school property tax rates. (Property tax rates and assessed valuations have all been equalized in this study to facilitate municipal comparisons. The state of New Jersey provides equalization data in its financial reports. Assessment ratios may be varied in this fiscal-impact model if desired.)

The principal focus of this cost-revenue model is on housing type and dwelling-unit size. Cost per dwelling unit varies according to the household size and school-age multipliers, together with the total property tax collections per capita or per pupil (which are used as estimates of average service costs since property taxation is the predominant source of local revenue). The household-size (the number of residents per unit) and school-age (the number of public school students per unit) estimates are a function of housing type and dwelling-unit size (measured in terms of bedrooms, rooms, or floor area), which also influence market value.[6] Housing types and dwelling-unit sizes are varied by simply changing market value and household multipliers. Each combination of these factors defines a different type or category of housing type and dwelling-unit size. The model can be used for any community by changing the tax rates and service cost parameters. The specific community under investigation defines property tax rates and property tax collections per pupil and per resident.

Net fiscal impact per acre ($)	=	net fiscal impact per unit ($)	X	dwelling units per acre
Net fiscal impact per unit ($)	=	tax revenue per unit ($)	−	tax cost per unit ($)
Tax revenue per unit ($)	=	property tax rates	X	market value per unit ($)
Tax cost per unit ($)	=	municipal costs per unit ($)	+	school costs per unit ($)
Municipal costs per unit ($)	=	household size	X	municipal costs per capita ($)
School costs per unit ($)	=	school-age children	X	school costs per pupil ($)

A sample of 176 suburban municipalities is used to evaluate the fiscal implications of local zoning ordinances. The sample includes all municipalities containing vacant, developable land located in the six study counties of chapter 3 (Bergen, Middlesex, Monmouth, Morris, Ocean, and Somerset).[7] The selection of these six counties was necessitated largely by restrictions on available data concerning new single-family construction. Neither census nor state housing reports contain any information on lot size. However Sagalyn and Sternlieb surveyed a sample of 529 new single-family units for sale between June 1, 1970, and July 1, 1971.[8] This sample is reported in table 3-12. Their data relate market value, dwelling-unit size (in terms of floor area and number of rooms), and lot description. The best data available were from the six study counties.

For each county, average estimates of market value and household size per dwelling unit have been developed for multifamily units and several single-family lot sizes (less than a quarter-acre, less than a half-acre, less than an acre, and one or more acres). The estimation procedure is straightforward for multifamily units. Market value is available by county from official state reports on multifamily construction in New Jersey. The years 1970 and 1971 were combined to reduce the possible effect of annual fluctuations.[9] These reports present monthly rental value by dwelling-unit size (measured as number of rooms). Monthly rental value was converted by the author to an equivalent market value.[10] Household size and school-age children were estimated from the 1970 Public Use Sample for New Jersey (5 percent sample) for housing constructed during 1960-1970. These estimates are available by dwelling-unit size in terms of number of bedrooms or rooms.[11]

All estimates in table 5-1 have been made on the basis of average dwelling-unit size measured as number of rooms.[12] There is a much greater variation in market valuation than in the household estimates. Bergen has very high market values compared with those of other counties. At $24,120 per unit, apartments are about $9,000 more than in Morris. Differentials are even larger for single-family homes on all lot sizes. Ocean generally has the lowest market values, although apartments are lower in Somerset. Household estimates roughly, but not entirely, correspond to differences in market values.

Such differences in market values have long been used as a principal linchpin in the argument that multifamily units are fiscally inferior to single-family homes (especially those on large lots with high values). The Hamilton and White models of fiscal zoning proceed from precisely this argument. The market values in table 5-1 reveal that a home on a one-acre lot may be priced as much as 50 percent higher than a home on a quarter-acre lot in New Jersey, while a quarter-acre home may be priced more than 100 percent higher than an apartment unit. At the same property tax rate, tax revenues would favor large-lot homes over small-lot homes over apartments.

However this analysis is strictly limited to the revenue side of the fiscal-impact model and ignores the fact that household size and school-age children (the cost side of the model) may also vary with housing type and dwelling-unit size. There is at least a fivefold to sevenfold difference in number of pupils per dwelling unit between apartments and even the smallest single-family home. Household size, however, is only half again as high. Both household size and school-age children increase with lot size, because dwelling-unit size is also increasing. Large-lot homes may have up to 50 percent more residents and between six to nine times as many pupils as apartments.

Table 5-1
Housing Unit Characteristics in the Study Counties (1970)

| County | Multi-family Units | Single-Family Homes on Lot Sizes of | | | |
		Less than 0.25 Acre	0.25-0.49 Acre	0.50-0.99 Acre	1.00 or More Acres
		Market Value per Unit			
Bergen	$24,120	$51,667	$60,217	$72,333	$91,667
Middlesex	15,480	40,556	48,824	46,667	52,172
Monmouth	15,552	31,280	37,222	42,222	58,636
Morris	15,768	29,918	40,600	50,972	80,588
Ocean	14,112	28,023	31,957	35,000	41,329
Somerset	13,464	30,000	40,000	66,667	60,652
		Household Size per Unit			
Bergen	2.590	3.938	4.265	4.590	4.573
Middlesex	2.427	4.263	4.434	4.573	4.619
Monmouth	2.556	4.242	4.176	4.480	4.476
Morris	2.478	4.376	4.376	4.501	4.662
Ocean	2.474	3.632	3.987	3.948	4.027
Somerset	2.504	4.242	4.176	4.428	4.395
		School-age Children per Unit			
Bergen	0.278	1.213	1.500	1.698	1.706
Middlesex	0.173	1.499	1.611	1.706	1.901
Monmouth	0.246	1.432	1.433	1.634	1.638
Morris	0.199	1.535	1.572	1.662	1.757
Ocean	0.196	1.040	1.291	1.277	1.497
Somerset	0.223	1.432	1.433	1.623	1.592
		Weighted School-age Children per Unit[a]			
Bergen	0.293	1.239	1.527	1.742	1.746
Middlesex	0.178	1.526	1.647	1.746	1.778
Monmouth	0.252	1.507	1.462	1.672	1.676
Morris	0.205	1.623	1.604	1.698	1.802
Ocean	0.200	1.061	1.318	1.304	1.364
Somerset	0.225	1.507	1.462	1.654	1.625

Sources: Market value is developed using dwelling unit size distributions calculated from the 1970 Public Use Sample for New Jersey (5 percent sample). For apartments, values are averaged from New Jersey Department of Community Affairs, Division of Housing and Urban Renewal, *New Multi-Family Dwellings in New Jersey* (Trenton, N.J., 1970 and 1971). For single-family homes, lot size and market values are calculated from the original survey data used for Lynne B. Sagalyn and George Sternlieb, *Zoning and Housing Costs: The Impact of Land-Use Controls on Housing Price* (New Brunswick, N.J.: Center for Urban Policy Research, Rutgers University, 1972). Household size and school-age children are calculated from the 1970 Public Use Sample for New Jersey (5 percent sample), using the dwelling unit size distributions.

aThese estimates are weighted by differences in per pupil costs on a grade-level basis, using weights developed by the New Jersey Education Association: 0.5 kindergarten; 1.0 elementary; and 1.2 secondary. New Jersey Education Association, *Basic Statistical Data of New Jersey School Districts, 1971 Edition* (Trenton, N.J., July 1971), Research Bulletin A71-2, p. 18.

Merely looking at the revenue side (market value per dwelling unit) is insufficient. The revenue and cost sides must be looked at simultaneously. One convenient way to examine the trade off between the costs and revenues of a particular housing type is to compute the ratio of its market value to school-age children or household size. This simple procedure measures the taxable valuation per pupil or per resident. We divide market value by household size or number of pupils. These computations have been carried out in table 5-2 for each of the study counties. Only statewide estimates of household size and school-age children are available for townhouses and duplexes, because room distributions by county are not available. As a result this study will focus largely on garden apartments and single-family homes. Generally garden apartments show the highest valuation per pupil. Valuation per pupil rises with lot size. However even large-lot homes fall considerably below garden apartments, as much as 50 percent or more. Valuation per resident shows a very different pattern. Garden apartments show the poorest ratio, while the largest lot sizes show the best ratio. Valuation per resident tends to rise steadily with lot size.

Comparison of the Study Counties

We may roughly compare the fiscal impact of various housing types using average county data (that is, for the average community in each county). Market value per dwelling unit, household characteristics, property tax rates, and service costs are varied for each county. Basic fiscal data for the six study counties,

Table 5-2
Market Value per Pupil and per Resident in the Study Counties (1970)

Housing Type	Bergen	Middlesex	Monmouth	Morris	Ocean	Somerset
	Market Value per Pupil					
Garden apartment	$86,763	$89,480	$63,220	$79,236	$72,000	$60,377
Single-family						
0-0.24 acre	42,594	27,055	21,844	19,491	26,945	20,950
0.25-0.49 acre	40,145	30,307	25,975	25,827	24,754	27,913
0.50-0.99 acre	42,599	27,355	25,840	30,669	27,408	41,076
1.00 or more acres	53,732	27,445	35,797	45,867	27,608	38,098
	Market Value per Resident					
Garden apartment	$ 9,313	$ 6,378	$ 6,085	$ 6,363	$ 5,704	$ 5,377
Single-family						
0-0.24 acre	13,120	9,513	7,374	6,837	7,716	7,072
0.25-0.49 acre	14,119	11,011	8,913	9,278	8,015	9,579
0.50-0.99 acre	15,759	10,205	9,425	11,325	8,865	15,056
1.00 or more acres	20,045	11,295	13,100	17,286	10,263	13,800

Source: Table 5-1.

computed as averages across each county's constituent municipalities, are reported in table 2-1. The market value and household characteristics are taken from table 5-1. The fiscal impact of various housing types in each county is analyzed in table 5-3 using the average-cost model introduced earlier. Per dwelling unit estimates are converted to a per acre basis using the platting coefficients introduced in chapter 3.

This simple exercise reveals two important results that can be anticipated from the market valuations per resident and per pupil presented in table 5-2. First, garden apartments had a positive or neutral fiscal impact in all six counties. The positive impact is fairly marked, given that all municipal and school costs have been loaded implicitly onto residential property, with no cost allocation to commercial and industrial property. The positive impact is considerably improved, except in Bergen County, when we add in housing density (at a typical fourteen dwelling units per acre in suburban New Jersey). The fiscal benefit of single-family housing declines on a per acre basis. This result is contrary to the conventional wisdom that favors single-family homes. Second, the net fiscal impact varies tremendously, even on average, among the study counties. For garden apartments, it ranges from a low of $224 per acre in Bergen to $2,240 per acre in Middlesex. Single-family homes constructed on lot sizes smaller than one acre show negative fiscal impact in every county. Fiscal impact is positive on lot sizes over one acre only in Monmouth and Morris. The principal

Table 5-3
Sample Cost-revenue Calculations for the Study Counties (1970)

Housing Type	Bergen	Middlesex	Monmouth	Morris	Ocean	Somerset
			Per Dwelling Unit			
Garden apartment	−$ 16	$160	$149	$101	$ 36	$ 50
Single-family						
0-0.24 acre	−544	−240	−437	−885	−441	−669
0.25-0.49 acre	−699	−123	−252	−632	−589	−407
0.50-0.99 acre	−700	−250	−280	−443	−499	107
1.00 or more acres	−357	−255	222	258	−546	−20
			Per Acre[a]			
Garden apartment	−$224	$2,240	$2,086	$1,414	$ 504	$ 700
Single-family						
0-0.24 acre	−1,316	−581	−1,058	−2,142	−1,067	−1,619
0.25-0.49 acre	−1,258	−221	−454	−1,138	−1,060	−733
0.50-0.99 acre	−707	−253	−283	−447	−504	108
1.00 or more acres	−154	−110	95	111	−235	−9

Sources: Table 5-1 for household characteristics and table 2-1 for fiscal data. Platting coefficients are taken from Franklin J. James and James W. Hughes, *Modeling State Growth: New Jersey 1980* (New Brunswick, N.J.: Center for Urban Policy Research, Rutgers University, 1973), p. 92.

[a]Platting coefficients are fourteen garden apartments; quarter-acre lots 2.42; half-acre lots 1.80; acre lots 1.01; larger lots 0.43 units per acre.

difference between Ocean and the other counties are its low market values and tax rates.

One might argue from the per unit results that an appropriate fiscal (cost-revenue) zoning strategy would be large lot zoning in Bergen, Monmouth, and Morris. Garden apartments would be admissible, but inferior, residential land uses. However such a zoning strategy ignores the effects of housing density on fiscal impact. Let us pursue a narrow cost-revenue policy based on average costing. Such a perspective is perfectly appropriate, if we are considering the development of an additional acre of vacant land (which is very unlikely to vitiate our average cost assumptions by affecting the quality of public services or overloading the capacity of existing public facilities). Using the platting coefficients assumed in table 5-3, the fiscal impact per unit is recomputed as fiscal impact per acre for all housing types.

In Morris County lot sizes under one acre have their negative impact magnified (although lot sizes between one-half and one acre are left essentially unchanged due to the platting coefficient of 1.01). The positive fiscal position of the largest lot sizes is cut more than in half from $258 per unit to $111 per acre (due to the platting coefficient of 0.43). Garden apartments show a strong jump in fiscal attractiveness from $101 per unit to $1,414 per acre. Roughly the same pattern occurs in the other study counties. Generally fiscal advantage rises with lot size for single-family housing types.

It is also a simple exercise to calculate the approximate break-even market values dictated by the household characteristics and fiscal conditions prevailing in each county. Dividing the costs of educational and municipal services to a particular housing type by the property tax rate yields the market value required to cover those costs. These break-even values are reported in table 5-4. The break-even values should be compared with the existing market values already reported for each county in table 5-1. It will be observed that in every county, garden apartments already have market values at or above the break-even level, especially in Middlesex and Monmouth counties.

Table 5-4
Break-even Market Values in the Study Counties (1970)

County	Multi-Family Units	Single-Family Homes on Lot Sizes of			
		Less than 0.25 Acre	0.25-0.49 Acre	0.50-0.99 Acre	1.00 or More Acres
Bergen	$24,977	$81,728	$98,826	$110,990	$111,370
Middlesex	8,954	50,317	53,837	56,813	62,531
Monmouth	10,719	45,478	45,400	51,319	51,421
Morris	12,020	62,696	63,992	67,400	71,057
Ocean	12,649	46,100	56,072	55,473	63,700
Somerset	11,512	55,710	55,643	62,556	61,441

Sources: Tables 5-1 and 2-1.

The Effects of Community Wealth

The results of these cost-revenue computations can be generalized by carrying out another very simple exercise. We restrict our example to a single county to eliminate the variations present in the previous calculations due to market values and household demographics. This procedure permits an investigation into community characteristics that affect the fiscal impact of residential development. There appears to be more variation among communities in property tax base than in market values or household demographics. First, let us take a county with high service levels financed at low tax rates against high taxable valuation. Each community is assumed to spend $800 per pupil and $75 per resident out of local property tax revenues. Table 5-5 examines the fiscal impact per unit and per acre of garden apartments and single-family homes.

Community 1 has a relatively poor property tax base of $20,000 in ratables per pupil and $7,500 per resident. Given the assumed service levels, these figures imply a 4 percent school property tax rate and a 1 percent municipal property tax rate. In such a community all housing types show a positive fiscal balance. Per unit, large-lot homes are fiscally superior ($2,875 over an acre and $1,914 over a half-acre). Garden apartments are least attractive at $789, only about half the figure even for smaller homes. However per unit and per acre fiscal strategies are reversed, because of differences in density per acre among housing types. Garden apartments are extremely profitable at $11,046 per acre. All the single-family lot sizes fall under $3,200 per acre. Large-lot homes are most profitable per unit at $2,875 but least profitable per acre at $1,236.

Community 2 has an average property tax base of $40,000 in ratables per pupil and $15,000 per resident. The service levels are held constant for comparison. These figures imply a 2 percent school property tax rate and a 0.5 percent municipal property tax rate. Expenditures are the same as in Community 1, but doubled average valuation cuts tax rates, and hence revenues, in half. Large-lot homes now show $584 per unit. Garden apartments are ahead of smaller lot sizes, and at least one lot size shows a negative balance, −$15. The results are again reversed per acre. Garden apartments are superior at $2,604 (which is a tremendous drop from Community 1). The single-family lot sizes again fall well behind. As before, large-lot homes are most profitable per unit at $584 but least profitable per acre at $251.

Community 3 has a relatively wealthy property tax base of $80,000 in ratables per pupil and $30,000 per resident. The service levels are again held constant. These figures imply a 1 percent school property tax rate and a 0.25 percent municipal property tax rate. Expenditures are the same as in Community 1, but quadrupled average valuation cuts tax rates, and hence revenues, to a fourth. All housing types now produce a fiscal deficit. The deficit per unit is highest for smaller single-family lot sizes, followed by the largest lot size. The least damaging housing type is the garden apartment. These results are again reversed per acre. Density drives up strongly the fiscal deficit of garden

Table 5-5
Fiscal Impact of Residential Development in Three Hypothetical
Communities of a Relatively Wealthy County

		Single-Family Homes on Lot Sizes of			
	Garden Apartments	Less than 0.25 Acre	0.25-0.49 Acre	0.50-0.99 Acre	1.00 or More Acres
Community 1: Relatively poor property tax base[a]					
Fiscal impact per housing unit					
Revenues	$ 1,206	$2,583	$3,011	$3,617	$4,583
Expenditures	417	1,266	1,520	1,703	1,708
Difference	789	1,317	1,491	1,914	2,875
Fiscal impact per acre	11,046	3,187	2,684	1,933	1,236
Community 2: Above average property tax base[b]					
Fiscal impact per housing unit					
Revenues	603	1,292	1,505	1,808	2,292
Expenditures	417	1,266	1,520	1,703	1,708
Difference	186	26	−15	105	584
Fiscal impact per acre	2,604	63	−27	106	251
Community 3: Very wealthy property tax base[c]					
Fiscal impact per housing unit					
Revenues	302	646	753	904	1,146
Expenditures	417	1,266	1,520	1,703	1,708
Difference	−115	−620	−767	−799	−562
Fiscal impact per acre	−1,610	−1,500	−1,381	−807	−242

Source: Market value and household characteristics are taken from table 5-2 for Bergen County.

Notes: Each of these three communities is assumed to spend $800 per pupil and $75 per capita out of local property tax revenues. Housing densities are defined per gross acre of land zoned for various uses. These densities (in housing units per gross acre) are multifamily units, 14; single-family units on lot sizes of less than 0.25 acre, 2.42; 0.25-0.49 acre, 1.80; 0.50-0.99 acre, 1.01; 1.00 or more acres, 0.43.

[a]Community 1 was assumed to have $20,000 of property tax ratables per pupil and $7,500 per capita. These figures imply a 4 percent school property tax rate and a 1 percent municipal property tax rate.

[b]Community 2 was assumed to have $40,000 of property tax ratables per pupil and $15,000 per capita. These figures imply a 2 percent school property tax rate and a 0.5 percent municipal property tax rate.

[c]Community 3 was assumed to have $80,000 of property tax ratables per pupil and $30,000 per capita. These figures imply a 1 percent school property tax rate and a 0.25 percent municipal property tax rate.

apartments to $1,610. Smaller lot sizes are equivalent to garden apartments. The fiscal deficit of large-lot homes is cut more than half from $562 per unit to $242 per acre.

We may contrast this county with a second county characterized by lower service levels, financed at high tax rates against lower taxable valuation. Each hypothetical community is assumed to spend $300 per pupil and $40 per

Table 5-6
Fiscal Impact of Residential Development in Three Hypothetical
Communities of a Relatively Poor County

	Garden Apartments	Single-Family Homes on Lot Sizes of			
		Less than 0.25 Acre	*0.25-0.49 Acre*	*0.50-0.99 Acre*	*1.00 or More Acres*
Community 1: Relatively poor property tax base[a]					
Fiscal impact per housing unit					
Revenues	$ 890	$2,332	$2,807	$2,683	$3,000
Expenditures	149	620	661	695	755
Difference	741	1,222	2,146	1,988	2,245
Fiscal impact per acre	10,374	2,957	3,863	2,008	965
Community 2: Above average property tax base[b]					
Fiscal impact per housing unit					
Revenues	446	1,168	1,406	1,344	1,503
Expenditures	149	620	661	695	755
Difference	296	56	743	647	745
Fiscal impact per acre	4,144	136	1,337	653	320
Community 3: Very wealthy property tax base[c]					
Fiscal impact per housing unit					
Revenues	223	584	703	672	750
Expenditures	149	620	661	695	755
Difference	74	−36	41	−24	−5
Fiscal impact per acre	1,036	−87	74	−24	−2

Source: Market value and household characteristics are taken from table 5-1 for Middlesex County.

Note: Each of these three communities is assumed to spend $300 per pupil and $40 per capita out of local property tax revenues. Housing densities are defined per gross acre of land zoned for various uses. These densities (in housing units per gross acre) are multifamily units, 14; single-family units on lot sizes of less than 0.25 acre, 2.42; 0.25-0.49 acre, 1.80; 0.50-0.99, 1.01; 1.00 or more, 0.43.

[a]Community 1 was assumed to have $8,000 of property tax ratables per pupil and $2,000 per capita. These figures imply a 3.75 percent school property tax rate and a 2 percent municipal property tax rate.

[b]Community 2 was assumed to have $16,000 of property tax ratables per pupil and $4,000 per capita. These figures imply a 1.88 percent school property tax rate and a 1 percent municipal property tax rate.

[c]Community 3 was assumed to have $32,000 of property tax ratables per pupil and $8,000 per capita. These figures imply a 0.94 percent school property tax rate and a 0.5 percent municipal property tax rate.

resident out of local property tax revenues. Table 5-6 examines the fiscal impact per unit and per acre of garden apartments and single-family homes. Community 1 has a relatively poor property tax base of $8,000 in ratables per pupil and $2,000 per resident. Given the assumed service levels, these figures imply a 3.75 percent school property tax rate and a 2 percent municipal property tax rate. In such a community all housing types show a positive fiscal balance. Per unit, single-family homes show marked advantages over garden apartments, with large-lot homes leading at $2,245. The pattern is reversed per acre with garden apartments at about $10,000. All single-family lot sizes are grossly inferior, with large-lot homes producing $965 per acre. Thus far, the picture is not much different from Community 1 in the first county.

Community 2 has an average property tax base of $16,000 in ratables per pupil and $4,000 per resident. Since the service levels are held constant, these figures imply a 1.88 percent school property tax rate and a 1 percent municipal property tax rate. Revenues are cut in half, due to lower tax rates. Now, although the same patterns per unit and per acre occur as in the first county, there are marked differences between the two counties. In the first county at least one lot size showed a deficit. For the second county every housing type shows a much better fiscal picture per unit and per acre precisely because the county is poorer. Even the differences between single-family lot sizes are marked. These differences are due to the greater wealth of the first county compared with the second.

This conclusion is reinforced in Community 3, which has a relatively wealthy property tax base of $32,000 in ratables per pupil and $8,000 per resident. Since the service levels are held constant, these figures imply a 0.94 percent school property tax rate and a 0.5 percent municipal property tax rate. Revenues are cut to a fourth, due to lower tax rates. In the first county all housing types produced negative balances at this point. In the second county the largest lot size is essentially neutral in fiscal impact per unit. Per acre, the smallest lot size (under a quarter-acre) shows a small deficit. The other housing types still show positive balances, although the next largest lot size is below $100 per acre.

Holding expenditure levels constant, Hamilton uses precisely such an argument (cited in chapter 2) to show that fiscal incentives are important in local zoning policies. Increasing average valuation will cut tax rates or support additional services. However we can obtain the following fiscal strategies from these simple examples. On a per unit basis, poor communities would presumably zone large lots in and zone garden apartments out; but wealthy communities ought to do exactly the opposite. The per acre results completely reverse the per unit findings. Poor communities would presumably zone garden apartments in and zone large lots out, while wealthy communities ought to do exactly the opposite. It becomes difficult to see how communities would go about using these conflicting fiscal results to design their zoning ordinances. This example is necessarily artificial, because it holds service costs constant regardless of tax base. Wealthy communities also provide higher expenditure levels, which would inflate the cost side and deflate net revenue.

There is a fiscal strategy that we can identify under these conflicting conditions. The largest lot sizes often (although not uniquely) have the dual property of maximizing net revenue per unit or at least minimizing fiscal impact per acre. Hence uncertainty over fiscal impact would be relieved by large lot zoning. It appears from the zoning information reviewed in chapter 3 that most suburban communities zone large lots in and zone apartments out, despite a wide variation in property tax bases, tax rates, and expenditure levels. White's conclusion was that such a strategy maximized fiscal-squeeze transfers. It may be the case that such a strategy simply minimizes fiscal uncertainty.

Fiscal Evaluation of Sample
Suburban Municipalities

To escape the somewhat artificial nature of the previous examples, we now examine the fiscal impact of garden apartments and single-family homes in the suburban sample of 176 municipalities in the six study counties. Results are reported per dwelling unit and per acre in table 5-7.[13] Per unit, large lot sizes over an acre show the best fiscal results, followed by garden apartments. Losses are imposed in 69 municipalities by garden apartments, in 155 by quarter-acre homes, in 150 and 138 by the next larger lot sizes, and in 90 by large-lot homes. The three smallest lot sizes show strongly negative results, concentrated in the category of $500 loss or greater (between 71 and 102 of the sample). About one-quarter of the largest lot sizes show over $300 gain. Nearly half of the garden apartments are concentrated in the category under $200 gain.

As in the county examples these per unit results are deceptive, because they ignore housing densities per acre. When the results are converted to per acre data, garden apartments become highly attractive. The fiscal attractiveness of the largest lot sizes is reduced (almost 60 percent using a 0.43 platting coefficient). Smaller lot sizes increase their negative impact. Garden apartments show net revenue of over $1,000 in 73 municipalities and net loss of over $1,000 in 46. Large-lot homes never show a gain or loss (except in one municipality) greater than $1,000 and are almost evenly divided between gain and loss. The smaller lot sizes are strongly concentrated as before in the loss categories; the loss over $1,000 steadily declines as lot size rises.[14]

The results for both apartments and smaller lot sizes again indicate the possibility of considerable fiscal uncertainty for local decision makers under property taxation. While garden apartments can produce substantial gains, they can also produce substantial losses. Smaller lot sizes are strongly weighted toward substantial deficits, which apparently decline with lot size. The largest lot sizes show much less variation. They impose gains and losses about equally in the developing communities, but these balances are (except for one municipality) less than $1,000.

Hamilton and White implicitly assume fiscal certainty in their formulations. Actually, large lots show much less fluctuation in fiscal impact than smaller lots or apartments. Given the wide variation in apartment results, large lot zoning

Table 5-7
Fiscal Impact of Residential Development in the Sample Suburban Municipalities (1970)

Net Fiscal Gain (Dollars per Year)	Garden Apartments		Single-Family Homes on Lot Sizes of							
			0-0.24 Acre		0.25-0.49 Acre		0.50-0.99 Acre		1 or More Acres	
Per dwelling unit										
-$500 or more	5	2.8%	102	58.0%	81	46.0%	71	40.3%	48	27.3%
-$250 to -499	13	7.4	26	14.8	45	25.6	31	17.6	13	7.4
-$1 to -249	51	29.0	27	15.3	24	13.6	36	20.5	29	16.5
$0 to 199	86	48.9	12	6.8	13	7.4	15	8.5	21	11.9
$200 to 299	18	10.2	3	1.7	4	2.3	5	2.8	10	5.7
$300 or more	3	1.7	6	3.4	9	5.1	18	10.2	55	31.3
Total	176	100.0	176	100.0	176	100.0	176	100.0	176	100.0
Per acre[a]										
-$1,000 or more	46	26.1%	111	63.1%	67	38.1%	31	17.6%	1	0.6%
-$1 to -999	23	13.1	44	25.0	83	47.2	107	60.8	89	50.6
$0 to 999	34	19.3	17	9.7	22	12.5	35	19.9	86	48.9
$1,000 to 2,499	47	26.7	4	2.3	4	2.3	3	1.7	–	–
$2,500 or more	26	14.8	–	–	–	–	–	–	–	–
Total	176	100.0	176	100.0	176	100.0	176	100.0	176	100.0

Sources: Market value and household characteristics are taken from table 5-1; municipal and school fiscal data from New Jersey Department of Community Affairs, *Thirty-Third Annual Report of the Division of Local Government Services, 1970: Statements of Financial Condition of Counties and Municipalities* (Trenton, N.J., 1971).

[a]Platting coefficients are taken from Franklin J. James and James W. Hughes, *Modeling State Growth: New Jersey 1980* (New Brunswick, N.J.: Center for Urban Policy Research, Rutgers University, 1973), p. 92.

may reduce uncertainty over the fiscal impact of land development. If we add to this cost-revenue consideration the fiscal implications of the fact that multifamily development permits a much larger population on the same land area with possibly more rapid scale effects in terms of service costs, we can see that fiscal uncertainty might lead local decision makers toward large-lot requirements and exclusion of multifamily development. However this fiscal strategy is designed not to maximize profit but to minimize risk.

Fiscal Efficiency of Single-Family Zoning

On purely cost-revenue grounds multifamily development would be most efficient in a large majority of suburban municipalities when considered on a per acre basis to incorporate the effects of housing density. While multifamily zoning is virtually nonexistent in suburban New Jersey, such restrictions may mean little, because developers typically apply for variances or rezonings. This informal process gives local governments a good deal of control over the scale effects and opportunity costs of multifamily development (incorporated in White's formula as $PCT \cdot Q_A$). About 40 percent of approved residential construction in New Jersey is multifamily. The problems of fiscal uncertainty, scale effects, and opportunity costs make it difficult to evaluate the fiscal wisdom of suburban land use policies.

However we may examine the efficiency of lot size requirements in single-family districts. White suggests that suburban communities concentrate single-family land in one or two large lot sizes in order to maximize fiscal-squeeze transfers. The data reported in table 5-7 do show a tendency for fiscal advantage (whether gain or reduced loss) to rise with lot size. While these results lend support to White's argument, they should be examined more closely. We may test the efficiency of single-family zoning by looking at the actual zoning ordinances in the sample municipalities adopted in comparison with what would be fiscally optimal according to the average-cost model.

The results of this comparison are shown in table 5-8. There is no significant relationship between fiscal incentives and actual zoning patterns in the sample municipalities. In the six counties overall, the actual zoning was close to the fiscal ideal. Of the approximately 554,700 vacant acres zoned for single-family residential use, about 420,200 were zoned for one-acre minimum lots. If the fiscal ideal were followed, about 422,400 acres would have been zoned for one-acre minimum lots. But this apparently close fit breaks down when we consider each lot size category separately. Of about 28,400 acres that should have been zoned for under a quarter-acre, 88.2 percent was zoned over an acre. Communities that would gain the most from small lot sizes zone just about the same as communities where large lots would be most favorable. An important factor should be remembered in considering these results. To a large extent, though not exclusively, the largest lot sizes are fiscally superior even per acre

Table 5-8
Comparison of Actual Single-Family Zoning of Vacant Land to Fiscally Optimal Zoning in the Sample Suburban Municipalities (1970)
(in acres and percentages)

Fiscally Optimal Lot Size	Actual Zoning for Single-Family Lot Sizes									
	Less than 0.25 Acre		0.25-0.49 Acre		0.50-0.99 Acre		1 or More Acres		Total	
Less than 0.25 acre	672	2.4%	1,254	4.4%	1,428	5.0%	25,043	88.2%	28,397	100.0%
0.25-0.49 acre	518	1.2	3,915	8.8	11,599	26.2	28,240	63.8	44,272	100.0
0.50-0.99 acre	1,255	2.1	2,131	3.6	12,656	21.2	43,580	73.1	59,622	100.0
1 or more acres	27,940	6.6	27,566	6.5	43,561	10.3	323,339	76.5	422,406	100.0
Total	30,385	5.5	34,866	6.3	69,244	12.5	420,202	75.8	554,697	100.0

Source: Franklin J. James with Oliver Duane Windsor, "Fiscal Zoning, Fiscal Reform, and Exclusionary Land Use Controls," *Journal of the American Institute of Planners* 42 (April 1976), table 5, p. 136, reprinted with permission.

Note: This table is restricted to 161 municipalities with single-family zoning.

among single-family types. While individual zoning ordinances do not particularly adhere strictly to their fiscal incentives, the overall results look like fiscal zoning, because municipalities typically zone for large lots regardless of the specific fiscal incentives that would be calculated using typical cost-revenue procedures.

For each municipality in the suburban sample I have computed an index of zoning efficiency which compares minimum lot size requirements in actual zoning ordinances with what would be fiscally efficient (on a per acre basis). The zoning efficiency index is defined as

$$I = \frac{AVG - MIN}{MAX - MIN}$$

where,

   MIN = net annual fiscal cost per acre of land zoned in the lot size category imposing the greatest net fiscal cost or offering the least net fiscal benefit per acre.

   MAX = net annual fiscal cost per acre of land zoned in the lot size category imposing the least net fiscal cost or offering the greatest net fiscal benefit per acre.

   AVG = average annual fiscal balance per acre of actual zoning for single-family homes in the municipality.

The index varies between zero and one.[15] An index value of one represents complete zoning efficiency and means that all single-family residential land in the municipality has been zoned in the lot size category giving the greatest fiscal advantage (MAX), so that $AVG = MAX$ and $I = (MAX - MIN)/(MAX - MIN) = 1$. A value of zero represents a total lack of zoning efficiency and means that all single-family residential land has the least favorable zoning (MIN), so that $AVG = MIN$ and $I = (MIN - MIN)/(MAX - MIN) = 0$. The average fiscal balance per acre of land zoned for single-family use in each zoning ordinance (AVG) was determined by multiplying the number of acres of land zoned in each lot size category against the net fiscal impact per acre of that category, summing over all lot size categories, and then dividing by the total number of vacant acres zoned for single-family homes.

Two types of municipalities had scores above 0.50 on the zoning efficiency index: (1) communities that had recently adopted or revised their master plans, and (2) those with large quantities of vacant residential land. The implication is that single-family zoning seems to be more fiscally efficient in such communities. Scores above 0.50 were not particularly found, however, for communities that had recently adopted or revised their zoning ordinances. Table 5-9 reports

Table 5-9
Fiscal Efficiency of Single-Family Zoning in the Sample Suburban Municipalities by Date of Adoption of Master Plan and Zoning Ordinance (1970)

Zoning Efficiency Index	Year of Adoption of Current Master Plan									
	No Master Plan		Pre-1960		1961-1965		1966-1971		Total	
0-0.10	11	29.7%	9	20.9%	3	12.0%	6	10.7%	29	18.0%
0.11-0.50	5	13.5	7	16.3	5	20.0	12	21.4	29	18.0
0.51-0.90	12	32.4	13	30.2	4	16.0	12	21.4	41	25.5
0.91 or more	9	24.3	14	32.6	13	52.0	26	46.4	62	38.5
Total	37	100.0	43	100.0	25	100.0	56	100.0	161	100.0

Zoning Efficiency Index	Year of Adoption of Current Zoning Ordinance									
	Pre-1960		1960-1964		1965-1969		1970 or Later		Total	
0-0.10	2	22.2%	3	30.3%	18	16.8%	6	17.2%	29	18.0%
0.11-0.50	1	11.1	1	10.0	19	17.8	8	22.9	29	18.0
0.51-0.90	3	33.3	2	20.0	28	26.2	8	22.9	41	25.5
0.91 or more	3	33.3	4	40.0	42	39.3	13	37.1	62	38.5
Total	9	100.0	10	100.0	107	100.0	35	100.0	161	100.0

Sources: The zoning efficiency index is computed from data in table 5-7. Master plan data are taken from the original data set used for Robert W. Burchell, *Planned Unit Development: New Communities American Style* (New Brunswick, N.J.: Center for Urban Policy Research, Rutgers University, 1972). Zoning ordinance data are taken from New Jersey Department of Community Affairs, "1970 Zoning Survey" (Trenton, N.J., 1971).

the efficiency indexes of single-family zoning by year of adoption of both current master plans and zoning ordinances. The proportion of scores above 0.50 rises as master plans are more recently adopted or revised. In communities with no master plan, 56.7 percent had scores above 0.50; this proportion rises to 62.8 percent, 68.0 percent, and 67.8 percent. The proportion under 0.10 drops by two-thirds. There is no marked pattern for scores above 0.50 with regard to year of adoption of zoning ordinance. The scores decline from 66.6 to 60 percent, rise to 65.5 percent, and decline again to 60 percent. But scores below 0.10 do decline for zoning ordinances adopted after 1964.

There is a marked rise in zoning efficiency as the quantity of vacant residential land increases, as reported in table 5-10. Under 500 acres, only 41.3 percent of municipalities had scores above the 0.50 level. This proportion rises to 66.7 and then 93.9 percent, followed by a slight drop to 86.2 percent above 7,500 acres. The fiscal efficiency of zoning also rises with the proportion of total vacant land zoned for residential use, to 70 percent when 60 percent or more of the land is zoned residential and to 66.3 percent above 80 percent zoned residential.

Fiscal Incentives under State School Aid

Hamilton argues that fiscal reform, in the guise of compensatory state aid to public education, is the proper strategy for correcting suburban exclusionary zoning. We now consider the possible effects on local fiscal zoning in New Jersey of the Robinson strategy. The New Jersey Supreme Court essentially adopted a modified Bateman Act formula, with guaranteed valuation set at about $47,300 (roughly 1.3 times the state average equalized valuation per pupil). We can compute the local fiscal implications of this financing scheme. Each school district is guaranteed a minimum valuation per pupil. When guaranteed valuation is equal to the district's actual equalized valuation, no equalization aid is provided and state aid is set at a flat subsidy (for which $182 per pupil will be used here).[16] Equalization aid is provided according to the following formulas:

$$\text{Tax rate} = \frac{\text{local tax expenditure per pupil}}{\text{guaranteed equalized valuation per pupil}}$$

$$\text{Equalization aid} = \text{tax rate} \times \left(\begin{array}{ccc} \text{guaranteed} & & \text{local} \\ \text{equalized} & - & \text{equalized} \\ \text{valuation} & & \text{valuation} \\ \text{per pupil} & & \text{per pupil} \end{array} \right)$$

Table 5-10
Fiscal Efficiency of Single-Family Zoning in the Sample Suburban Municipalities
by Amount and Proportion of Vacant Residential Land (1970)

Zoning Efficiency Index	Acres of Vacant Land Zoned for Residential Use									
	Less than 500		500-1,499		1,500-7,499		7,500 or More		Total	
0-0.10	25	33.3%	1	4.2%	—	—	3	10.3%	29	18.0%
0.11-0.50	19	25.3	7	29.2	2	6.1%	1	3.4	29	18.0
0.51-0.90	18	24.0	7	29.2	8	24.2	8	27.6	41	25.5
0.91 or more	13	17.3	9	37.5	23	69.7	17	58.6	62	38.5
Total	75	100.0	24	100.0	33	100.0	29	100.0	161	100.0

Zoning Efficiency Index	Proportion of Vacant Land Zoned for Residential Use									
	Less than 40 Percent		40 Percent-59.9 Percent		60 Percent-79.9 Percent		80 Percent or More		Total	
0-0.10	5	27.8%	4	17.4%	6	15.0%	14	17.5%	29	18.0%
0.11-0.50	3	16.6	7	30.4	6	15.0	13	16.3	29	18.0
0.51-0.90	6	33.3	3	13.0	13	32.5	19	23.8	41	25.5
0.91 or more	4	22.2	9	39.1	15	37.5	34	42.5	62	38.5
Total	18	100.0	23	100.0	40	100.0	80	100.0	161	100.0

Sources: The zoning efficiency index is computed from data in table 5-7. Zoning ordinance data are taken from New Jersey Department of Community Affairs, "1970 Zoning Survey" (Trenton, N.J., 1971).

State School Aid in the Study Counties

This procedure has been used to compute the average state aid per pupil in the six study counties. Aid per pupil multiplied by the number of pupils for each housing type in each county yields aid per dwelling unit, which is reported in table 5-11. Aid per unit is added to the revenue side, increasing the fiscal attractiveness of *all* housing types. The situation under local property taxation is thus adjusted in table 5-12 for state school aid. Because single-family homes have more pupils per unit relative to household size than garden apartments, the former generate more state school aid per unit, even though aid per pupil is constant within each county.

There are now two dramatic changes in the local fiscal picture reported earlier in table 5-3. First, smaller lot sizes had produced substantial cost-revenue deficits in all counties. These deficits have been converted with state school aid to substantially positive balances in Middlesex and Monmouth counties. In Ocean County the deficits have been sharply reduced. However the relative attractiveness among lot sizes has not been significantly affected. Second, where there were already positive balances for single-family homes, the differential between them and garden apartments has been sharply increased. In Middlesex, for example, state school aid increases the fiscal gain per apartment only $68; it

Table 5-11
State Assistance for Public Education under the Robinson Strategy (1970)

Housing Type	Bergen	Middlesex	Monmouth	Morris	Ocean	Somerset
			Aid per Pupil			
	$182	$ 392	$ 449	$ 429	$229	$ 422
			Aid per Unit			
Garden apartment	51	68	108	85	45	94
0-0.24 acre	221	588	630	659	238	604
0.25-0.49 acre	273	632	631	674	296	605
0.50-0.99 acre	309	669	719	713	292	685
1 or more acres	310	745	721	754	343	672
			Aid per Acre[a]			
Garden apartment	714	952	1,512	1,190	630	1,316
0-0.24 acre	535	1,423	1,515	1,595	576	1,462
0.25-0.59 acre	491	1,138	1,136	1,213	533	1,089
0.50-0.99 acre	312	676	726	720	295	692
1 or more acres	133	320	310	324	147	289

Sources: Table 5-1 for household characteristics and table 2-1 for fiscal data. Platting coefficients are taken from Franklin J. James and James W. Hughes, *Modeling State Growth: New Jersey 1980* (New Brunswick, N.J.: Center for Urban Policy Research, Rutgers University, 1973), p. 92.

[a]Platting coefficients are fourteen garden apartments; quarter-acre lots 2.42; half-acre lots 1.80; acre lots 1.01; larger lots 0.43 units per acre.

Table 5-12
Fiscal Implications in the Study Counties of State Assistance for Public
Education under the Robinson Strategy (1970)

Housing Type	Bergen	Middlesex	Monmouth	Morris	Ocean	Somerset
			Per Unit			
Garden apartment	$ 35	$228	$ 257	$ 186	$ 81	$ 144
0-0.24 acre	−323	348	193	−226	−203	−65
0.25-0.49 acre	−426	509	379	42	−293	198
0.50-0.99 acre	−391	419	439	270	−207	792
1.00 or more acres	−47	490	943	1,012	−203	652
			Per Acre			
Garden apartment	490	3,192	3,598	2,604	1,134	2,016
0-0.24 acre	−781	842	457	−547	−491	−157
0.25-0.49 acre	−767	917	682	75	−527	356
0.50-0.99 acre	−395	423	443	273	−209	800
1.00 or more acres	−21	210	405	435	−88	280

Sources: Tables 5-3 and 5-11.

increases the fiscal gain per large-lot home by $745 (almost doubling the fiscal gain). Previously each large-lot home produced something over double the fiscal gain of a garden apartment in the same county; state school aid doubles the difference again to four times the fiscal gain.

These effects are buried in table 5-12 by housing density in the per acre conversion. Garden apartments still come out ahead strongly in every county. However three important factors should be borne in mind. First, it appears that fiscal zoning is widely discussed in per unit, not per acre, terms. Second, it is probable that additional compensation is widely demanded for the scale effects, opportunity costs, and externalities expected from multifamily housing. The fiscal profitability of such housing must be sufficiently high to offset other considerations. In effect cost-revenue dollars are weighted differently by housing type. Third, fiscal impacts are uncertain in character. This uncertainty is minimized by single-family zoning. State school aid reinforces this reduction of fiscal uncertainty.

Per acre, the fiscal balance of smaller lot sizes has jumped as much as $535 (from −$1,316 to −$781) in Bergen, $1,423 in Middlesex (from −$581 to $842), $1,515 in Monmouth (from −$1,058 to $457), $1,595 in Morris (from −$2,142 to −$547), $576 in Ocean (from −$1,067 to −$491), and $1,462 in Somerset (from −$1,619 to $157). Smaller lot sizes are now typically as favorable or more favorable than large lot sizes per acre, except in Ocean. Garden apartments have not shown that much improvement. The fiscal balance for apartments rose $51 in Bergen, $952 in Middlesex, $1,512 in Monmouth, $1,190 in Morris, $630 in Ocean, and $1,316 in Somerset.

The fiscal balance has probably turned more in favor of single-family homes with state school aid. This picture becomes clearer when we examine the state school aid implications directly in table 5-11. The table shows aid per pupil, per dwelling unit, and per acre for each study county. On a per unit basis, aid generally rises with lot size and is considerably higher for single-family than for multifamily units. These effects are reversed somewhat by density when we convert to a per acre basis. However in several counties the smaller lot sizes are still receiving more aid in dollar terms than multifamily units even per acre. Because of the effects of density, the aid per acre declines with lot size. In Bergen and Ocean counties multifamily units fare better than single-family units, but the difference is minimal, particularly if cost-revenue dollars are in fact weighted by housing type.

State School Aid in the Sample
Suburban Municipalities

These fiscal effects can be traced in the suburban sample of 176 developing municipalities. The fiscal implications per dwelling unit are reported in table 5-13. All housing types show a definite improvement in net fiscal impact over the results under local property taxation reported in table 5-7. No municipality now shows a deficit of more than $249 for garden apartments. The number with positive balances for garden apartments of more than $300 has jumped from 3 to 51. But the single-family lot sizes have shown the greatest improvement per unit. Under local property taxation, between 102 and 48 municipalities showed deficits of over $500, which decrease with lot size. With state school aid these deficits are cut in half or better. Between 49 and 113 municipalities now show positive balances over $300, which increase with lot size. The number of municipalities with such positive balances for lot sizes over one acre literally doubles from 55 (31.3 percent of the sample) to 113 (64.2 percent).

As before, these effects are buried by housing density in the per acre conversion. Fully two-thirds of the municipalities show positive balances for garden apartments over $2,500 with state school aid, compared with only about 14.8 percent under local property taxation. But the single-family lot sizes, while not increased so dramatically in dollar value, are raised substantially into the positive categories. The deficits over $1,000 are cut in half or better. Under local property taxation about half of the municipalities incurred deficits for the largest lot sizes; with state school aid that proportion is cut to 25 percent. For the next smaller lot sizes, the shift is from about 78 percent to 34 percent with deficits.

State assistance tends to relieve the uncertainty of deficits for single-family lot sizes, as well as for multifamily housing. The largest lot sizes are virtually guaranteed a positive balance. Although the balance will be under $1,000 per acre compared with over $2,500 per acre for garden apartments in two-thirds of

Table 5-13
Fiscal Impact of Residential Development in the Sample Suburban Municipalities under the Robinson Strategy (1970)

Net Fiscal Gain (Dollars per Year)	Garden Apartments		Single-Family Homes on Lot Sizes of							
			0-0.24 Acre		0.25-0.49 Acre		0.50-0.99 Acre		1 or More Acres	
Per dwelling unit										
−$500 or more	–	–	55	31.3%	26	14.8%	24	13.6%	15	8.5%
−$250 to −499	–	–	12	6.8	17	9.7	16	9.1	11	6.3
−$1 to −249	12	6.9%	24	13.6	24	13.6	19	10.8	18	10.2
$0 to 199	54	30.7	24	13.6	29	16.5	22	12.5	9	5.1
$200 to 299	59	33.5	12	6.8	10	5.7	13	7.4	10	5.7
$300 or more	51	29.0	49	27.8	70	39.8	82	46.6	113	64.2
Total	176	100.0	176	100.0	176	100.0	176	100.0	176	100.0
Per acre										
−$1,000 or more	4	2.3	59	33.5	23	13.1	6	3.4	–	–
−$1 to −999	8	4.5	32	18.2	44	25.0	53	30.1	44	25.0
$0 to 999	8	4.5	45	25.6	68	38.6	98	55.7	132	75.0
$1,000 to 2,499	37	21.0	38	21.6	41	23.3	19	10.8	–	–
$2,500 or more	119	67.6	2	1.1	–	–	–	–	–	–
Total	176	100.0	176	100.0	176	100.0	176	100.0	176	100.0

Sources: Tables 5-7 and 5-11.

the sample, we must keep in mind the complicated fiscal and nonfiscal environment of local decision makers. Is an additional $1,500 an acre sufficient compensation for the possible scale effects and opportunity costs of population growth and the expected externalities of multifamily development? How certain are the potential fiscal gains from multifamily development? There is no final evidence to answer this question, but the fiscal picture for single-family homes has been markedly improved, per unit or per acre. If local zoning practices tend to ignore the direct cash-flow effects under local property taxation, why will the shift to state aid to local education alter that fact?

Relationship between School and
Municipal Functions

The results just presented should also be considered in light of the relationship between school and municipal functions under the local property tax. The analysis thus far has combined these functions. Only school costs are subsidized under the Robinson strategy. In fact, the fiscal burdens of these functions have very different distributions among municipalities in New Jersey. Therefore we should examine separately the fiscal impact of housing development on the two functions. This separation is carried out in table 5-14 using county data for garden apartments and the four single-family lot sizes. Negative balances for school functions are found primarily for the smaller lot sizes in Bergen, Monmouth, and Ocean. Garden apartments show substantial positive balances, strongly increased per acre, in all counties. However negative balances for municipal functions occur in the same three counties for garden apartments. The fiscal difference between communities is much larger for municipal functions than for school functions.

This separation of municipal and school cost-revenue balances is carried out for the 176 sample municipalities in tables 5-15 and 5-16. The first table contains a per unit analysis. For municipal functions, only 4 communities show a neutral or positive balance with garden apartments, all below $200 per unit. Single-family homes show a more positive picture generally; and the positive balances rise with lot size from about 11 percent to 44 percent of the sample communities. Large-lot homes show the best fiscal results per unit for municipal functions. Deficits occur in single-family homes for school functions. Here all but 16 communities show positive balances for garden apartments. (Large-lot homes still show the best fiscal results per unit in the sense that 51 communities have over $300 gain.)

Table 5-16 is a per acre analysis. Garden apartments show over $1,000 loss per acre in 143 municipalities (about 81 percent of the sample) for municipal functions; a positive fiscal picture is found in only 4 municipalities. The smaller lot sizes are similarly very unattractive, but between 73 percent and 81 percent

Table 5-14
Comparison of Fiscal Impact of Residential Development on School and Municipal Functions in the Study Counties (1970)

Housing Type	Bergen	Middlesex	Monmouth	Morris	Ocean	Somerset
			Per Dwelling Unit			
School functions						
Garden apartment	$ 168	$ 180	$ 179	$ 154	$ 99	$ 98
0-0.24 acre	−235	−272	−420	−803	−385	−616
0.25-0.49 acre	−358	−190	−274	−606	−533	−396
0.50-0.99 acre	−329	−300	−318	−466	−461	24
1.00 or more acres	13	−331	84	87	−535	−81
Municipal functions						
Garden apartment	$ −19	$ −20	$ −30	$ −53	$ −63	$ −48
0-0.24 acre	67	32	−17	−82	−56	−53
0.25-0.49 acre	100	67	22	−26	−56	−11
0.50-0.99 acre	155	50	38	23	−38	83
1.00 or more acres	280	76	138	171	−11	61
			Per Acre			
School functions						
Garden apartment	$2,352	$2,520	$2,506	$2,156	$1,386	$1,372
0-0.24 acre	−569	−658	−1,016	−1,943	−932	−1,491
0.25-0.49 acre	−644	−342	−493	−1,091	−959	−713
0.50-0.99 acre	−332	−303	85	88	−540	−82
1.00 or more acres	6	−142	36	37	−230	−35
Municipal functions						
Garden apartment	$−266	$−280	$−420	$−742	$ 882	$−672
0-0.24 acre	162	77	−41	−198	−136	−128
0.25-0.49 acre	180	121	40	−47	−101	−20
0.50-0.99 acre	157	51	38	23	−38	84
1.00 or more acres	120	33	59	74	−5	26

Source: Table 5-3.

fall under a $1,000 loss. The largest lot sizes are split about evenly between gain and loss under $1,000 for municipal functions. In contrast only 16 municipalities show a fiscal loss on school functions for garden apartments. And 145 show a fiscal gain of over $1,000 per acre. The smaller lot sizes fall heavily into the loss category over $1,000. The loss declines with lot size, until in the case of the largest lot sizes, there is again a fairly even division between $1,000 loss or gain.

The explanation for this result is straightforward. Table 5-2 showed that garden apartments have high market value per pupil but low market value per resident compared with single-family homes. This pattern results from the low pupil estimates for garden apartments relative to household size, which is much closer among housing types than age composition. The overall results in table 5-7 are dominated by school functions, which are a very large component of local

Table 5-15
Comparison of Fiscal Impact per Unit of Residential Development on School
and Municipal Functions in the Sample Suburban Municipalities (1970)

Net Fiscal Gain (Dollars per Year)	Garden Apartments		Single-Family Homes on Lot Sizes of							
			0-0.24 Acre		0.25-0.49 Acre		0.50-0.99 Acre		1 or More Acres	
School Functions										
−$500 or more	—	—	81	46.0%	51	29.0%	50	28.4%	36	20.5%
−$250 to −499	1	0.6%	31	17.6	58	33.0	40	22.7	21	11.9
−$1 to −249	15	8.5	39	22.2	40	22.7	45	25.6	37	21.0
$0 to 199	97	55.1	15	8.5	13	7.4	20	11.4	20	11.4
$200 to 299	48	27.3	3	1.7	3	1.7	6	3.4	11	6.3
$300 or more	15	8.5	7	4.0	11	6.3	15	8.5	51	29.0
Total	176	100.0	176	100.0	176	100.0	176	100.0	176	100.0
Municipal Functions										
−$500 or more	3	1.7	9	5.1	8	4.5	8	4.5	8	4.5
−$250 to −499	16	9.1	53	30.1	36	20.5	32	18.2	23	13.1
−$1 to −249	153	87.0	95	54.0	106	60.2	91	51.7	67	38.1
$0 to 199	4	2.3	16	9.1	20	11.4	35	19.9	58	33.0
$200 to 299	—	—	2	1.1	3	1.7	7	4.0	10	5.7
$300 or more	—	—	1	0.6	3	1.7	3	1.7	10	5.7
Total	176	100.0	176	100.0	176	100.0	176	100.0	176	100.0

Source: Table 5-7.

Table 5-16
Comparison of Fiscal Impact per Acre of Residential Development on School and Municipal Functions in the Sample Suburban Municipalities (1970)

Net Fiscal Gain (Dollars per Year)	Garden Apartments		Single-Family Homes on Lot Sizes of							
			0-0.24 Acre		0.25-0.49 Acre		0.50-0.99 Acre		1 or More Acres	
School Functions										
-$1,000 or more	8	4.5%	93	52.8%	47	26.7%	15	8.5%	–	–
-$1 to -999	8	4.5	58	33.0	102	58.0	120	68.2	94	53.4%
$0 to 999	15	8.5	21	11.9	23	13.1	37	21.0	82	46.6
$1,000 to 2,499	67	38.1	4	2.3	4	2.3	4	2.3	–	–
$2,500 or more	78	44.3	–	–	–	–	–	–	–	–
Total	176	100.0	176	100.0	176	100.0	176	100.0	176	100.0
Municipal Functions										
-$1,000 or more	143	81.3	16	9.1	7	4.0	2	1.1	–	–
-$1 to -999	29	16.5	141	80.1	143	81.3	129	73.3	98	55.7
$0 to 999	2	1.1	18	10.2	26	14.8	45	25.6	78	44.3
$1,000 to 2,499	2	1.1	1	0.6	–	–	–	–	–	–
$2,500 or more	–	–	–	–	–	–	–	–	–	–
Total	176	100.0	176	100.0	176	100.0	176	100.0	176	100.0

Source: Table 5-7.

public expenditures in suburban communities. State aid to education may in effect give added significance to the municipal functions still funded almost exclusively at the local level. These municipal functions may become relatively more important to local governments with substantial population growth.

Fiscal Incentives under a Statewide School Property Tax

Another approach to examining this issue is to assume that the state provides full funding of school costs through a statewide property tax. For illustration we can set per pupil expenditures at the 1970 state average (local expenditure plus state school aid) of $978.[17] Such full funding would require a state property tax rate of $2.56 per $100 of equalized valuation. The net fiscal gain of housing development in the sample municipalities is computed in table 5-17 under these assumptions. This computation now includes only school functions. (Municipal functions would still be carried on the local property tax.) Net fiscal gain here will not be to municipal government, but to the state. Hence a positive fiscal balance constitutes surplus funds transferred to the state by the municipality; a negative fiscal balance constitutes deficit funds transferred to the municipality by the state.

This statewide taxation procedure may still have important fiscal zoning implications for local governments. Multifamily units produce substantial transfers to the state government in all 176 municipalities (over $2,500 per acre in 106 municipalities). Single-family lot sizes lead to transfers from the state government. Transfers would apparently decline with lot size, so smaller lot sizes are favored. One can foresee circumstances in which these computed cash flows may still affect local zoning decisions by subsidizing the exclusion of multi-family development. The state would, in effect, be directly subsidizing single-family homes, particularly if all properties were taxed at the same tax rate. The subsidy would be drawn from communities approving multifamily development.

Moreover full state funding at average figures would cause increased school tax rates in fully 80.8 percent of the municipalities, as shown in table 5-18. For about half of the communities tax-rate changes (positive or negative) would be within $0.50 of present tax rates. Tax rates would rise more than $1.00 in 113 municipalities (fully one-fifth). To a large degree this impact is due to the increase in per pupil expenditures required to raise many communities to the state average.

The distribution of these tax-rate changes is probably more important than the fact that most school tax rates would rise. Table 5-19 shows the distribution of the tax-rate changes among municipalities by population size (1960) and growth rate (1960-1970). The tax-rate changes show a marked pattern by growth rate. They rise rapidly from an average of $0.03 in declining communi-

Table 5-17
Fiscal Impact of Residential Development in the Sample Suburban Municipalities under a State Property Tax (1970)

Net Fiscal Transfer (Dollars per Year)	Garden Apartments		Single-Family Homes on Lot Sizes of							
			0-0.24 Acre		0.25-0.49 Acre		0.50-0.99 Acre		1 or More Acres	
Per dwelling unit										
−$500 or more	–	–	90	51.1%	–	–	32	18.2%	24	13.6%
−$250 to −499	–	–	42	23.9	132	75.0%	80	45.5	18	10.2
−$1 to −249	–	–	–	–	–	–	–	–	52	29.5
$0 to 199	70	39.8%	44	25.0	44	25.0	64	36.4	–	–
$200 to 299	62	35.2	–	–	–	–	–	–	–	–
$300 or more	44	25.0	–	–	–	–	–	–	82	46.6
Total	176	100.0	176	100.0	176	100.0	176	100.0	176	100.0
Per acre										
−$1,000 or more	–	–	114	64.8	–	–	–	–	–	–
−$1 to −999	–	–	18	10.2	132	75.0	112	63.6	94	53.4
$0 to 999	–	–	44	25.0	44	25.0	64	36.4	82	46.6
$1,000 to 2,499	70	39.8	–	–	–	–	–	–	–	–
$2,500 or more	106	60.2	–	–	–	–	–	–	–	–
Total	176	100.0	176	100.0	176	100.0	176	100.0	176	100.0

Source: Table 5-7.

Note: Per pupil expenditures are set at $978 and state property tax rate at $2.56 to correspond with 1970 state averages including both local tax levy and state aid as reported in table 2-1.

Table 5-18
Change in School Tax Rates among New Jersey Municipalities
Resulting from Imposition of a State Property Tax (1970)

Change in School Tax Rate	Number of Municipalities	Percentage
$1.00 or more	113	19.9
$0.50 to 0.99	140	24.7
$0 to 0.49	205	36.2
−$0.01 to −0.49	75	13.2
−$0.50 to −0.99	24	4.2
−$1.00 or more	10	1.8
Total	567	100.0

Source: New Jersey Department of Community Affairs, *Thirty-Third Annual Report of the Division of Local Government Services, 1970: Statements of Financial Condition of Counties and Municipalities* (Trenton, N.J., 1971).

Note: State property tax rate is set at $2.56 to incorporate both local tax levies and state aid.

ties to $0.56 or $0.57 in slowly or moderately growing communities (under 50 percent growth rate) and then drop to $0.47 and $0.43 (under 200 percent growth rate). There is then a very large drop to an average $0.07 in explosively growing communities (over 200 percent growth rate). Very small tax increases would thus be imposed on either declining or explosively growing communities. Tax-rate changes show no strong pattern by population size but are somewhat higher on average in communities over 10,000 population.

Tax rates fall primarily in small municipalities under 2,500 population with declining populations and in communities over 2,500 population with explosive growth (over 200 percent growth rate). State assumption of full school costs would bring tax relief for those municipalities. We should anticipate that rapidly growing suburban communities might be reinforced in their exclusionary practices by such tax relief. In general the highest tax rate increases would occur in municipalities over 50,000 with growing populations, and in small communities under 2,500 population with growth rates between 20 percent and 200 percent.

Conclusion

When we directly measure the fiscal impact of housing types, using an average-cost model, we find results contrary to the fiscal motive theory. Apartments are fiscally superior even to large-lot homes, particularly on a per acre basis. Fiscal benefit does appear to rise with lot size for single-family housing. The fundamental flaw of the fiscal zoning hypothesis is its assumption

Table 5-19
Distribution of School Tax Rate Changes among New Jersey Municipalities by Population Size and Growth Rate (1970)

Population (1960)	Declining	Growth Rate, 1960-1970 (percent)					Total
		0-19.9	20-49.9	50-99.9	100-199.9	200 or More	
				School Tax Rate Changes			
Less than 2,500	−1.07	0.52	0.78	0.67	0.71	0.53	0.47
2,500-4,999	0.47	0.39	0.52	0.46	0.43	−0.02	0.44
5,000-9,999	0.11	0.59	0.41	0.29	0.05	−0.29	0.42
10,000-24,999	0.58	0.64	0.45	0.28	0.01	−0.67	0.50
25,000-49,999	0.61	0.65	0.31	0.79	0.26	−	0.56
50,000 or more	0.27	0.72	0.60	−	−	−	0.52
Total	0.03	0.56	0.57	0.47	0.43	0.07	0.46
				Number of Municipalities			
Less than 2,500	19	51	56	29	14	3	172
2,500-4,999	16	37	31	25	14	3	126
5,000-9,999	9	46	37	19	5	1	117
10,000-24,999	16	42	26	13	4	1	102
25,000-49,999	5	19	6	1	2	−	33
50,000 or more	7	8	2	−	−	−	17
Total	72	203	158	87	39	8	567

Sources: Table 5-18; population data are taken from 1960 and 1970 Censuses of Population and Housing.

that taxable valuation per household is necessarily maximized in single-family housing.

School-age children are concentrated in single-family homes, not apartments. Taxable valuation per household is especially low in the smaller lot sizes. The higher the tax rate, the more profitable apartments will appear when compared with single-family homes. If we housed exactly the same population, large-lot homes would be fiscally superior due to market value, but such an example is artificial. Large amounts of land would be needed, reducing open space and affecting other environmental amenities perhaps as much or more than multifamily construction for the same population. It also appears that even single-family zoning is inefficient from the fiscal viewpoint. Suburban communities zone for large lots regardless of the specific cost-revenue implications.

The Robinson strategy may thwart implementation of the Mt. Laurel strategy of least-cost zoning by increasing the fiscal pressures for exclusionary zoning practices. *Robinson* formula aid increases the fiscal benefit for all housing types by providing property tax relief. However aid per dwelling unit rises with the number of school-age children. On this basis, the fiscal benefit is much larger for single-family than for multifamily development and rises with lot size. On a per acre basis multifamily development still comes out strongly ahead because of density. However in four of the six study counties, the changes are more dramatic for single-family housing.

Since single-family housing becomes strongly positive in virtually all counties, *Robinson* formula aid will relieve the fiscal pressures for exclusionary zoning (rather than increasing them) only if we assume that suburban voters simply count property tax dollars on a per acre basis and consider nothing else. If they demand compensation for multifamily development and poorer households, state school aid may simply tip the fiscal balance further in favor of single-family housing. Voters may be more impressed with the per unit fiscal implications than with the per acre results. Moreover state school aid reduces the fiscal uncertainty associated with single-family development, especially for large lot requirements on a per unit basis. The municipal functions still borne almost entirely by local government—and hardly supplemented by state aid—markedly disfavor multifamily development, because household size varies less with housing type than with schoolchildren.

Full state funding of public education under a state property tax would increase school tax rates in 81 percent of municipalities—more than $1.00 in 20 percent. Tax relief would occur largely in declining and very rapidly growing communities. The highest tax-rate increases would occur in municipalities over 50,000 with growing populations and in small communities under 2,500. Tax-rate increases would not be imposed on the typical suburban community. It also appears that multifamily development would cause a larger outflow of tax dollars to the state treasury than single-family development so that a state property tax would subsidize the latter.

Notes

1. This argument has been presented elsewhere by the author with Franklin J. James. The first part of this chapter draws substantially on that joint work. See "Local Land Use Controls in New Jersey: Their Effects on Housing Costs and Community Fiscal Advantage," in *New Dimensions of Urban Planning: Growth Controls,* ed. James W. Hughes (New Brunswick, N.J.: Center for Urban Policy Research, Rutgers University, 1974), chap. 7, pp. 97-121; "Fiscal Zoning, Fiscal Reform, and Exclusionary Land Use Controls," *Journal of the American Institute of Planners* 42 (April 1976): 130-141; "Breaking the Invisible Wall: Fiscal Reform and Municipal Land Use Regulation," in *Urban Problems and Public Policy,* ed. Robert L. Lineberry and Louis H. Masotti (Lexington, Mass.: Lexington Books, D.C. Heath and Co., 1975), chap. 9, pp. 87-105.

2. New Jersey County and Municipal Government Study Commission, *Housing and Suburbs: Fiscal and Social Impact of Multifamily Development* (Trenton, N.J., October 1974), chap. 5, "Leadership Perceptions and Local Decisions," pp. 75-100.

3. John F. Kain, *Urban Form and the Costs of Urban Services* (Cambridge, Mass.: M.I.T.-Harvard Joint Center for Urban Studies, Program on Regional and Urban Economics, May 1967, revised).

4. See New Jersey County and Municipal Government Study Commission, *Housing and Suburbs,* chap. 3, "The Housing Development Balance Sheet," pp. 30-47, and appendix II, "Techniques for the Evaluation of the Cost/Revenue Impact of Multifamily Housing Development," pp. 145-158; New Jersey Department of Community Affairs, *Evaluating the Fiscal Impact of the Planned Unit Development* (Trenton, N.J., 1975); George Sternlieb et al., *Housing Development and Municipal Costs* (New Brunswick, N.J.: Center for Urban Policy Research, Rutgers University, 1973), chap. 1, "Housing Development and Municipal Costs: A Summary," pp. 1-57.

5. For a detailed examination of the difference, see Duane Windsor and Franklin J. James, "Statewide Multipliers for Municipal Cost-Revenue Analysis," paper presented at the national conference of the American Institute of Planners, Denver, Colo. (October 1974).

6. See New Jersey County and Municipal Government Study Commission, *Housing and Suburbs,* chap. 1, "Overview of the Fiscal Impact of Housing Development," pp. 1-12; Sternlieb et al., *Housing Development and Municipal Costs,* chap. 3, "The Impact on Public Education," pp. 85-126; Thomas Muller, *Fiscal Impacts of Land Development: A Critique of Methods and Review of Issues* (Washington, D.C.: Urban Institute, 1975), p. 7. In conducting this study, a slight change was made in the pupil estimates for multifamily units reported in previous studies, which may have overstated those estimates somewhat. The effect was simply to deflate the net revenue for multifamily units in those studies, since school costs were inflated. The practical effect is unimportant, since multifamily units still showed a strong positive fiscal balance, despite the cost inflation.

7. Previous studies reported by the author used a sample of 175. In conducting this study, it was discovered that an additional municipality could have been included in the sample. The difference is unimportant.

8. Lynne B. Sagalyn and George Sternlieb, *Zoning and Housing Costs: The Impact of Land-Use Controls on Housing Price* (New Brunswick, N.J.: Center for Urban Policy Research, Rutgers University, 1972), appendix A, "Sampling Procedures and Sample Characteristics," pp. 71-80. The original data set from this survey was made available to the author.

9. New Jersey Department of Community Affairs, Division of Housing and Urban Renewal, *New Multi-Family Dwellings in New Jersey: 1970* (Trenton, N.J., n.d.); *New Multi-Family Dwellings in New Jersey: 1971* (Trenton, N.J., n.d.).

10. Monthly contract rent was multiplied by 72 (12 months' rent multiplied by a factor of 6), which is a standard estimating procedure in New Jersey. The procedure is arbitrary but corresponds roughly to local assessment practices in New Jersey, where tax bills for apartments are computed not from an assessment of market value but directly from the rent roll. See New Jersey County and Municipal Government Study Commission, *Housing and Suburbs,* pp. 146-147.

11. U.S. Department of Commerce, Bureau of the Census, *Public Use Samples of Basic Records from the 1970 Census: Description and Technical Documentation* (Washington, D.C., 1972). For a detailed explanation of how these multipliers are estimated, see Windsor and James, "Statewide Multipliers for Municipal Cost-Revenue Analysis." These estimates were checked against a large sample survey of housing developments in suburban New Jersey conducted during 1972-1973 by the author and reported in both the paper cited and Sternlieb et al., *Housing Development and Municipal Costs,* chap. 3, "The Impact of Public Education," pp. 85-126, and appendix A, "Survey Methodology," pp. 316-360. See also George Sternlieb and Robert W. Burchell, "The Numbers Game: Forecasting Household Size," *Urban Land* 33 (January 1974):3-20.

12. The pupil estimates were originally computed from the census data by grade level. Weighted pupil estimates were also computed to adjust these original figures for differences in cost per pupil by grade level using weights recommended by the New Jersey Educational Association, *Basic Statistical Data of New Jersey School Districts, 1971 Edition* (Trenton, N.J., July 1971), Research Bulletin A71-2, p. 18. These weights are 0.5 kindergarten, 1.0 elementary, and 1.3 secondary. Relatively little difference is introduced by the weighting procedure. The effect of weighting would be to increase school costs per dwelling unit for single-family homes, which in New Jersey have more children in secondary grades. See Muller, *Fiscal Impacts of Land Development,* p. 54.

13. For New Jersey, school financial data are available on both municipality and school district bases. Although school property taxes are levied by municipality, school districts and municipalities do not necessarily correspond. All data presented in this study have been placed on a municipal basis for comparison with governmental authority for land use regulation. Number of pupils, however, is reported only by school district, not by municipality. Per pupil expenditures were developed by estimating school enrollment for each municipality. Where a school district did not match a municipality, pupil enrollment was allocated to the constituent municipalities on a proportional basis according to municipal population in the 1970 Census of Population. Enrollment figures were dated September 30, 1971, and were taken from New Jersey Education Association, *Basic Statistical Data of New Jersey School Districts, 1972 Edition* (Trenton, N.J., July 1972), Research Bulletin A72-2.

14. The method used in this study loads all municipal and school costs of residential development onto each residential unit, as if commercial and industrial land uses were completely independent of residential land uses. This assumption has been criticized by Julius Margolis, "On Municipal Land Policy for Fiscal Gains," *National Tax Journal* 9 (September 1956): 247-257; and Ruth L. Mace, *Municipal Cost-Revenue Research in the United States* (Chapel Hill, N.C.: Institute of Government, University of North Carolina, 1961), chap. 1, "Background and Preview," pp. 1-27. For a different view, see Muller, *Fiscal Impacts of Land Development,* "Choice of Allocation Approach," pp. 16-18. Ruth L.

Mace and Warren J. Wicker, *Do Single-Family Homes Pay Their Way?: A Comparative Analysis of Costs and Revenues for Public Services* (Washington, D.C.: Urban Land Institute, 1968), appendix, "Methodological Details," pp. 39-46, suggests allocating service costs to land uses according to the relative proportion of property valuation constituted by the particular land use. The author has corrected the results of table 5-7 using a specific procedure recommended by the New Jersey County and Municipal Government Study Commission, *Housing and Suburbs,* appendix II, "Techniques for the Evaluation of the Cost/Revenue Impact of Multifamily Housing Development," pp. 145-158. Per unit, all housing types would show a more favorable fiscal picture. The improvement is most favorable in the case of garden apartments, where only three municipalities would now show a loss. This relative improvement is greatly magnified by per acre conversion, where 157 municipalities would now show a gain of over $2,500 for garden apartments. These two approaches together should serve to provide the boundaries for the fiscal-impact estimates.

15. A similar index, reversed in direction, was employed in the three studies cited in note 1.

16. These figures are derived from the New Jersey Supreme Court's opinions in Robinson v. Cahill. In 351 A.2d 713 (1975), the supreme court ordered provisional remedy for school year 1976-1977 in accordance with the incentive equalization aid formula of the 1970 Bateman Act. Essentially that same formula was adopted in the Public School Education Act of 1975, which set the guaranteed valuation per pupil for equalization aid at 1.3 times the state average valuation and was approved in 355 A.2d 129 (1976). There are two problems in this derivation. First, the equalization aid formula varies according to type of school district. Therefore the maximum aid categories of $165 minimum support aid and $43,000 guaranteed valuation per weighted pupil have been used in this study. Second, a pupil weighting factor (for differences in school costs by grade level) must be introduced. Justice Botter's opinion, 287 A.2d 187 (1972) adopts a weighting factor of 1.1 as a state average. His sample calculations proceed by weighting both minimum support aid and guaranteed valuation by this factor. This same procedure has been followed here, yielding $182 and $47,300. Within reason, the actual figures used are relatively unimportant.

17. This approach is suggested in Polly Roberts, "Making dollars and sense out of fiscal impact analysis," *Planning* 42 (August 1976):21. She argues that a statewide property tax will make school-age children fiscally attractive to suburban communities, as well as transferring the financial burden of public education to low-tax jurisdictions.

6

Policy Conclusions

This study considers certain problems in the design of public policy to deal with suburban exclusionary practices. It examines the twin strategies of state aid to public education and least-cost zoning adopted by the New Jersey Supreme Court in the landmark cases of *Robinson, Mt. Laurel,* and *Madison.* Those strategies appear to rest on three fundamental assumptions which form a widely accepted theory of fiscal zoning. The exclusionary zoning hypothesis argues that metropolitan housing supplies and costs are significantly affected by restrictive zoning practices. Although we have little idea of the actual empirical magnitude of these housing market effects, they are then linked to the income segregation and fiscal disparities that are evident in major metropolitan areas. These effects are to be relieved through least-cost zoning under the Mt. Laurel strategy. The fiscal zoning hypothesis assumes that such exclusionary zoning is based on strong and well-defined fiscal incentives specifically created by the system of local property taxation prevalent in New Jersey and other states. The Robinson strategy is partly predicated on the assumption that state aid to public education will significantly relieve the underlying fiscal incentives for exclusionary zoning, as well as compensating for fiscal disparities in local tax base.

These three assumptions have been investigated, drawing on extensive zoning, fiscal, census, and construction data for New Jersey. A sample of 176 developing municipalities with vacant land in six rapidly growing suburban counties of northern and central New Jersey was used to test the fiscal impact of alternative housing types, the fiscal efficiency of local zoning ordinances, and the fiscal implications for local zoning practices of the Robinson strategy of state aid to public education. The fiscal implications of land development and population growth were investigated by a cross-sectional analysis of the 567 municipalities in New Jersey.

The study looked at a number of specific conditions that are necessary to the fiscal motive theory of suburban zoning. For the exclusionary zoning hypothesis to be valid, local restrictions must be widespread enough to affect metropolitan housing markets and must be binding, without simply reflecting developers' preferences (and hence market demand). For the fiscal zoning hypothesis to be valid, income segregation and residential location decisions ought to be significantly influenced by local fiscal variables, and such fiscal considerations ought to outweigh nonfiscal factors. The fiscal implications of alternative land uses must be well known or calculable, with the specific result that large lot zoning is fiscally superior to multifamily development.

The argument that local zoning practices affect metropolitan housing supplies and prices is a reasonable one. However it is dubious that the Mt. Laurel strategy of least-cost zoning will particularly alleviate this problem for low- and moderate-income households. Urban economic analysis suggests that income segregation and fiscal disparities are explainable through market forces without much reference to local zoning practices. Exclusionary zoning may reinforce these market-determined patterns, but it is not a necessary factor. There is some evidence that exclusionary zoning practices may actually reduce the cost of land for single-family construction on large lots. There is little evidence that least-cost zoning will lead private developers to supply new construction in suburban locations for such households. New suburban construction of such housing may well require substantial direct subsidies to developers or consumers. Housing is supplied for the low- and moderate-income markets largely by the filtering process. Expanded supplies and reduced costs may assist these markets indirectly through the same process. However we have virtually no idea of the effect of suburban zoning practices on this filtering process. The issue requires additional investigation.

The principal conclusion of this study is that the exclusionary zoning practices of suburban communities involve more complicated fiscal and nonfiscal considerations than are assumed in the standard formulation of the fiscal motive theory. The typical cost-revenue studies prepared for municipal governments are not a very accurate measure of these considerations. It is likely that suburban communities attempt to practice some form of fiscal mercantilism.[1] However the Hamilton or White fiscal zoning mechanism is an inadequately formulated model of those fiscal practices. The basic problem is that their underlying assumptions appear to have relatively limited empirical application. The same criticism may be leveled against the Robinson strategy of the New Jersey Supreme Court, insofar as that strategy is aimed at altering local fiscal incentives for exclusionary zoning.

Contrary to the fiscal motive theory, it appears that other factors outweigh fiscal variations that may exist among housing types. The principal fiscal considerations are population growth, development standards for site improvements, spatial distribution of new development with respect to existing capital facilities and infrastructure having excess capacity (a factor that is often mislabeled "urban sprawl"), and what has been called public-goods zoning (which is closely associated with the problem of placing subsidized housing in suburban communities). These factors are ignored in cost-revenue studies and in the fiscal motive theory. This study indicates that contrary to the assumptions of the Hamilton or White models, multifamily housing of lower value per dwelling unit is often fiscally superior and that suburban communities may ignore the direct cash-flow implications of development alternatives in their zoning ordinances.

The fiscal mercantilism of such municipalities is more properly characterized as a combination of growth management (rather than fiscal zoning in the strict cost-revenue sense), reduction of fiscal uncertainty, preservation of environmental amenities, and anticipation of negative externalities or opportunity costs associated with poor households and multifamily development. Suburban zoning ordinances are built around holding devices intended to prevent or retard the development of vacant land. A principal fiscal objective is to regulate population growth in order to avoid scale effects and opportunity costs and to postpone the lump sum expenditures required for capital facilities and infrastructure. Whether showing a deficit or profit, large lot zoning reduces fiscal uncertainty. Manipulation of land markets through exclusionary zoning may also lower the cost of land for single-family construction. Although cost-revenue studies are not a particular accurate measure of fiscal impact, voters do not have to compute their tax bills. Rather voters and suburban officials act on general expectations about the fiscal and nonfiscal implications of alternative housing types, land development, and population growth.

Lacking an accurate picture of the fiscal stakes confronting developing suburban communities, the New Jersey Supreme Court may have adopted mutually conflicting strategies in *Robinson* and *Mt. Laurel.* The supreme court confuses fiscal zoning with growth management. It is not housing type that matters, but the amount, pace, and density of population growth permitted. The *Robinson* strategy of state aid to public education may alter local fiscal incentives further in the direction of exclusionary practices. It is not the source of revenue (local property taxation versus state income taxation), but the formula for state aid distribution that is crucial to the fiscal zoning hypothesis.

The New Jersey County and Municipal Government Study Commission has advocated a very different approach to the problem of exclusionary practices in New Jersey.[2] This approach is based on a different view of the fiscal stakes involved in local zoning practices and the expectation that private housing production will not respond to zoning and fiscal reform without heavy subsidy of low- and moderate-income housing. The commission's report redirects the objective of zoning and fiscal reform. Such reform should be aimed directly at reducing zoning barriers and fiscal objections to subsidized housing, together with land costs. The report is based on the conviction that direct or indirect subsidy of low- and moderate-income housing construction will be required to affect metropolitan housing markets.

The commission report distinguishes the fiscal burden of providing new facilities and infrastructure due to population growth from the cost-revenue balance of particular housing types, especially low- and moderate-cost units of three or more bedrooms. It is critical to recognize that such units probably involve more public-goods zoning, in the sense meant by Mills and Oates, than fiscal zoning in the sense meant by Hamilton or White. The commission proposed to meet these two fiscal burdens with different strategies. The first strategy is to have the state directly assume the local service deficits imposed by subsidized housing.[3] The second strategy is to have the state partly finance facilities and infrastructure required by population growth. State aid would thus rise with population and be tied to subsidized housing. Funds would be transferred from low-growth to high-growth communities, especially those accepting subsidized housing. Both municipal and educational services would be included.[4] These fiscal recommendations have not been adopted in New Jersey.

Hamilton favors retention of local zoning to achieve efficiency objectives in land use. The commission report recommended abandoning traditional or Euclidean zoning, to be replaced by direct development planning (on the Ramapo model). This recommendation is based on the conclusion that most multifamily development in suburban New Jersey occurs not directly through zoning but indirectly through variances that permit detailed control over the physical, social, and fiscal impact of such development. This approach endorses the view that municipalities ought positively to regulate the fiscal impacts of development within certain broad guidelines subject to state, regional, or county review. The report strongly recommended the use of the Planned Unit Development Act of 1966 as a framework for cost-revenue balancing. In other words communities ought to mix housing types in planned unit developments, guided in part by fiscal balancing.[5] Although none of the fiscal recommendations of the commission have been adopted, the Municipal Land Use Law of 1975 ordered the creation of new development plans. The law required the rewriting of all land use ordinances in the state to meet this requirement.

This study is not opposed to the objectives pursued by the New Jersey Supreme Court in *Robinson, Mt. Laurel,* and *Madison.* The Mt. Laurel strategy should break down the zoning barriers to subsidized housing.[6] Least-cost zoning may have some effect on low- and moderate-income housing costs through the filtering process. But it will not provide low-cost housing construction. The Robinson strategy may have to be incorporated into a very different fiscal strategy for the reduction of suburban resistance to such housing.

Notes

1. This term is taken from Dick Netzer, "Fiscal Mercantilism," in *Economics of the Property Tax* (Washington, D.C.: Brookings Institution, 1966), pp. 131-132.

2. New Jersey County and Municipal Government Study Commission, *Housing and Suburbs: Fiscal and Social Impact of Multifamily Development* (Trenton, N.J., October 1974), pp. 117-136; *Housing and Suburbs: Fiscal and Social Impact of Multifamily Development. Summary of Findings, Conclusions and Recommendations* (Trenton, N.J., June 1974), pp. 17-22.

3. The report suggests financial aid diminishing over time from 100 percent (first year) to 50 percent (second year) to 25 percent (third year). Aid would be discontinued after the third year. *Housing and Suburbs,* p. 127.

4. Funds for these purposes would be raised either from general state revenues or by a property tax surcharge on communities with net revenue from development each year. Poor communities would be exempted from the surcharge permanently; communities receiving funds would be exempted for three years. Ibid., pp. 127-128.

5. Ibid., pp. 120-121.

6. Exclusionary zoning may be a principal barrier to subsidized construction. Massachusetts passed a law under which the state housing agency may override local zoning ordinances by appealing to a state review board. This approach was specifically rejected by the New Jersey County and Municipal Government Study Commission, ibid., p. 120. A similar view of this approach's effectiveness is taken by Nathan Glazer, "On 'Opening Up' the Suburbs," *The Public Interest,* no. 37 (Fall 1974):89-111. A more positive endorsement is made by Dorothy Altman, "Anti Snob Law Produces Low Income Housing," *Practicing Planner* 6 (December 1976):31-33, 9.

Index

About the Author

Duane Windsor is assistant professor of administrative science in the Jesse H. Jones Graduate School of Administration at Rice University. He received the Ph.D. in political economy and government from Harvard University. He was previously instructor of urban and regional planning at the University of Iowa and research associate at the Center for Urban Policy Research of Rutgers University. He is coauthor of *Housing Development and Municipal Costs* (1973). Dr. Windsor has contributed articles or reviews to the *Journal of the American Institute of Planners* and *The Annals of the American Academy of Political and Social Science.*